AF328667

World
Competitiveness

World Competitiveness

Rewriting the Rules of Global Prosperity

Stéphane Garelli

WILEY

Registered Office(s)
John Wiley & Sons, Inc., 111 River Street, Hoboken, NJ 07030, USA
John Wiley & Sons Ltd, New Era House, 8 Oldlands Way, Bognor Regis, West Sussex, PO22 9NQ
John Wiley & Sons Singapore Pte. Ltd, 134 Jurong Gateway Road, #04-307H, Singapore 600134

For details of our global editorial offices, customer services, and more information about Wiley products visit us at www.wiley.com.

Wiley also publishes its books in a variety of electronic formats and by print-on-demand. Some content that appears in standard print versions of this book may not be available in other formats.

Library of Congress Cataloging-in-Publication Data is Available:

ISBN 9781394366798 (Cloth)
ISBN 9781394366804 (ePub)
ISBN 9781394366811 (ePDF)

Cover Design: Wiley
Cover Image: © Asim-Backgrounds/stock.adobe.com
Author Photo: Courtesy of Stephane Garelli

Set in 10/13.5pt Bembo Std by Straive, Chennai, India

To my wife, Joséphine,

my son, Stéphane,

"The day will come when there will be no battlefields other than markets opening to trade and minds opening up to ideas."

—**Victor Hugo**
Peace Congress, 1849
Stele, Waterloo battlefield

Contents

Why This Book?

In his book *The Economic Consequences of Peace*,[1] published in 1919, John Maynard Keynes described globalization before its time. By the end of the 19th century, the wealthy Londoner could order products from all over the world from his home and have them delivered to his door.

When Philéas Fogg circumnavigated the globe in 80 days in Jules Verne's novel, he never showed his passport or changed money.[2] The same was true of Sherlock Holmes. In the second half of the 19th century, wealthy citizens of the UK could travel throughout the empire freely, using the pound sterling as a universally accepted means of payment.

The Hold of Empires

Empires have always been based on two fundamental principles: territorial expansion and administrative unification of conquered lands. The aim was, among other things, to facilitate travel and trade within the conquered territories.

In Egypt and Mesopotamia, kings often issued safe-conducts for their envoys on significant missions.[3] In 221 BCE, Emperor Qin Shi Huangdi unified China, establishing a single administration and ensuring everything was surveyed, named,

---

[1] Keynes, J. M. (1919). "The Economic Consequences of the Peace." London: Macmillan.

[2] Verne, Jules. *Around the World in Eighty Days.* Translated by William Butcher. Oxford: Oxford University Press, 1995.

[3] There is a passage in the Bible where King Artaxerxes I of Persia (5th century BCE) gave such a letter of recommendation to Nehemiah for his return trip to Judea.

and registered. The Roman Empire not only exported its legions but also Roman law. The "Pax Romana" was based on similar rules that applied to all parts of the empire, encompassing everyone's public and private lives.[4]

In 13th-century China, under the Mongolian Yuan dynasty, Emperor Kubilai Khan[5] combined Mongolian traditions with Chinese law to govern his empire. He issued passes that allowed envoys to travel safely and freely across the empire, offering them assistance and protection. Marco Polo took advantage of this system. By the 15th century, King Henry V of England established a passport system allowing citizens to travel overseas.[6]

Globalization Is Not an Empire

Yet the British empire described by Keynes had marked differences with what would later become globalization. The world then was limited to the British Empire (already considerable) and did not include all countries. It was centered on the country of origin, Great Britain. Most products converged on London and the major cities.

Therefore, the rest of the empire was a supplier of goods to the center and rarely a consumer. Finally, only the very wealthy section of the population could take advantage of this trade.

Globalization has changed this. Now, nearly any country can buy, sell, or travel with ease, benefiting many. People in China, the US, and Brazil can trade similarly and enjoy lower prices, thus raising living standards. This accessibility, along with job creation and skill development from decentralized production, has enhanced quality of life.

Shared Prosperity as an Objective

This phase of "pure" globalization spanned only four decades. It started with Deng Xiaoping's "Open Doors" policy in China in 1978 and ended in 2018; definitively with the onset of the COVID pandemic in 2020. The objective was prosperity for all, especially for those who did not benefit from the formidable economic and technological expansion that took place after World War II.

The opening up of the world was a considerable success. Prosperity may have been perceived differently depending on each person's aspirations but it was real,

---

[4] It is thought to have lasted around 207 years, from 27 BCE to 180 CE. It began with the reign of Emperor Augustus, who established a period of relative peace and stability throughout the Roman Empire, and ended with the death of Emperor Marcus Aurelius.

[5] Born in 1215 and died in 1294, he was emperor of China from 1271.

[6] McHugh, Jenny M. (2021). "The Passport's Medieval Forebear: Grants of Safe-conduct in Medieval Britain." *Epoch Magazine*, November 30, 2021.

even if not always equally distributed. Prosperity is a fundamental objective for nations and individuals: it is both material and intangible. Prosperity is not just about accumulating wealth, it also means developing attitudes and a system of values. It is additionally based on progress and a reasoned hope for a better future. The ultimate goal is *well-being* for individuals and *living well together* for a community or a nation.

Globalization and Competitiveness

When I was managing director of the World Economic Forum and the Davos Annual Meetings, I was struck by the growing number of business and country leaders referring to "national competitiveness." For most, it was simply an extension of companies' competitiveness. However, in practice, countries also compete by improving government policies and developing their economic and social infrastructures.

Globalization implies a transition from an economy primarily driven by trade to one focusing on foreign investment. Establishing a physical presence in another country involves understanding its policies, laws, and value system. It also requires comparing countries to choose the best location.

When I became a professor of World Competitiveness at IMD and the University of Lausanne, I decided to investigate further and expand the concept of national competitiveness. It gave rise to the World Competitiveness Yearbooks, which quickly established themselves as the reference in this field. Then, with the support of IMD, I founded the World Competitiveness Center.

In the early days of globalization, research on world competitiveness was scarce, and there were very few books available in libraries, if any. To understand this revolution, the only option was to travel to countries where it took place and meet government and business leaders driving it. My professional career provided me with this opportunity. I had the chance to live through 40 extraordinary years and those before and after. Before this era, we had seen many countries that were closed and intolerant, especially on the other side of the Iron Curtain. That was half of humanity. I first visited Russia in 1968 and China in 1981 and retained an impression of dullness from these early trips to another world. Everything was gray: buildings, clothes, people's expressions, and probably their hopes. However, in 1978, because of Deng Xiaoping's open-door policy in China, and later the fall of the Berlin Wall in 1989, life changed – and color returned.

New ideas were experienced "on-site" before they could be analyzed, connected, and theorized later. Thus, a parallel is made in this book between encountering leaders and their various national strategies and the resulting theories on competitiveness. They illustrate successful or failed policies.

A Fractured World

Four decades later in 2018 – and then in 2020 when the world came to a halt because of a small virus – openness turned into vulnerability. The incredibly small[7] was destroying the immensely large. Geopolitical tensions threatened an already fragile world. Security became an obsession.

As a consequence, our world is fracturing once more, a victim of ideologies and ancestral fears. Victim, too, of a kind of collective amnesia that prompts a new generation to erase from its memory or rewrite the dramas of the past. The world is still global, but it is not united anymore. What does this mean for nations, companies, and people?

There is something tragic about the disappearance of an open world, of which economic globalization has been a symbol for 40 years. As Honoré de Balzac wrote in his book *Illusions Perdues*, we are living: "The moment when the reality of life is at odds with one's hopes."[8] However, it is unlikely that an open world will disappear entirely. The desire of people to meet, trade, innovate, and exchange ideas is the result of a long history that has spanned several millennia. It is probably in our DNA.

The world's relentless march towards openness will continue, albeit differently. The determination of leaders to achieve this goal remains essential to ensure the prosperity of nations, the well-being of people, and peace. The long journey is not over, but it will need new strategies.

This is the subject of this book.

---

[7] The size of this virus varies between 60 and 140 nanometers, i.e. 1,000–2,000 times smaller than the diameter of a human hair.

[8] Balzac, Honoré de. *Illusions Perdues*. Paris: Gallimard, 1971.

Introduction

A New Knowledge: Competitiveness

The word is a tongue twister. It often makes people uncomfortable. It carries the idea that competitiveness is the law of the strongest: that there is no other aim than winning at all costs. But is this true?

> *What Is World Competitiveness?*
> *What the MIT Department of Economics and Nobel Prize Winners Have to Say*
> *What Politicians Have to Say*

What Is World Competitiveness?

All knowledge stems from two roots: curiosity and frustration.

I was curious to understand how a country generates prosperity and why some nations achieve greater success in this than others.

Why, on the same island – Hispaniola – where Christopher Columbus landed in 1492, is one of the world's poorest countries, Haiti,[1] on one side of a 390 km-long border, and one of the most dynamic economies in the Caribbean and Latin America, the Dominican Republic, on the other?

---

[1] According to the IMF, in 2023, Haiti ranked 148th worldwide for its GDP per capita ($2,125), while the Dominican Republic ranked 78th ($11,242).

How is it possible that Mongolia and the Democratic Republic of Congo (DRC),[2] both blessed with immense natural resources, generate less prosperity than Singapore or Switzerland – which have none?

My frustration stemmed from studying economics at university, which did not address these questions. As a human or moral science, economics was not considered equal to exact sciences like physics, chemistry, or mathematics.

Scholars privileged quantitative studies and convoluted mathematical formulas that did not seem to explain much but demotivated most students. I was left with the impression that the economy was like plumbing: products and money flowed through pipes; along the way, there were taps – taxes or interest rates – to regulate the flow; mathematical formulas tried to gauge the speed of circulation.

It was intellectually stimulating (well, for some) but did not answer my questions. Alfred Marshall (1842–1924), in his *Principles of Political Economy*, published in 1890,[3] noted that economics should be "a study of mankind in the ordinary affairs of life." It was time to take the problems that affected people daily seriously. Gary Becker's (1930–2014) research first gave economic credentials to subjects such as discrimination, minorities, crime, or the economics of the family.[4] He is the leading theorist on human capital and was awarded the Nobel Prize in 1992.[5]

And at the national level I wanted to know whether was it possible to integrate a country's various economic and social policies, from macro- and micro-economic perspectives, to determine which lead to greater prosperity?

When I was managing director of the World Economic Forum and the Davos Annual Meetings from 1974 to 1986,[6] we were struck by the growing number of business and country leaders beginning to use the term "national competitiveness." But nobody was talking about the same thing. Moreover, countries were perceived to compete in the same way as companies.

But this is not the whole story. Countries also compete by implementing government policies and building economic and social infrastructures. A nation's competitiveness involves much more than just the collective competitiveness of its companies. Furthermore, governments have a longer term perspective than companies subject to immediate profitability pressures by publishing quarterly results.

---

[2]According to the same source, Mongolia was ranked 111th worldwide ($5,348) and the DRC 180th ($675).

[3] Marshall, Alfred. *Principles of Economics*. London: Macmillan, 1890.

[4] Becker, Gary. *A Treatise on the Family,* Harvard University Press, 1981.

[5] Daniel Kahneman (1934–2024), professor at Princeton University and winner of the 2002 Nobel Prize in Economics, has also conducted extensive research on cognitive bias and the economics of happiness.

[6] 1974–1986.

We therefore felt it necessary to clarify the subject, especially as we had all the major players in globalization and the competitiveness of companies and nations within Davos.

We decided to follow two parallel paths: the first was to measure and compare all aspects of the competitiveness of nations. This gave rise to the World Competitiveness Reports,[7] which quickly established themselves as the benchmark in this field.

Second, we aimed to create a theory of national competitiveness using a "holistic" approach.[8] This was primarily done through IMD's Center for World Competitiveness and my professorships at this business school and the University of Lausanne in Switzerland.

In short, since I was not good at plumbing, I decided to focus my attention on the competitiveness of nations.

It was not easy. Paul Krugman, the future Nobel Prize winner in economics, wrote in *Foreign Affairs* magazine in 1994 that the concept of competitiveness was "simply wrong" and nothing more than "a new name for productivity."[9]

We were off to a bad start …

What Is Competitiveness?

Many different and obscure definitions fail to clarify the concept. I have always told my students that once you've mastered a concept, you should be able to define it in one line.

From a generic point of view, here is my definition:

Competitiveness is the ability to solve problems better than others.

It may be an oversimplification, but it gets to the core of the matter.

"Better" can mean faster, cheaper, higher quality, or more innovative. In general, anything that helps you stand out from the competition and provides better value to users.

Thus, competitiveness lies in the plumber who quickly repairs your sink, the doctor who cures you, the politician who wins an election, the entrepreneur who turns a profit, or the government that enhances the nation's wealth and its citizens' prosperity.

At a national level, competitiveness encompasses the management of all the resources – material, financial, and human – that create collective prosperity and improve living standards for everyone.

---

[7] There are two: IMD's World Competitiveness Yearbook and the World Economic Forum's Global Competitiveness Report. I used to be responsible for both.

[8] In other words, as a global, interconnected system.

[9] Krugman, P. (1994). "Competitiveness: a dangerous obsession." *Foreign Affairs*, 73(2), 28–44. 10.2307/20045917

You Cannot Compete Alone

Competitiveness inherently suggests rivalry since nations compete to gain or create these resources. Thus, you cannot be competitive in isolation. Competitiveness always involves a comparison with others.

Suppose I run 100 m in 15 seconds (a hypothesis) and, after much effort and training, I improve my time to 13 seconds. In that case, I can be proud of my performance. However, with that time, I will still finish last in the Olympic 100 m final.

Similarly, a government or business leader can boast 3% growth from the previous year. But if their competitors grow at 5%, they are losing at competitiveness.

This was not always easy for politicians to understand. How could their country's economic growth accelerate, yet in our competitiveness rankings, they were losing ground?

The answer was that other countries were accelerating their growth even faster. And this deserved better explanation and a more solid theoretical approach.

What the MIT Department of Economics and Nobel Prize Winners Have to Say

In the early 1980s, I had the chance to visit the Massachusetts Institute of Technology (MIT) Department of Economics. For an economist, it is the temple of knowledge in the field and where you meet the largest number of Nobel Prize winners.

Paul Samuelson

My first visit was to Paul Samuelson, winner of the Nobel Prize in 1970, whose book *Economics*[10] has inspired generations of economists. It has been reprinted more than 20 times. It was one of the most terrifying meetings of my career. He was sitting behind his desk, with his hair cut into a brush, small glasses, and a piercing gaze.

For 30 minutes, he fired questions at me, practically without giving me time to answer. By the end, I felt like my back was against the wall and that the next question would be: "How do you justify your existence on this earth?"

Paul Samuelson liked to say that he did not need any power other than writing textbooks that would influence the management of the economy. He belonged to that generation of economists who believed that economic laws could be created based on mathematics.

---

[10] Samuelson, P. A., & Nordhaus, W. D. (2010). *Economics* (19th). New York: McGraw-Hill.

This was not new to me since my Alma Mater, the University of Lausanne, had welcomed Leon Walras[11] and Vilfredo Pareto,[12] who became famous for their economic equations. However, I have never met a head of government or a business leader who made a decision by referring first to a mathematical formula or a chapter in an economics textbook.

Franco Modigliani

Shortly afterward, I had an appointment with Franco Modigliani,[13] who also won the Nobel Prize in Economics in 1985. This meeting was precisely the opposite experience. He was friendly, empathetic, and smiling, as Italians of the highest intelligence often are.

That was precisely my problem. He was so clever that I am unsure I understood everything he told me, especially since his specialty was finance.

However, I remember one of his comments:

Economists cannot predict the future because every time they give an opinion, they impact the environment and change it.

The development of quantum physics probably inspired this comment. According to the uncertainty principle, enunciated by Werner Heisenberg in 1927,[14] we cannot know both the speed and position of a fundamental particle. More precisely, the act of observing modifies what we observe.

The same applies to the economic environment. When a leading CEO or economist expresses an opinion on equities, interest rates, or the economic outlook, the market will react accordingly. John Maynard Keynes summed up this effect concerning the stock market:

Successful investing means anticipating the expectations of others.

---

[11] Walras, Léon. *Elements of Pure Economics, or the Theory of Social Wealth.* Translated by William Jaffé. Homewood, IL: Richard D. Irwin, 1954.

[12] Pareto, Vilfredo. *Manual of Political Economy: A Critical and Variorum Edition.* Translated and edited by Alberto Zanni and John S. Chipman. Oxford: Oxford University Press, 2014.

[13] Modigliani, Franco. The life cycle hypothesis of saving: aggregate implications and tests. *American Economic Review* 53, 1 (1963): 55–84.

[14] Professor at the University of Leipzig (aged 26), he was awarded the Nobel Prize in Physics in 1933 "for the creation of quantum mechanics."

Rudiger Dornbush: the Dissident

Continuing my visits, I met Rudiger Dornbusch. He was the "enfant terrible" of the house. His great specialty was the study of finance in developing countries. He also wrote an essential economics textbook, *Macroeconomics*,[15] co-edited with Stanley Fischer (who became vice-president of the US Federal Reserve).[16]

He advised us to continue our research regardless, as the anthill occasionally needs a kick. He was a follower of Sir Karl Popper's theories and the principle of falsification. According to Karl Popper, a theory can never be verified by a finite number of observations. On the other hand, it can be falsified by a single contradictory observation. Yet, this principle is not easy to apply. In the academic world, you must document everything extensively to support your ideas and cite authors. But how can you do this when you are a pioneer in a field and, by definition, there is no one to quote?

Subsequently, I have tried, along with my colleagues, to apply the following approach:

> We should pursue our work diligently and honestly and document our research. Then, we should not be afraid to come up with new ideas. At this stage, we can assume that it is no longer up to us to prove that we are right but up to others to prove that we are wrong.

And if others find a flaw in our ideas, we should accept it and modify our approach accordingly. It is not a very modest approach, but a very powerful principle when you want to innovate and push back the boundaries of established thinking.

Who to Believe?

I came away from these visits both overwhelmed and confused. Economics can also be a science influenced by the opinions of illustrious personalities. But they rarely agree with each other.

On my return to Europe, I could not help but think of the words of John Kenneth Galbraith[17] (Harvard professor, ambassador to India, and economic advisor to President Kennedy), who said with characteristic humor:

> Economics is the only science where two people can win the Nobel Prize and say the exact opposite of each other.

He was right. And I have spent my professional career experiencing this.

---

[15] Dornbusch, R., Fischer, S., & Startz, R. (2014). *Macroeconomics* (12th). New York: McGraw-Hill.

[16] The central bank of the United States.

[17] Galbraith, John Kenneth. *The Affluent Society*. Boston: Houghton Mifflin, 1958.

What Politicians Have to Say

Two other people influenced my research.

Raymond Barre

Barre was vice-president of the European Commission and prime minister of France from 1976 to 1981. But, above all, he was the author of economics textbooks,[18] like Paul Samuelson, and as such, had trained generations of economists. When French President Giscard d'Estaing appointed him to head his government, he called him France's best economist.[19]

As he defined himself, he was a square man with a round body. His physical appearance did not do justice to his clarity of thought and determination. From the outset, he supported our research into the competitiveness of nations. The reason was probably that his European culture made the role of the state central to a country's prosperity.

In the United States, on the other hand, the role of the state has long been regarded as peripheral. One of the great American professors on the competitiveness of companies and nations, Harvard's Michael Porter, devised a system known as the "Diamond."[20] According to him, the forces that interacted with a country's competitiveness were demand, factors of production, competition, and shared value chains. However, the role of the state was an external factor to his model, as was chance.

In the United States, the role of the state in the economy, at both federal and local levels, has historically been less prominent than in other countries. However, this situation has changed over time, and Michael Porter has refined his theory accordingly.

Edward Heath

Heath had also been prime minister of his country from 1970 to 1974. He was not an economist but a politician at heart, having graduated from Oxford and been trained by student debating societies. He also chaired the Davos Annual Meetings, and I often had the opportunity to meet him, notably at his private residence in London's Wilton Street.

---

[18] Barre, Raymond. *Économie politique*. Paris: Presses Universitaires de France, 1956.

[19] His wife, Eva Barre, had a unique tradition of having everyone at the table sign the menu during meals. Somewhere, there must be an impressive collection of menus autographed by the most influential leaders of that time.

[20] Porter, Michael E. *The Competitive Advantage of Nations*. New York: Free Press, 1990.

Edward Heath, Prime Minister of Great Britain, 1970–1974

"Sir, you have to go back, it is dangerous!"

The policeman was worried. We were standing on the sidewalk in front of his private residence on London's Wilton Street. He had insisted on walking me back to his doorstep. But he was also on the IRA's hit list.

He was the epitome of a British politician. An Oxford graduate, trained in rhetoric through student debates, a Member of Parliament for 51 years and, above all, the man who brought the United Kingdom into Europe.

His talents were manifold. Three of his books retrace them: *Travels, Music,* and *Sailing.* He was also probably the best public speaker I have ever known. I once asked him his secret: "You have to talk to people, not give them speeches – if you talk to them, they will forgive you any errors."

He also had an extraordinary capacity for attention. When I spoke with him, he would stare at me intently, making me feel like the most important person in the world. He once told me he had learned this from President Eisenhower.

"Sir, you must not stay here." The policeman insisted. I insisted, too. If the sniper missed, Switzerland could lose a good economist …

Source: Travels, Music, Sailing, all published by Sidwick and Jackson, London 1977.

He also supported research into the competitiveness of nations and the role of the state. He had probably fallen victim to it during his political career. He had called early elections in 1974 to force voters to decide whether the government or the unions, especially the miners' unions, should run the country.

He lost and had to resign.

Later, Margaret Thatcher continued the battle during Arthur Scargill's 1984 miners' strike,[21] emerging victorious. Margaret Thatcher and Edward Heath were not fond of each other.

However, Edward Heath understood that you could not run a country without managing its economic strategy. That is why he brought Britain into the European Union in 1973.

---

[21] Milne, Seumas. *The Enemy Within: The Secret War Against the Miners.* London: Verso Books, 1994.

Chapter Takeaways

One might have believed, as I did, that such advances would consolidate a world open and accessible to everyone. Perhaps this was an illusion…

The concept of globalization and competitiveness analyzed in this book is referred to as "world competitiveness." It underlines that the gradual opening of the world has fundamentally changed how nations, people, and companies compete and how, by doing so, they increase their prosperity and well-being.

World competitiveness was not initially developed through research in libraries or publications. It stemmed from direct experience and discussions with government and business leaders "in the field." It was mainly achieved through meetings such as the World Economic Forum gatherings, teaching and research at IMD business school, the University of Lausanne, and numerous international conferences.

This "bottom-up" approach led to the accumulation of many facts and ideas. Subsequently, the objective was to connect the dots and develop a theoretical framework.

Part I of this book therefore focuses on traveling through time and across nations to highlight where and how the fundamentals of world competitiveness emerged and what we have learned from these.

Part II highlights the challenges raised by a world that may be deglobalizing once more or at least fracturing. It assesses the implications for nations' policies and companies' strategies.

Part III emphasizes the "so what" of world competitiveness. Why does it matter to all of us; and, particularly, what is the ultimate goal?

In summary, the book aims to shed light on one of the most important concepts in contemporary economics, affecting our lives more than any other.

Competitiveness is everywhere, yesterday and today, near to us and globally.

Where Next?

The opening up of the world and its impact on competitiveness stems from a rich history that extended over a long time.

Its development has not always been linear or stable. Nevertheless, since the birth of agriculture and the first settlements, many structures and mentalities that still exist today have emerged and almost relentlessly expanded over the centuries. Evidence can be found in virtually every country.

Thus, world competitiveness cannot be understood without delving deeper into other disciplines such as anthropology, history, and sociology. Competitiveness is also the result of a long journey that sheds light on today's events and mindsets.

This is the subject of the next chapter.

PART

I

1 | The Premise of an Open World

In the early 1980s, the world began to change: China opened up, and the Soviet Union collapsed. Half of humanity – which until then had lived in a closed environment – decided, politically and economically, to become part of the rest of the world. Economic development, and therefore the competitiveness of their nations, was the means to achieve this.

If the great adventure of markets opening up took off rapidly at this time, this was because of a long history. And if we don't understand that history, we cannot understand what is happening today.

Traveling Through Time and Geography
Messages from the Past to Help Understand Today
The Foundations of Modern Competitiveness

Traveling Through Time and Geography

From the second half of the 20th century onwards, air and sea transport developed faster than the convergence of economies. Travelling far away from home also meant travelling through space and time.

Into the Future

My first trip to the United States in 1966, specifically to New York, felt like a leap into the future. The televisions were in color, cars were huge, and skyscrapers towered impressively. For foreigners, the American dream was almost like entering a sci-fi movie. It was also a glimpse of what our lives would become on the old European continent and beyond. We could go home with a few novelty products and enjoy unrivaled prestige: we knew what the future held.

Into the Past

Conversely, when I first went to China – to Beijing in 1981 – it was like stepping decades back in time. There were practically no cars. On Chang' an, the capital's main central avenue and the one that passes in front of the entrance to the Forbidden City, a tiny lane was reserved for cars. The rest belonged to bicycles.

Of course, there were no multistory buildings because of the risk of earthquakes. Dinner was served at 5:30 in the evening, as we had to live with the setting and rising sun to save electricity. From 8 p.m. onwards, the city fell into an immense silence.[1]

In the Present

Now, cars are everywhere; and Beijing is noisy and never sleeps. It is the same elsewhere. Whether it is Shanghai, Hong Kong, Singapore, Tokyo, or Dubai, one is struck by a new uniformity: the same skyscrapers, cars, stores, clothes, and restaurants.

New York is no longer unique, and globalization has standardized ways of living and thinking. New products like smartphones and cutting-edge technologies like artificial intelligence are now marketed globally and available at the same time all over the world.

Today, we travel almost freely in geographic space and practically in real-time. People can fly to the other side of the world in just a few hours. Even there, a true change of scenery is increasingly hard to find. Whereas in the past, travel was reserved for the education of the elite, today, it is available to everyone.

Travel to Learn and Compare

Since ancient times, philosophers, artists, and politicians have traveled. Ionia and Mesopotamia were favored destinations, though sometimes, as with Herodotus, Egypt was also part of their travels.

---

[1] Even the sound of birds disappeared. Very few were left, as most of them had been eradicated by the 1962 campaign to protect the crops.

These trips were seldom relaxing. For instance, after visiting Denys of Syracuse, Plato fell victim to pirates and endured six months of enslavement before friends paid his ransom — in what might be considered the best investment in human thought.

Similarly, Julius Caesar was kidnapped by Cilician pirates in 75 BCE. This was sadly not a good idea for them — because after buying his freedom, he returned to execute them.

Elite Tourism: The Grand Tour

Thomas Hobbes (1588–1679) ranks among Britain's most prominent philosophers. His work *Leviathan*, published in 1651,[2] stands as a strong rejection of the scholastic ideas of Thomas Aquinas and promotes materialism and rational thought. He believed that men are by nature wicked and violent, but also equal. The only way to live in peace is to transfer their power to an absolute sovereign who can enforce the law. Today, this is a bit controversial …

However, one can be one of the most brilliant minds of one's time and still have to work for a living. And in Thomas Hobbes' case, he was attached to the Cavendish family as a "travelling tutor."

As such, he accompanied two of the house's sons — William Cavendish I and II — on an educational tour of Europe: the Grand Tour. The idea was to perfect young aristocrats' education by traveling through much of Europe, especially France and Italy. Later, all the great intellectuals took advantage of this tradition: Montaigne, Locke, Montesquieu, Voltaire, Diderot, Goethe, Alexandre Dumas, Lord Byron, and many others. To be an educated gentleman, you had to travel. And this tradition of the Grand Tour gave us the word: "tourism."[3]

A World Accessible to All

Gradually, the world became accessible to all. An expanding economy and widespread affluence allowed more individuals to travel, educate themselves, or at least engage with the world's diversity and cultures.

I have always been struck by the fact that as soon as a country liberalizes, the first reaction of people who can do so is to travel. For example, since China opened up to the rest of the world, approximately 135 million Chinese tourists visit foreign

---

[2] Hobbes, Thomas. *Leviathan, or the Matter, Forme, and Power of a Commonwealth Ecclesiasticall and Civil.* London: Andrew Crooke, 1651.

[3] Lassels, Richard. *The Voyage of Italy, or a Compleat Journey Through Italy.* Edited by a Modern Hand. London: Richard Wellington, 697. (Google Books).

countries annually. On the other hand, when a country descends into dictatorship, the first decision of the new tyrants is precisely to ban travel and close the borders. The aim is to prevent the population from learning and comparing.

And yet, over time, the trend has been towards opening up countries and markets and comparing ideas. Those who have been able to travel, as I have, have thus been able to complete their education.

Messages from the Past to Help Understand Today

Without the past, however distant, it is impossible to understand the present and anticipate the future.

Anthropology should be part of an economics education. Without it, we cannot understand some of the most profound behaviors that influence our environment. This is not a new idea. Studying anthropology to better understand economic structures was initiated 100 years ago with the work of Poland's Bronislaw Malinovski[4] and France's Marcel Mauss.[5] They focused on economic exchanges in primitive societies as they believed, as Claude Levi Strauss[6] later did, that this would shed light on our modern social behaviors. If we are talking about globalization today, it is probably because there is in our DNA an insatiable need to look further, beyond our traditional horizon of life and thought.

Anthropology to Better Understand the Present

The history of *homo sapiens* resembles a branching tree with multiple species coexisting simultaneously. These species were mobile within their territories and also ventured into others'. This movement led to interbreeding, which did not always involve conflict.[7]

---

[4] Bronislaw Malinowski, *Argonauts of the Western Pacific: An Account of Native Enterprise and Adventure in the Archipelagoes of Melanesian New Guinea* (London: Routledge, 1922).

[5] Marcel Mauss, *The Gift: Forms and Functions of Exchange in Archaic Societies*, translated by Ian Cunnison (New York: W.W. Norton, 1967).

[6] Claude Lévi-Strauss, *Tristes Tropiques*, translated by John Weightman and Doreen Weightman (New York: Penguin Books, 1973).

[7] *Homo Sapiens* did not deliberately exterminate Neanderthals through warfare, as has often been claimed. If the two species competed, they also have intermingled in Europe, Asia, and, probably earlier, in Africa. Today, 2–4% of our DNA comes from the Neanderthal.

A Long History of Travel ...

Hominid specimens recently found at Jebel Irhoud in Morocco are over 315,000 years old. In Omo-Kibish, Ethiopia, they could be 233,000 years old, and in the Rising Star cave in South Africa, the so-called Naledi man is said to be 200,000 years old.

However, these hominids soon began to travel — and not just in Africa.

Genetic analyses carried out by the Max Planck Institute for Anthropology in Leipzig and Oxford University show that man had already reached New Guinea 140,000 years ago.

New species such as Homo floresiensis, discovered in Indonesia in 2003, and Homo luzonensis, excavated in the Philippines in 2010, indicate that despite their very small size, especially their brain, these hominids appear to have survived until 45,000 years ago.

Other discoveries also prove that man reached America over 50,000 years ago.

We also crossed paths with a Denisovian hominid whose remains have been found in Siberia. His DNA makes up around 5% of that of Melanesian populations. Recently, the remains of an individual whose mother was Neanderthal and whose father was Denisovian were excavated in Siberia.

Our history is thus made up of constant migration and interbreeding.

Competing, but Also Cooperating

Our history is also about sociability and cooperation. Numerous Paleolithic burials have revealed the remains of humans of advanced age or profoundly handicapped by injuries. Their tribe appears to have cared for them even beyond the age of procreation. This might signal the early stages of a humane society. Alternatively, it might be part of a utilitarian approach that used elders to care for grandchildren while the parents were hunting or gathering food.

Even at this time, we were probably torn between the need for power, cooperation, and sociability to ensure our survival. Today we have an expression for this: "Frenemy," which is the conjunction of "friend" and "enemy."

A Larger Horizon, Geographically and Mentally

Dunbar's Number

It seems that our brain has been programmed to manage a maximum number of relationships: 150, according to Robin Dunbar, an anthropologist at Oxford University, and his colleague Russel Hill.

To find this out, they analyzed a widespread tradition in the UK at Christmas: sending greetings cards to one's closest relations.

Since it represents a major personal effort, a choice has to be made on essential relationships. The result: 153.5 cards.

This number, rounded to 150, seems to have been imprinted on our brains since the dawn of time. Anthropologists estimate that the first villages comprised 150 people.

From a military point of view, the company is the smallest administrative unit in many armies, with a staff of approximately 150.[8]

For most of our history, our ancestors' geographical and mental horizons did not exceed a distance of 30 km. This was the distance one could cover in a day, either on foot or on horseback. It was also considered the optimum marching day for armies, until Napoleon pushed it to 45 km.

It was within this geographical horizon that life's major events took place. It constituted the backbone of the organization of states. It was also within this range that temples or churches were built, and most information was gathered concerning the birth, marriage, or death of populations.

Mobility encouraged trade. In many prehistoric tombs, one can find artifacts hundreds of kilometers from their origin, such as shells or pieces of amber. The development of economics is, therefore, inseparable from mobility.

Trade on land and sea, transportation, and technology have constantly pushed back our physical and mental barriers. As discoveries have been made, our geographical and time horizons have continued to both expand and harmonize.

---

[8] Dunbar, Robin. 2010. *How Many Friends Does One Person Need?: Dunbar's Number and Other Evolutionary Quirks*. London: Faber & Faber.

Agriculture Changed Everything

Throughout history, fundamental inventions have profoundly impacted our economic societies, with enduring effects today. A notable example is the shift from a hunter-gatherer society to one centered around agriculture and animal husbandry.

Since the emergence of agriculture, the world's population has grown steadily. In 10,000 BCE, it was estimated at between 1 and 10 million individuals. Today, it is over 8 billion.

One of the reasons for this exponential growth is that agriculture enabled people to store crops and move away from a hand-to-mouth economy.[9] Storing and saving led to the accumulation of capital and, hence, capitalism. And if savings have been made, people can then invest in the future.[10]

Drawbacks   Agriculture also created several problems, including nutritional deficiencies in Neolithic bones, especially teeth. Shifting from hunting-gathering to farming led to lower protein intake and a diet focused on a few cereals. Raising livestock to compensate for protein shortages then spread new diseases to humans. Human history has thus been marked by epidemics, from the plague to measles.

Another school of thought, exemplified by Jean-Jacques Rousseau, links the emergence of agriculture to specialization and consequent social inequality. This in turn initiated a significant debate about economic growth and its effects on society, employment, and property. This debate influenced the French and Russian revolutions and 19th-century social theories from thinkers like Proudhon, Fourrier, and Marx. Today, it continues to shape discussions on inequality and discrimination.

Tribal Spirit

Another demon from the depths of time: tribal spirit. At 45, and for the first time in his life, Desmond Morris, the British zoologist and author of the bestseller The *Naked Ape*,[11] attended a soccer match. It was in Malta, and the game never finished as it was interrupted by violence and riots.

---

[9] Early grains like spelt could be kept for long periods, leading to stocks that needed to be preserved and stored. This may have contributed to the foundation of early cities such as Çatalhöyük in Anatolia around 7500 BCE.

[10] Every economics student learns this from the formula I = S (Investment = Saving).

[11] Morris, Desmond. *The Naked Ape: A Zoologist's Study of the Human Animal*. New York: McGraw-Hill, 1967.

He wondered what could drive otherwise quiet and rational people he knew well to such a level of passion. In his book *The Soccer Tribe*[12] he concluded that it was the ancestral sense of the tribe that was reappearing. In the tribal system, ancient or modern, a sense of belonging takes precedence over rationality. Leaders insist on absolute loyalty while external criticism is perceived as calling into question the tribe's identity.

You may never change your tribal alliance. Even a losing soccer team keeps its supporters. However, people now have the choice of belonging to several tribes at once. We can be Apple or Microsoft, Samsung or Google, Facebook or LinkedIn, Amazon or Alibaba, Manchester United or Paris Saint-Germain.

Tribalism, Technology, and Politics   New technologies – such as the Internet and social networks – make it possible to create virtual tribes of people who have never met. The concept thus goes beyond the territorial, ethnic, or religious sphere to include universal ideologies, such as the environment or biological diversity – at best – or terrorism, at worst.

However, the impact remains the same. When Barack Obama was asked why the Democrats lost the 2006 election to Donald Trump, he replied: "We probably overlooked the tribe effect."

Some of these examples may seem trivial, but they underline the extent to which we are heirs to this long history, even in our everyday lives.

Behaviors Influenced by our Distant Past

If we are prepared to spend a fortune on high-definition televisions or high-performance cameras, it is because we are intuitively captivated by colors. The reason behind this is the fact that our primate ancestors were frugivores. And the best way to tell when a fruit becomes edible is when it changes color.

Our urge to dance might be traced back to our ancestors who swung from branches to attract mates. Today, we still move rhythmically in clubs for similar reasons. Singing likely comes from our habit of shouting together to scare away beasts at night or muster courage while hunting. Talking evolved from the need to share stories of gathering and hunting and boast about achievements.

Our current behaviors, therefore, have much deeper origins than we think. They sometimes change form, but the mechanisms and motivations have been ingrained in us for millennia. Technologies can change appearance. But in the end, understanding our distant past helps us to grasp today's attitudes better.

---

[12] Morris, D. (1981). "*The Soccer Tribe.*" London: Jonathan Cape.

The Foundations of Modern Competitiveness

Accounting, statistics, commerce, taxes, and banking laid the foundations for a new world and the birth of enterprises.

While globalization of the economy stems from two critical historical factors: war and trade.

War as a Means of Enrichment

For an extended period, war was the dominant factor. It was a way for the victors to gain wealth by seizing it from others. Mesopotamian cities, and later the Egyptian, Babylonian, Assyrian, and Persian empires, seized nearby treasures, often depicting enslaved people offering their tribute in frescoes.

Caesar's triumphs also showcased the spoils taken from the defeated. The Roman Empire thrived on goods obtained from its conquered territories for centuries.

The war economy still exists today.[13] It has the disadvantage of concentrating the bulk of economic, technological, human, and financial resources on one sector of the economy – the military – to the detriment of all others.[14] Moreover, it feeds itself: a wartime economy must keep engaging in conflict to maintain its existence.[15]

Gross Domestic Product (GDP) only accounts for products subject to a financial transaction.[16] It does not show how much a war economy destroys material and human assets that cannot be replaced quickly.

A war-driven economy can still display growth, as GDP measures spending without considering its impact on national well-being. People living in such an economy would probably choose to invest in health and education rather than military equipment. Ultimately, empires built solely through force do not endure over time; they have all vanished throughout history.

Trade as a Source of Wealth

Trade became vital for a nation's economic and political longevity for two primary reasons. First, in trade, keeping the other party alive is more beneficial than

---

[13] According to the Stockholm-based SIPRI institute, global military spending reached $2.8 trillion in 2023, up 7% on the previous year. The United States and China account for 49% of global spending. Stockholm International Peace Research Institute (SIPRI).

[14] *SIPRI Yearbook 2023: Armaments, Disarmament and International Security.* Oxford: Oxford University Press. Available at: https://www.sipri.org/publications/sipri-yearbook

[15] A further development of this concept is presented in Chapter 4.

[16] John Maynard Keynes used to say: "Do not marry your cleaning lady, it lowers the GDP" – assuming, of course, that the new wife would continue to do the housework, but for free …

eliminating them. Recurring transactions generate wealth by allowing products to be sold multiple times.[17]

Second, commerce is an activity where size plays a lesser role than the military. Even small nations or individuals can become great successes.

From the Bronze Age onwards (3300–1200 BCE), trade routes became essential for developing countries, even if warfare continued in parallel. These routes were primarily concerned with trading minerals. Among the most important were the copper and tin routes (notably from Cornwall in England) needed to make bronze. The iron route, dominated by the Hittites in Anatolia, enabled them to rule the Levant (and led to conflicts with Egypt).

Apart from metals, trade in agricultural products – such as olive oil and wine, wheat, and spelt – developed from Anatolia and the shores of the Pont-Euxin (the Black Sea). The route for frankincense and myrrh began in Yemen and extended to the Levant and Europe; while the Silk Road connected Xi'an to Rome via land and sea. Additionally, the New World's gold and silver passed through Spain and Portugal, and the spice route flourished from the Moluccas – eventually triggering a conflict between England and the Netherlands.

The Exchange of Products and Ideas

When not at war, major empires kept trade relations from afar. The Han Dynasty in China and the Roman Empire were aware of each other. The Romans imported silk, while China received Italian glass. However, trade occurred through intermediaries like the Parthians. Direct commercial contact only came later. It was not until the travels of the Jesuit fathers in the 13th century, followed by those of Marco Polo, that the first regular commercial contacts were made.[18]

These political and trade routes also facilitated the exchange of technologies and ideas. The Greek triremes, Viking ships, and Chinese junks showcased the progress in design, materials, and navigational tools essential for maritime dominance. In Alexandria, the Ptolemies' library copied valuable parchments from travelers, keeping the originals and providing copies, underscoring early discussions about the increasing value of knowledge.

Trade's significant impact on global economic integration lies in fostering related activities like accounting, logistics, finance, and business law, a trend still relevant today.

---

[17] Montesquieu (1689–1755) had already made this point: "The natural effect of trade is to bring about peace" because "two nations that negotiate together make themselves reciprocally dependent." This is the theory of the so-called "gentle commerce."

[18] Alain Peyrefitte, *The Immobile Empire*, translated by Jon Rothschild (New York: Alfred A. Knopf, 1992).

The Rise of Accounting

Accounting likely represents the earliest form of economic knowledge. In ancient Mesopotamia, Egypt, the Indus Valley, and Rome, it was initially used to count crops and livestock, followed by tax calculations.

The first known accountant, "Kushim,"[19] is named on a cuneiform tablet from the Uruk period (3400–3000 BCE), which documented transactions involving goods like spelt or barley. Even today, all ports and major commercial cities are home to large accounting, auditing, and consulting firms.[20]

The Origin of Statistics

The etymology of the word "statistics" goes back to the Italian word "statista," meaning "statesman" or "politician."

This term was used to designate a person involved in the affairs of government or state management.

In the 18th century, the term "Statistik" was introduced into German by Gottfried Achenwall (1719–1772), a professor at the University of Göttingen, although elements of the concept can be traced back to the Italian Giovanni Botero (1544–1617).

Gottfried Achenwall used "Statistik" to refer to the systematic analysis of state data, such as populations, territories, or economic resources, with the aim of informing government decisions.

The Rise of Statistics

The vast accumulation of accounting data that could be kept led administrations to track its evolution over time.[21] They assumed that a better understanding of past cycles would enable them to anticipate the future.

Understanding requires measurement. Managing a state's social and economic progress hinges on having an accurate and up-to-date statistical system. The speed

---

[19] Nissen, Hans Jörg, Peter Damerow, and Robert K. Englund. *Archaic Bookkeeping: Early Writing and Techniques of Economic Administration in the Ancient Near East*. Chicago: University of Chicago Press, 1993.

[20] As we'll see in Chapter 3.

[21] For example, the British Museum holds over 130,000 cuneiform tablets, many of which relate to accounting operations.

of data publication varies widely between countries. Singapore, Hong Kong, and China typically release quarterly GDP figures 10–15 days after the period ends. The US follows in 15–17 days, Europe around 20 days, while Denmark and Switzerland can take up to six weeks.

To address this lag, some economists use shortcuts, like monitoring electricity or copper consumption to gauge a country's economic activity, as copper is prevalent in traditional and modern industries. One of the most famous alternatives is the Li Keqiang Index, named after the Chinese Prime Minister, who was in office from 2013 to 2023. It combines electricity consumption, rail freight, and bank loans to estimate China's economic activity.[22]

Statistical Problems Statistical problems culminate in a small footnote in national statistics cleverly named "Errors and Omissions." Errors include data collection, processing, or estimation due to imperfect surveys or reporting errors. Omissions involve transactions that are not recorded because they have been forgotten or overlooked. Ideally, global exports should match global imports, but they do not.[23]

Online Statistics GDP statistics are updated up to 18 months after the first publication – and one might question the utility of such late-breaking information for the day-to-day running of a nation. However, introducing new technologies should speed up and refine the collection of statistics. For example, Google's Mobility Report[24] offers a series of online statistics, by country, about what people are doing. These include changes in business from grocery stores and pharmacies to public transport or time spent in the office.[25]

Payment with a cell phone offers unparalleled access to information, allowing companies and states to monitor consumers' purchases, locations, and prices in near real-time. However, this raises concerns about data privacy.

---

[22] Norland, Erik. "China's Li Keqiang Index." *The Hedge Fund Journal*, March 2018.

[23] World Bank data reveals a discrepancy ranging from $2,500 to $3,000 billion between the two, depending on the year. This gap accounts for roughly 5–6% of the world's trade, valued at an average of $45,000 billion. A detail …

[24] Google. *"Community Mobility Reports."* https://www.google.com/covid19/mobility/ (accessed May 14, 2025).

[25] In addition, PriceStats provides daily inflation statistics for more than 20 countries by aggregating online data. SpaceKnow also provides statistical series, including economic data, this time using satellite imagery. Eurocontrol shows aircraft movements. Flightradar24 shows the exact position of aircraft, enabling some to track the movements of company directors negotiating contracts or celebrity meetings for social occasions. Vesseltracker and Vesselfinder can track ships worldwide and assess port congestion.

The Rise of National Accounts

Collecting data of all kinds soon raised the question of its use at a national level. At first, governments were mainly interested in statistics for tax collection or troop mobilization. To do this, creating an accounting system that could be implemented at the state level and later aligned with international practices was essential. As we have observed, being competitive also involves making comparisons with others.

In modern times, the first works on national accounting can be traced back to the Englishman William Petty (1623–1687)[26] and the Frenchman François Quesnay (1694–1794).[27] Adam Smith and Karl Marx also tackled this issue.

Simon Kuznets (1901–1985) in the US is credited with advancing modern national accounting and published "National Income (1929–1932)"[28] for the government to monitor war planning. This work established the basis for national accounting systems.[29]

Following the war, Richard Stone (1913–1991), a professor at Cambridge University in England,[30] gained recognition for his groundbreaking work in creating national accounting systems. He was crucial in developing the first System of National Accounts (SNA) released by the United Nations in 1953. His contributions established formal methods for measuring and reporting domestic and international economic activities.[31]

The Evolution of Money

In the early days of trade, barter was the primary payment method. But it was impractical as it involved exchanging goods of uncertain value. The invention of money expanded accounting from tracking products by number to monitoring their value too.

According to Herodotus, the first coins were minted in Lydia in the 6th century BCE.[32] Aristotle believes it was a little earlier, in the 8th century, under the reign of

---

[26] Petty, William. *A Treatise of Taxes and Contributions*. London: [Publisher], 1662.

[27] Tableau économique, published in 1758 or Quesnay, F. (1972). *"Tableau Économique"* (Critical edition by Marguerite Kuczynski and Ronald Meek). Paris: Macmillan.

[28] Kuznets, Simon. *National Income, 1929–1932*. Senate Document No. 124, 73rd Congress, 2nd Session. Washington, D.C.: U.S. Government Printing Office, 1934.

[29] Kuznets had a unique view of GDP, arguing it should only include data that enhanced societal well-being, excluding advertising, armaments, and much of finance.

[30] Stone, Richard, and Giovanna Stone. *National Income and Expenditure*. 10th London: Bowes & Bowes, 1977.

[31] Both were awarded the Nobel Prize in Economics, Simon Kuznets in 1971 and Richard Stone in 1984.

[32] Herodotus. *The Histories*. Translated by Aubrey de Sélincourt. Revised with an introduction and notes by John M. Marincola. London: Penguin Books, 2003.

King Midas of Phrygia. These coins did not indicate a value, which depended on the metal content (they had to be weighed) and the issuer's credibility. Coins from Athens were more sought-after than those from other cities, with fewer quality guarantees.[33]

The development of accounting and money through trade brought about banking institutions. Ships full of goods enabled investments to be funded and goods to be monetized before resale. However, the necessity to store money arose from two additional functions: securing accumulated wealth and financing transactions, requiring trusted intermediaries.

The Creation of Banks

In ancient times, temples and individuals alike acted as guardians of wealth. It was the rise of trade between cities and then states that encouraged the exchange of currencies. As a result, commercial banks as we know them today often developed around major ports, notably Genoa, Venice, Bruges, Antwerp, Hamburg, Lübeck, Seville, Lisbon, and London.

The word "bank" comes from the Italian "Banca."[34] Initially, Lombard bankers worked in open spaces, sitting on benches. They not only exchanged money but also lent it out, which led to the invention of interest rates. The word credit comes from the Italian "credo," to believe, which implies having confidence that the borrower will repay its debt. If not, the bank would go bankrupt, in Italian "banca rotta," meaning that the bank where transactions were made had to be broken down.

Isaac Newton's Other Career

In 1699, Isaac Newton was appointed Master of the Royal Mint and, as such, oversaw a series of measures to eradicate counterfeiting.

He had the old, worn or cropped coins withdrawn from the market and replaced by new ones with special markings to make them more difficult to imitate.

He improved manufacturing techniques by using better coining methods and special, uniform, high-quality alloys that were difficult to imitate.

---

[33] Kroll, John H. *The Athenian Agora. Volume XXVI: The Greek Coins.* Princeton: The American School of Classical Studies at Athens, 1993.

[34] Goldthwaite, Richard A. Banks, *Places and Entrepreneurs in Renaissance Florence.* Aldershot, Hampshire: Variorum, 1995.

He set up a system for monitoring suspect manufacturing using advanced metallurgical and chemical analyses. He was also very active in the legal pursuit of counterfeiters.

Isaac Newton held this position until his death in 1727. England then had one of the best currencies in Europe, which would serve as the basis for its industrial expansion.

During the Renaissance, one of the greatest innovations in banking was double-entry bookkeeping, which records the origin of funds on the one hand and their destination on the other. However, it was already commonly used by many bankers in Genoa and Florence by the Medici.[35]

And the Creation of Bankers   In the 15th and 16th centuries, notable European banking families emerged outside Italy, particularly within the Holy Roman German Empire. The Fuggers[36] were the most renowned among them. They pioneered financing commercial deals and mining ventures and provided funds to European rulers, especially the Habsburgs and the Pope.

Private bankers amassed significant influence, extending their power from economics into politics. This led states to recognize the necessity of establishing their own financial institutions to handle money and credit: central banks.

The world's oldest central bank is the Bank of Sweden, founded in 1668 with 20 employees. The Bank of England followed in 1694, and the Bank of Scotland a year later. Spain's central bank was created by King Charles III in 1782, and France's by Napoleon in 1800. The Federal Reserve Bank of the United States came into being in 1913, and the People's Bank of China in 1948.

Cistercian Abbeys and Management

Founded by Robert de Molesme in 1098 with the Abbey of Cîteaux near Dijon in France, they enjoyed considerable success and spread throughout Europe.

In the 13th century, there were 742 abbeys, stretching from the Balkans to Ireland, from Sweden to Castile. They were all linked by a formidably efficient logistical and organizational network.

(continued)

---

[35] It was codified by Luca Pacioli at the end of the 15th century in his book *Tractatus XI particularis de computibus et scripturis*, published in Venice in 1494.

[36] Steinmetz, Greg. *The Richest Man Who Ever Lived: The Life and Times of Jacob Fugger.* New York: Simon & Schuster, 2015.

> (*continued*)
>
> Approximately every 30 km, there were "granges," which were specialized farms administered by lay monks (lay brothers) that produced all the substances needed to feed the praying monks (Order of Saint Benedict): cereals, wine, oil, and livestock.
>
> They also served as relays for monks on their travels. Each abbey had to send a representative to the "General Chapter," a kind of General Assembly of the abbeys, where all major decisions were discussed. There were plenary sessions, commissions, votes, and elections.
>
> Production, maintenance, logistics, cooperation, transport, and decision-making – the Cistercian abbeys anticipated modern management. And what company today manages over 700 subsidiaries in this way?

However, the financial risks in business escalated as products came from countries farther away. Operational risks, like contract durations and travel uncertainties, were hard for individuals or small groups to handle alone. Thus, organizations shared trade risks and profits with financial institutions, and this led to the establishment of companies. Initially localized, these companies soon expanded globally.

The Internationalization of Companies

Let's take the Hanseatic League[37] as an example. It was created in 1241 by a mutual assistance treaty between Hamburg and Lübeck. It soon became an association of merchants trading all around the Baltic Sea, where it had established trading posts. Management rules and accounting principles were standardized. Major decisions were taken at an annual meeting, the Hanseatic Diet, the forerunner of our current shareholder meetings.

Meanwhile, in 1288, Bishop Peter of Falun[38] in Sweden founded a company with seven business partners (including the King of Sweden) to exploit the copper mine on

---

[37] Dollinger, Philippe. *The German Hansa*. Translated by D.S. Ault and S.H. Steinberg. London: Routledge, 1970.
[38] Also known by the Latin name Petrus Philippi de Falcone.

the Kopparberg mountain. The company was incorporated in 1347 under the name Stora Kopparberg. It soon enjoyed considerable success and took on an international dimension. In the 17th century, it was the leading supplier of copper to Europe.[39]

New Legal Structures

These different company initiatives, combined with the Industrial Revolution in the 19th century, prompted states to control the expansion of companies and introduce new legal structures.

The limited partnership was an early predecessor of contemporary companies.[40] It separated the roles of an investor, who provided essentials for maritime transport like a vessel, gear, and funds, from the ship's captain, who offered his expertise and risked his life. Upon the ship's return, both parties divided the expedition's profits.

This legal structure democratized investment and diversified risk-taking in maritime adventure. In Venice, Bruges, Amsterdam, Lübeck, and London, it fostered, among other things, the creation of a prosperous and increasingly powerful bourgeoisie.

The concept of a "legal entity" was developed in Europe and the United States[41] during the 19th century. It enabled companies to be recognized as entities distinct from their owners or shareholders. Legal entities can benefit from corporate rights and responsibilities similar to individuals, such as the ability to own property, sign contracts, sue, and be sued.

A New Tax Concept: Free Zones

The Laws of Livorno

Favorable taxes are not the only prerequisite for success.

For example, in 1591, Ferdinand of Medici promulgated the "Laws of Livorno," which offered a series of privileges and incentives for this Italian city.

(continued)

---

[39] Today, it is the oldest European industrial company still in operation. It has kept copies of almost all its board minutes. In 1998, it became Stora Enso following its merger with Stora Oyj of Finland.

[40] Doe, John. *The Evolution of Limited Partnerships in Renaissance Europe.* Cambridge: Cambridge University Press, 2020.

[41] In 1886, the recognition of corporations as legal entities was confirmed by the Supreme Court's decision in *Santa Clara County vs. Southern Pacific Railroad.* Although this was a tax case on its merits, the Supreme Court recognized in its ruling that corporations had rights as "persons" under the Fourteenth Amendment to the US Constitution. They thus became "legal persons."

> *(continued)*
>
> They included freedom of religion, tax exemption for foreign merchants, and the right for them to settle in the city and do business.
>
> The aim was to provide Tuscany with a port. The success was considerable, as these laws had a unique character. They offered asylum and protection to various persecuted groups in Europe, such as Jews and Muslims, who brought with them their skills and contacts.
>
> Whether for a port or a country, success also depends on attracting skills.

Free ports and free zones were established to facilitate trade by exempting goods from customs duties until they were sold or exported. This created areas where goods could be stored, handled, and sometimes processed. During the storage period in free zones, goods are not subject to the usual import and export taxes. Taxes only apply if the goods enter the host country, but not if they are re-exported.

This concept has been an essential factor in the prosperity of numerous ports: Venice in the Middle Ages; Singapore — founded in 1819 by Sir Stamford Raffles;[42] Hong Kong, which ceded to the British in 1842, just like Gibraltar in the 18th century; or Hamburg, which became a free port in 1888.[43]

The Imperative of Efficient Logistics

The success of the international trade industry depends not just on goods or financing but also on efficient logistics and effective management. From the late Middle Ages, European ports began operating like modern enterprises. Venice was a prime example of an exceptional organization.

In the 12th century, the Venetian shipyard was capable of arming 100 galleons in seven weeks! The standardization of production meant that identical parts could be manufactured and stored in all Mediterranean ports, enabling ships to be repaired quickly, wherever they were.[44]

---

[42] Glendinning, Victoria. *Raffles and the Golden Opportunity*. London: Profile Books, 2012.

[43] Such was their success that today, free ports have multiplied, as in Dubai (Jebel Ali), Shanghai, or Panama (Colon). There are even free ports on land, such as Geneva, or those adjacent to airports, like Changi in Singapore, Zhengzhou in China, or Incheon in South Korea.

[44] In 1571, at the Battle of Lepanto, which saw the defeat of the Turkish armada, more than half of the Christian vessels had been built in the Venetian arsenal.

Maritime transport continues to be crucial for globalization, with the OECD estimating that over 90% of global trade is conducted by sea. Of the world's ten largest ports, seven are Chinese. Singapore is in second place, after Shanghai. Busan, in South Korea, is in sixth place, and Rotterdam and Jebel Ali in Dubai vie for tenth. A country's economic power can also be gauged on the seas.[45]

This applies even to landlocked nations. Switzerland boasts the world's largest inland merchant fleet. Additionally, Geneva is a global hub for maritime trade and raw materials management.

A Focus on Added Value

Over time, technological, legal, and financial advances have established a fundamental principle: a nation's prosperity and competitiveness depend on its ability to turn resources into final products or services, creating added value. Many countries have driven this revolution towards economic globalization. I have had the privilege of visiting many of them and witnessing these changes, often before fully grasping their impact.

Chapter Takeaways

- Since antiquity, our perception of time and geography has changed profoundly. As communication improved and the world opened, people met and trade expanded.
- Over the centuries, trade has created an infrastructure and legal system that is still pervasive today. It has become a critical means of enrichment for nations, more than war and looting.
- Reviewing this history helps to understand the institutions and behaviors that continue to shape modern competitiveness – albeit sometimes in the background.

Where Next?

The next cluster of chapters takes us on a discovery trip to nations that have experienced the many aspects of competitiveness. Appropriately, it starts with Britain and the Industrial Revolution since this established many of the principles that would come to shape world competitiveness. It was also a revolution led by formidable entrepreneurs.

---

[45] United Nations Conference on Trade and Development (UNCTAD). (2022). *"Review of Maritime Transport 2022."* Geneva: United Nations. Available at: https://unctad.org/webflyer/review-maritime-transport-2022

2 | Countries That Made Their Mark on Competitiveness: Great Britain

Principle: Through innovation and engineering, a nation can convert its resources into products, fostering economic growth and the rise of an entrepreneurial middle class.

The Industrial Revolution

My father told me as a child that mastering English would ensure I never went hungry. Therefore, in the summers of the early 1960s, for three years in a row, I stayed with an English family as a "paying guest." They operated a center for young asthmatics in Devonshire, located in the southwest English countryside.

The summer days were calm. In the mornings, I worked on learning English and its measurements. Back then, there were pence, shillings, pounds, guineas, feet, and ounces. It was pretty bewildering for someone used to the metric system (and likely vice versa).

At lunchtime, we had to get used to English meals[1] and especially desserts. These inevitably took the form of a transparent, colorful jelly pudding that, once on the table, wriggled for an interminable time. At night in the dormitory, after lights out, we tuned into a radio and listened to new music from another world — the Beatles, the Rolling Stones, or the Beach Boys — broadcast by Radio Caroline from a ship off the British Isles.

The afternoon was devoted to fishing. But not just any fishing: river trout fishing by hand. The technique consisted of spotting a sunbathing trout near a rock, gently taking it under the belly, inserting a finger in the mouth, bringing it out through a gill, and pulling. In theory, it is simple; in practice, it is a little more complicated.

The problem was that many of these trout also took refuge in excavations found all along the rivers. These took the form of long, black, rocky tunnels. You had to dig deep here to catch the famous fish. Except that eels often inhabited these excavations! And they had a nasty habit of violently biting our fingers, perhaps to feed before their final journey to the Sargasso Sea.

The Great Canals

On the other hand, as I traveled up these rivers and many others in England, I was fascinated by the number of locks one could encounter. At the time, I was told they were there to allow pleasure boats to navigate the rivers and canals. It seemed to me, however, that all this work for pleasure boats was a little suspect.

For example, according to British Waterways, the government body responsible for most of Britain's waterways before being replaced by the Canal and River Trust in 2012,[2] there are over 2,000 locks in England. The same organization manages around 3,200 km of navigable canals in England and Wales. At one time, there were more than twice that number. I discovered later that the locks, canals, and even tunnels through which these pleasure barges meandered once had another function: they were the backbone of Britain's Industrial Revolution.

The first coal mines were developed in the Midlands around Newcastle, particularly in Derbyshire, Nottinghamshire, and Staffordshire counties. But to extract the coal, and before transporting it by barge on canals, a fundamental problem had to be solved: water!

Indeed, while the weather in England is, to use the local expression, quite "moist," the uninformed tourist does not realize that there is probably even more

---

[1] Somerset Maugham said that to eat well in England you had to eat "three breakfasts a day."
[2] Canal & River Trust (2013). *Annual Report & Accounts 2012/13*. Canal & River Trust.

water underground than above. The same applies to Wales and, of course, Ireland. I remember visiting an Anglo Base Metal zinc and lead mine in Lisheen, Ireland. The first operating cost item was to pump water from the mine into an adjacent artificial lake.[3]

Charles Dickens and Trains

On June 9, 1865, the famous English writer Charles Dickens was returning from Paris by train. At Staplehurst, England, 14 m of track was being repaired. The workmen forgot to signal this to the oncoming train.

The accident was inevitable. All the first-class carriages fell into the ravine, except for Charles Dickens's carriage. There were 10 dead and 50 injured. Charles Dickens spent the day comforting the wounded and dying. He became a hero and wrote many times of the horror of a train accident.

Charles Dickens was a celebrity, and his drama became that of a nation. Thanks to his genius for writing, it was as if everyone had had a train accident. Some called for trains to be banned.

Yet the government preferred to increase rail safety provisions, and engineers looked for new ways to increase brake efficiency. The world of rail transport changed.

It was a positive time for progress. When there was a problem, we solved it. Today, we tend to want to ban new technologies.

But can we really block innovations on a global scale, or isn't it more reasonable to work on making them safer?

A similar challenge occurred in Great Britain during the early Industrial Revolution in the 18th century. James Watt (1736–1819) addressed this by patenting a steam engine with a piston in 1769, making water pumping more efficient.[4] This innovation is often credited with kickstarting the Industrial Revolution and enabling large-scale coal extraction. But once the coal or iron ore had been extracted from the mine it had to be transported to factories or ports. That is where canals came in.

Perhaps the oldest is the Sankey Canal, opened in 1757 to transport coal from the St Helens' mines to Liverpool. It is sometimes referred to as the first canal of the

---

[3] The water would be returned to the mine later when operations were completed.
[4] Russell, Ben. *James Watt: Making the World Anew*. London: Reaktion Books, 2014.

industrial age. However, it was initially built as an improvement on a natural water-course. A few years later, in 1761, the Bridgewater Canal was opened. It is often regarded as Britain's first actual canal of the modern era. The Duke of Bridgewater[5] commissioned it to transport coal from his mines in Worsley to Manchester.[6]

A New World of Entrepreneurs

Richard Arkwright is best known for inventing the "Water Frame" in 1769, a revolutionary machine for spinning cotton. This invention made it possible to spin several strands of cotton simultaneously, considerably increasing efficiency and productivity compared to hand-spinning. He also created the first large factory. His spinning mills, powered by water (hence the name Water Frame), employed hundreds of workers.[7]

In 1775, Mathew Bolton joined forces with James Watt, inventor of the modern steam engine. Together, they founded Boulton & Watt to produce the steam engines at the heart of the Industrial Revolution. He played a pivotal role in advancing coin production methods. He secured a significant contract with the Royal Mint to manufacture high-quality coins in large quantities using steam-powered presses.

Joshua Wedgwood[8] eventually implemented enhanced manufacturing techniques, allowing for more efficient and large-scale production of high-quality ceramics. He created several new types of ceramics, such as Black Basalt and Jasperware, which became extremely popular due to their unique style and superior finish.[9]

The Greatest Engineer   The Industrial Revolution was driven by entrepreneurs who were often engineers and had a flair for marketing. Perhaps the most fascinating of these was Isambard Kingdom Brunel (1806–1859).[10] He was chief

---

[5] Malet, Hugh. Bridgewater: The Canal Duke, 1736–1803. Manchester: Manchester University Press, 1977.

[6] Then there was the Trent and Mersey Canal, which was begun in 1766 and was completed in 1777. It was designed by James Brindley to link Derbyshire, where coal was mined, with the Mersey and Trent, enabling faster transport.

[7] In 1760, Great Britain imported 1,000 tons of cotton to keep its spinning mills running; by 1850, production was so high that imports had soared to 220,000 tons!

[8] Hunt, Tristram. *The Radical Potter: The Life and Times of Josiah Wedgwood.* New York: Metropolitan Books, 2021.

[9] Joshua Wedgwood was among the first manufacturers to apply standardized production methods and strict quality control in his factories. It enabled him to ensure consistent quality and reduce production costs. The brand is still present today.

[10] Buchanan, R. Angus. *Brunel: The Life and Times of Isambard Kingdom Brunel.* London: Hambledon and London, 2002.

engineer of the Great Western Railway, a rail network linking London with western England and Wales. His innovations included wider gauge tracks and revolutionary engineering of roads and bridges for trains.[11]

He also revolutionized shipbuilding. He launched three gigantic ships: the Great Western, Great Britain, and Great Eastern. For the first time, ships of this size were built with steel hulls and powered by steam and propellers. The Great Eastern, for example, could sail from Great Britain to Australia with over 4,000 passengers on board.

The Trials and Tribulations of The Thomas Lawson

Competitors did not immediately recognize the magnitude of the steamship revolution introduced by Isambard Brunel.

In 1902, the Baltimore shipyard launched The Thomas Lawson, a prodigious sailboat with 7 masts and 25 sails.

Five years later, she sank in a storm off the Scilly Isles.

The shipyard's managers had wanted to address a fundamental paradigm shift with a strategy from the past and do more of the same.

It is often the same in the corporate world.

The English Industrial Revolution resulted in a considerable increase in the country's wealth and power. England would distance itself from the rest of the world in just a few years. To understand this, it is helpful to assess what other nations did.

Prosperity from the Perspective of Time

Angus Maddison and his successors at the University of Groningen in Holland produced the first estimates of GDP evolution over 2,000 years! They show a very different destiny for nations according to their relationship with trade and industrialization.[12]

---

[11] Among his most spectacular achievements are the Clifton suspension bridge in Bristol (still standing), a classic example of suspension bridge architecture, and the tunnel under the Thames in London.

[12] Maddison, A. (2010). "Historical Statistics of the World Economy: 1–2008 AD." Gröningen: University of Gröningen, Groningen Growth and Development Centre. Available at: https://www.rug.nl/ggdc/historicaldevelopment/maddison/

The Silver Manna

It is estimated that in 200 years, particularly after the discovery of the Potosi mine in Bolivia in 1545, Spain exported 200,000 tons of silver, or 80% of world demand.

What's more, the Chinese emperors of the Ming dynasty (1368–1644) demanded that, from then on, taxes be paid in silver money and not in kind.

In China, this was the case for provincial taxes in 1465, salt taxes in 1475, and exemption from corvée in 1485. World demand for silver exploded, with consequent inflation in Spain.

They assumed that China's GDP during the Han dynasty and Europe's in Roman times, in the year 1 CE were roughly identical, ranging from $600 to $800. China did not regain a similar level of wealth until 1963. Economic crises, wars, and epidemics have caused fluctuations throughout the country's history. The rapid population growth, up to the one-child policy, also absorbed much of China's increased agricultural and industrial productivity.[13]

In Europe, trends varied greatly from country to country. In 1300, Northern Italy was the wealthiest region, with a GDP per capita above $1,600. Textiles and maritime trade (mainly Venice, Genoa, and Florence) were the main reasons for this success. By 1600, the Netherlands had become Europe's leading country, with a GDP already exceeding $2,650 per capita, thanks in part to the spice trade (pepper and nutmeg, for example) and trade from Asia.

Great Britain supplanted the rest of the world, rapidly evolving from a trading nation in the 17th and 18th centuries to an industrial powerhouse. In 1820, Britain's GDP per capita was $1,706. Almost a century later, in 1913, it had risen to $4,921.

Some Countries Have Fallen Behind

Conversely, Spain did not take full advantage of its newfound riches. In 1600, the GDP per capita stood at $853. The influx of gold and silver (see insert) from the Americas significantly increased the wealth of the Spanish monarchy and the nobility, but not of the country. In 1820, Spain's GDP per capita was $1,000 and only improved to $2,056 by 1913, the lowest in Europe alongside Portugal. Wealth was not used to develop products or create a manufacturing industry, missing out on the Industrial Revolution.

---

[13] Today, China has caught up, and its GDP per capita exceeds $13,000.

Japan's industrial growth started late, taking off during the Meiji era (1868–1912). In 1820, its GDP per capita was $669, rising to $1,387 by 1913. After World War II, Japan saw massive industrial expansion, and today, its GDP per capita exceeds $40,000.

The Premise of a New Class

This divergence of destinies raises the question of the social conditions that enabled the Industrial Revolution in England and other parts of Europe but not elsewhere.

The standard explanation is that England had a bourgeoisie and a minor landed gentry willing to invest in a different developmental model. This explanation holds, but why did this social class emerge in England? One theory suggests that King Henry VIII helped create a middle class by seizing monasteries during his break from the Pope and the Catholic Church between 1536 and 1541 when the Crown took over monastic lands and properties.[14]

By distributing seized monastic lands, Henry VIII enabled the rise of a new class of wealthy landowners who could invest in agricultural improvements and early industrial ventures. These landowners had the capital to fund emerging industries, acting as precursors to the bourgeoisie before the Industrial Revolution.

The Emergence of the Bourgeoisie

In addition, the new landowners' estates were limited in size. They could not compete with the extensive agriculture developed by the established landed gentry, who had large estates. As they couldn't expand horizontally, they began to look vertically, underground, towards minerals and their extraction.

This rising social class gained wealth through international maritime trade. By the 18th century, London had become the world's top port, having replaced Venice as much of the Oriental trade shifted outside the Mediterranean, for example, around the Cape of Good Hope. London subsequently overtook its rival Amsterdam as trade with the North American colonies grew, challenging the Spanish and Portuguese galleons returning from their South American territories.

Later, London would have to compete with its former colonies in North America. In 1820, the per capita GDP in the United States was $1,257. By 1913, it had increased to $5,300. Today, GDP per capita is over $78,000. Within a century, despite experiencing two world wars, the United States emerged as the foremost economic power globally.

---

[14] The National Archives. *Dissolution of the Monasteries 1,536–1,540.* https://www.nation alarchives.gov.uk/help-with-your-research/research-guides/dissolution-monasteries-1536-1540/ (accessed March 1, 2025).

Brexit: The Voluntary Fracture of an Economy

Following the referendum on June 23, 2016, the United Kingdom formally exited the European Union on February 1, 2020. It is one of the rare examples of an economy voluntarily deciding to separate from its main economic partners.

Besides regaining political sovereignty, the economic goal was to boost British growth through numerous free trade agreements with countries like the former Commonwealth and the US.

Negotiating a free-trade agreement can be a lengthy process. For instance, the discussions between the European Union and Canada lasted over seven years (2009–2016). The negotiations for the agreement between the United States and South Korea took more than four years (2006–2010). Similarly, the talks between the European Union and Mercosur started in the late 1990s and were concluded in 2024.

Some agreements were completed more quickly, such as the free trade agreement between the UK and Australia in 2021, which took only a year and a half. The treaty ratifying Brexit between the European Union and the United Kingdom in 2020 was negotiated in less than a year. It is sometimes easier to separate than to join.

Economic impacts are challenging to measure. A 2024 study by Cambridge Econometrics for the Mayor of London[15] estimated that Brexit has cost the British economy $300 billion, with London losing 290,000 jobs and the country losing 2 million jobs.

Another study by the London School of Economics calculated that over 16,400 companies would have stopped exporting to the European Union, representing a loss of exports of $35 billion.[16]

An Emotional Decision?

Political factors and national pride may have influenced the vote. Still, a country that separates from its main economic partners often faces negative consequences. Economists have long argued against the illusion that a country, even a large one, can thrive in isolation.

The 2016 referendum resulted in 51.89% of voters favoring Brexit, while 48.11% opposed it. It is noteworthy that a simple majority determined such a significant decision. In contrast, corporate status changes typically require a qualified majority, often needing the approval of at least two-thirds of shareholders.

---

[15] Cambridge Econometrics (2024). Cambridge Econometrics Report: https://www.camecon.com/what/our-work/londons-economy-after-brexit-impact-and-implications (accessed May 14, 2025).

[16] London Business School, Center for Economic Performance (2024). Deep Integration and Trade, UK Firms in the Wake of Brexit. Available at: https://cep.lse.ac.uk/pubs/download/dp2066.pdf

While it is understandable that every country should be able to ask its people to choose their future, it may seem dangerous that such a fundamental decision could be made at the spur of the moment and by a simple majority of voters.

Chapter Takeaways

- Britain's Industrial Revolution emphasized the importance of transforming raw materials into finished products that could be exported worldwide.
- It was initiated by entrepreneurs, often engineers, who developed break-through technologies. They arose from a new social class: the bourgeoisie.
- Thus, Britain founded an industrial empire that is a prime example of globalization. However, unlike today, commercial and financial flows were directed mainly towards the center of the empire, London, and the large cities.

Where Next?

Cultural and linguistic proximity enabled the US to initiate its own Industrial Revolution based on the same policies as Great Britain but in a different environment and with a new mindset.

In just a few decades, the US became the most formidable industrial, technological, and financial power the world has ever seen. It has lasted until today. How?

3

Countries That Made Their Mark on Competitiveness: The United States

Principle: A country's success stems from the competitiveness of entrepreneurs who dare to found companies to manage their innovations and technologies.

The Birthplace of Management

When I first visited the United States in 1966, I flew from Luxembourg to Reykjavik in Iceland with the national airline, which at the time was called Loftleidir (one of the first low-cost airlines in history). Then, from Reykjavik, we flew directly to New York or, if the weather was bad, to a stopover in Gander, Newfoundland.

The flight was on a propeller plane. I recall that most passengers were emigrants, and upon arriving in New York, everyone sang and celebrated their arrival in the New World. The country offered stark contrasts: business hubs like New York versus quaint white houses in New England; Florida's beaches versus Arizona's deserts; Illinois's bitter cold versus Nevada's heat; and the self-righteousness of Massachusetts versus California's avant-garde vibe.

Skyscrapers as a Landmark of Success

The first impression of arriving in New York at the time was of the skyscrapers. It is hard to imagine today how different it was from the rest of the world. Merv Griffin, who had a TV show for 21 years, used to say that you could tell a tourist in Manhattan by the sunburn on his tongue (from looking up at the skyscrapers …).

Why Are There So Few Skyscrapers in Europe?

In most cases, restrictions on skyscrapers in Europe are intended to preserve historical or cultural heritage.

In Rome, for example, no modern building can exceed the height of St. Peter's Basilica, for both aesthetic and religious reasons.

London has conservation areas where building heights are limited to preserve the city's iconic views, including sites such as Parliament, the Tower of London, and St. Paul's Cathedral.

In Paris, the construction of the Montparnasse Tower (210 m high) in the city center aroused such disapproval that it is now forbidden to build new towers within the city limits.

The Eiffel Tower (330 m) is thus likely to remain the tallest building in Paris for some time to come.

Today, there are 320 skyscrapers in Manhattan, i.e. buildings over 150 m.[1] Yet skyscrapers are no longer exclusive to New York. They are just as common in Hong Kong, Shenzhen, Pudong (Shanghai), Dubai, and all the world's megacities. Skyscrapers have become markers of a country's competitiveness – or rather of a city's. They are extraordinary concentrations of skills and energy in a small space.[2]

Manhattan became an English territory after the Treaty of Breda in 1667, when the Dutch traded New Amsterdam for Suriname and the Moluccan islands, known for their nutmeg production. At the time, the general consensus was that the agreement greatly benefited the Dutch, considering Manhattan offered little more than a few scattered furs traders.

---

[1] Wikipedia. *"List of cities with the most skyscrapers."* https://en.wikipedia.org/wiki/List_of_cities_with_the_most_skyscrapers (accessed February 25, 2025).

[2] More than 50,000 people worked every day in the World Trade Center towers in New York before the 2001 attacks.

Ports and Competitiveness

To grasp the economic success of New York, it is essential to consider the significance of ports in a nation's economic growth. Initially, the Manhattan estuary was home to four key ports: Port Elizabeth, Newark, Red Hook, and Howland Hook. In 1962, Port Elizabeth became the pioneering port globally to focus primarily on container traffic. Today, nearly all cargo traffic has shifted from Manhattan and is managed in New Jersey and Staten Island.

The Power of J. P. Morgan

On October 24, 1907, at 1:30 p.m., a very agitated man appeared at Wall Street number 23, in front of the office of the famous financier J. P. Morgan. It was Ransom "Pay Me" Thomas (quite a nickname …), president of the New York Stock Exchange. He did not beat around the bush: if he did not have $25 million by 2.30 p.m., 50 brokers would go bankrupt, and the exchange would close.

J. P. Morgan immediately summoned 14 presidents of major banks to his office. He gave them 10 minutes to raise the funds.

By 2.16 p.m., they had already raised $23 million. A few minutes later, J. P. Morgan heard thunderous applause from across the street at the stock exchange.

The American financial system was saved by the fortitude of one single man.

In line with the logic of large port centers, the same development process as in Europe evolved: accounting, finance, logistics, and company legal status. New York is where the leading accounting and auditing firms originated. These firms, which have grown into the world's largest, include Deloitte, PWC, Ernst & Young, and KPMG.

Impact on Finance

But it is above all in banking that New York has left its mark on the US and the rest of the world. For a long time, it was so powerful that it replaced the role of the state in the country's monetary affairs (see insert on J.P. Morgan).

Despite this success, it became clear to the US Congress that the management of the financial system of an economy as large as that of the United States could not be left in private hands. President Woodrow Wilson created the Federal Reserve (the Fed) on December 23, 1913.[3] In 2024, the Fed's assets exceeded $7,800 billion: 45% of the world's commercial transactions are in dollars, and 59% of the world's foreign exchange reserves. China alone holds over $760 billion in US currency. This predominance of the dollar on a global scale also creates a dependence of other countries on the Fed's monetary policy.[4]

These advances established the groundwork for contemporary corporate legal structures, fostering significant economic expansion and innovation. New York City hosts over 250,000 businesses, with 89% having fewer than 20 employees, and is the headquarters for 43 of the S&P 500 companies – more than any other city globally.[5]

Beyond the Megacities

While New York epitomizes American competitiveness, the nation's prosperity isn't solely reliant on megacities. A flight from New York to San Francisco reveals expansive agricultural lands that are crucial to the country's success.

The US is the world's leading oil producer, with 12 million barrels per day, more than Saudi Arabia.[6] It is also one of the world's largest producers of coal, bauxite (and, therefore, aluminum), iron, copper, and nickel. However, unlike other nations rich in raw materials, the US has transformed them into advanced products and technologies. To frame it another way, American bauxite and aluminum ended up on the Moon.

The US is a top global producer of corn, soybeans, barley, and oats. Beyond domestic use, it is also a leader in agricultural exports. Additionally, these crops support livestock, making the US the leading beef producer, with about 20% of the world's production.

The US's competitive edge stems from its remarkable diversity, including major cities, extensive agricultural areas, a mix of industries and services, raw materials, and cutting-edge technology. The US may be unique in its ability to possess and excel across such a broad range of resources.

---

[3] Meltzer, Allan H. *A History of the Federal Reserve, Volume 1: 1913–1951.* Chicago: University of Chicago Press, 2003.

[4] As John Connally, who served as President Nixon's Treasury Secretary (before that, he had also been wounded in President Kennedy's limousine when he was assassinated in Dallas in 1963), put it: "The dollar is our currency but is also your problem."

[5] New York State Department of State. *"Corporation and Business Entity Database."* https://apps.dos.ny.gov/publicInquiry/ (accessed March 1, 2025).

[6] On the other hand, Saudi Arabia remains the world's leading oil exporter (its production is 9 million barrels/day but could be increased to 12 million). The US consumes most of what it produces, and therefore exports less.

California

I first went to California in 1970 as a student-tourist. Like everyone, I took the road from San Francisco to Los Angeles, inland to Nevada and Las Vegas, the Death Valley, Palm Springs, and Indian Wells, the home of show-business celebrities.[7]

Although California, with its 40 million residents, is the world's fourth largest economy due to its technology companies, it is also the top agricultural state in the country, producing 13% of the nation's output. It leads in fruit, vegetable, and dairy production, and agriculture initially drove its prosperity. However, the 19th-century gold and oil rushes, followed by the cinema and computer industries in the 20th century, transformed its economy and image.[8]

The extraordinary freedom of expression and attitude during the 1960s was particularly striking. It was evident in the clothing trends (with the hippies) and the music scene (like the Beach Boys). Everything seemed not only possible but effortless. For Europeans traveling from a more regulated and complex environment, visiting California felt like a breath of fresh air, allowing technological innovations to thrive.

An Emblematic Company

I returned to California in the 1980s to work for Hewlett-Packard, which I saw as a model company blending innovation, competitiveness, and respect for customers and employees. Founded in the late 1930s by Stanford engineers Bill Hewlett and Dave Packard, HP started by making an audio oscillator for Disney's Fantasia.[9]

Astronaut John Glenn

John Glenn was a legend. He was the first American to orbit the Earth in 1962, and the oldest to return in 1998 at the age of 77. There was a time when little boys dreamed of being astronauts like him; today they want to be YouTubers.

John Glenn was also a senator (Democrat, Ohio) and I chaired a session with him in the "Mike Mansfield" room in the US Senate. There was a striking

(continued)

---

[7] Palm Springs has a Frank Sinatra Drive.

[8] Harris, Malcolm. *Palo Alto: A History of California, Capitalism, and the World*. New York: Little, Brown and Company, 2023.

[9] They worked out of their garage, creating a legendary narrative for entrepreneurs. Their Stanford professor noted that business was good if their car was outside; if it was inside, it wasn't. Today, the garage is a California State Historic Site.

> (*continued*)
>
> contrast between the old-English woodwork of this room and the presence of the man who embodied the technological success of the United States.
>
> He was as rational and logical as his profession — or rather, his professions — demanded. Because the American tradition allows everyone to decompartmentalize their skills.
>
> John Glenn had been in the army, a fighter pilot, an engineer, an astronaut, a businessman, and a politician.
>
> A senior member of the US administration can come from the private sector or the academic world, spend some time in Washington, then leave for other horizons. No one sees any conflict there.
>
> When he left the room, I felt we had touched a little piece of the American dream.

The company put innovation and people at the heart of its competitiveness. I met Bill Hewlett on several occasions. He insisted that the company's profits were born in laboratories and research. It was applied research that led to a product.[10]

One of the company's leading products was the pocket calculator. As an engineer, Bill Hewlett requested a calculator small enough to fit in his shirt pocket. The initial prototype was too large. Consequently, it was returned, and the engineers measured his shirt pockets to design a new product. This resulted in a major success. Known as "concurrent engineering," this process involves research, production, and marketing working together throughout development. This ensures that the product can be manufactured and sold effectively.

Investing in Skills

Another story underlines the importance of investing in skills. At the end of World War II, many engineers who had worked in the war effort found themselves unemployed and on the market. At the time, Dave Packard and Bill Hewlett decided to employ as many of them as possible, even though they had no immediate need. They felt the engineers' wartime skills would eventually lead, one day,

---

[10] Packard, David. *The HP Way: How Bill Hewlett and I Built Our Company*. New York: HarperBusiness, 1995.

to successful products. This indeed occurred, demonstrating that the success of American companies often results from a blend of innovation, talent, entrepreneurship, and management.

Innovators

The US is renowned as a country of innovation. In 2020, the US Patent Office granted 388,000 patents.[11] This figure conceals a very different reality like all those relating to a country's patents.

Foreign citizens can also receive patents in various fields, from pure invention to design improvements. Japan, known for holding many patents, mainly focuses on production processes that make its factories more efficient. After World War II, Japan's edge was its ability to produce existing inventions like radios and cars better, faster, and cheaper.

Management and Entrepreneurs

Success in the US stems not only from fundamental innovations but also from effective management. Inventors often build companies around their inventions rather than just selling patents. For example, with 1,093 patents, Thomas Edison[12] created multiple companies, including General Electric. Similarly, Elon Musk's 23 patents are crucial to his industrial strategies.

Entrepreneurship is often considered America's national pastime. I've noticed that even cab drivers possess impressive economic insights. I once learned that some of them are actually entrepreneurs between ventures. In the US, failure and non-fraudulent bankruptcy are not as stigmatized as in other places.[13]

The close relationship between innovators and company founders was also at the root of the Industrial Revolution in Europe and Japan. The great names of today's companies are those of entrepreneurs who decided to create a company to exploit their inventions: Siemens (submarine cable), Bayer (aspirin) in Germany, Matsushita (the battery-powered bicycle lamp), and Toyota (a mechanical loom) in Japan.

---

[11] United States Patent and Trademark Office. "U.S. Patent Activity Calendar Years 1790 to the Present." https://www.uspto.gov/web/offices/ac/ido/oeip/taf/h_counts.htm (accessed March 1, 2025).

[12] Israel, Paul. *Edison: A Life of Invention*. New York: John Wiley & Sons, 1998.

[13] Peter Drucker (1909–2005), the father of modern management, said: "The fundamental purpose of a company is to create a customer." It is an attitude that is still common in the US today. Anyone can try it – and often want to do so.

A Culture That Has Spread

The HP Way has set an example in Silicon Valley. Traces of it can be found today in most major companies, from Apple to Google and Microsoft.

For the record, Steve Jobs recounted that in 1967 — at the age of 12 — he called Bill Hewlett directly at home, because he was looking for an electrical component. Bill Hewlett kindly helped him and even found him a summer internship with the company in 1969.

It was there that he met Steve Wozniak. Later, the two went on to create Apple.

Nowadays, especially in Europe, young innovators often prefer to sell their start-ups rather than expand them. While this can financially benefit the entrepreneur, it harms a country's competitiveness. Renewing the industrial fabric requires both innovation and the growth of new companies that create jobs and generate taxes.

This creates social mobility, which is essential to a country's prosperity, according to Joseph Schumpeter (1883–1850).[14] He likened society to a hotel, where the best rooms are always occupied by successful people who, however, are constantly changing over time.

A Legendary Corporate Culture

What set Hewlett-Packard apart and made it a model in Silicon Valley was its unique culture known as "The HP Way." This philosophy can be encapsulated by the following statement: "In a supportive and respectful corporate environment, employees will naturally do a good job." This approach was documented in Douglas McGregor's book *The Human Side of Enterprise*, published in 1960.[15] He identified two distinct categories of managerial attitude.

According to McGregor, X managers think employees naturally dislike work and require strict oversight, viewing pay as the only incentive. Conversely, Y managers are optimistic, believing employees will work hard and succeed if given a chance, driven by higher aspirations once their basic needs are met.

Douglas McGregor followed in the footsteps of a famous psychologist, Abraham Maslow (1908–1970),[16] who features in every economics course and introduced the

---

[14] McCraw, Thomas K. *Prophet of Innovation: Joseph Schumpeter and Creative Destruction.* Cambridge, MA: Harvard University Press, 2007.

[15] McGregor, Douglas. *The Human Side of Enterprise.* New York: McGraw-Hill, 1960.

[16] Maslow, Abraham. *Motivation and Personality.* New York: Harper & Brothers, 1954.

concept of the value pyramid. When our fundamental needs are met, we become driven by higher values like belonging, self-fulfillment, or developing a sense of purpose.

Clusters: A Formidable Concentration of Talent

Silicon Valley, stretching from the San Francisco Bay Area to San José, is often considered a classic "cluster." Though similar setups existed before (like Detroit for cars or New York for finance), this concept became highly influential in economics.

A cluster[17] refers to a geographic area where companies in the same sector share technologies, skills, and a value chain but still compete and don't formally integrate due to competition laws. Other clusters in California besides information technology include film and media near Los Angeles, aerospace and defense in the south towards San Diego, and agriculture and viticulture in the center and north (Sonoma and Nappa for wine).

Clusters frequently emerge from a nation's economic background. Outside the US, notable examples include London for finance, Bavaria and Baden-Württemberg for automotive and electronic components, Milan and Florence for fashion, Basel and Galway for life sciences, Toulouse for aviation, and Copenhagen for renewable energies.

In Japan, Osaka is renowned for mechatronics, Nagoya for automotives, Kobe for biotechnology and food industries, and Tokyo for finance. Many clusters are more contemporary, driven by proactive government measures. Examples include Bangalore and Hyderabad in India for electronics and online services and Singapore for finance, port, and trade services.

The primary benefit of clusters for companies lies in providing access to a comprehensive ecosystem encompassing technology, finance, and expertise within the same sector. This facilitates interaction among value chains without merging them.

Clusters often emerge near hubs of technology or expertise. For instance, Silicon Valley originated from Stanford University in Palo Alto. Some clusters grow around military activities, like telecommunications in Omaha, influenced by the US Strategic Air Command at Offutt Air Force Base.

In Israel, the defense sector has led to several tech clusters in cybersecurity, AI, drones, and biotechnology. The country also helps retired military personnel start businesses. The Unit 8200 Innovation and Entrepreneurship Support Program fosters innovation using alumni skills and networks.[18]

Dubai is notable for its successful cluster policies in various sectors: finance with DIFC, tourism with luxury hotels and conferences, trade and logistics via

---

[17] Perry, Martin. *Business Clusters: An International Perspective.* London: Routledge, 2005.

[18] Rousseau, J. Peter. *The History and Impact of Unit 8,200 on Israeli Hi-Tech Entrepreneurship.* Athens, OH: Ohio University, 2017.

Jebel Ali Port and Dubai International Airport, technology through Dubai Internet City and Dubai Silicon Oasis, and healthcare with Dubai Healthcare City. Similarly, Saudi Arabia aims to develop clusters in its Vision 2030 strategy, including petrochemicals in Jubail, finance and healthcare in Riyadh, commerce in Jeddah, mining in Ras-al-Khair, and business and tourism in Neom. Clusters attract foreign companies by providing a familiar environment, known competitors, and appropriate legislation and infrastructure.

However, clusters can create problems, too. They can destabilize the economy, especially for small and medium businesses, by concentrating major investments and top firms in specific areas. It often leads to the best jobs and highest salaries being limited to those clusters.[19]

Tariffs also Fracture an Economy

When President Trump took office in January 2025, he famously declared that "tariffs are the most beautiful word in the dictionary," adding "more than love and more than respect." A series of executive orders have supported this policy of fragmenting global trade and, consequently, supply chains.

The return to the Monroe Doctrine[20] can be partially attributed to the US trade deficit, which is projected to reach $918 billion by 2024. China accounts for $361 billion of this deficit. The European Union, Mexico, Vietnam, and Ireland follow in the list of contributors. Mexico and Canada are particularly affected as over 75% of their exports are directed to the United States.

This is also a reminiscent of the mercantilism theory[21] of the 18th century. Nations sought to export more goods than they imported. Accordingly, the state intervened to protect national industries, regulate trade, and introduce customs duties. Governments favored local industries and manufacturing to reduce dependence on imports. Sound familiar?

---

[19] To counteract this, some countries require foreign investors to establish skills and training centers to transfer technology to local employees and partners.

[20] US President James Monroe declared on December 2, 1823 "The American continents … are henceforth not to be considered as subjects for future colonization by any European powers." In exchange, the US pledged not to intervene in European affairs or conflicts. This doctrine guided the US administration until World War I.

[21] The earlier influencers were Thomas Mun (1571–1641) in England, and Jean-Baptiste Colbert (1619–1683), Louis XIV's minister of finance. However, it was Sir James Steuart (1712–1780) in England who theorized mercantilism in his book *An Inquiry into the Principles of Political Economy* (1767).

Adam Smith denounced the system's absurdity: "The wealth of a nation is not measured by the quantity of gold and silver in its treasury but by the total of its production and commerce. The maxim of every prudent master of a family is never to attempt to make at home what it will cost him more to make than to buy."[22]

A Challenge for Customs Authorities

Distinguishing the origin of a product from its ownership or, more precisely, from the country responsible for the greatest added value, presents challenges. For instance, an iPhone entering the US is categorized as a Chinese product. However, it is merely assembled in China, mainly by Foxconn near Shenzhen, and the Chinese value-added contribution does not exceed 6–7% of the total value.

Likewise, numerous imports from Mexico and Vietnam originate from American companies that either source or assemble products in these nations. Additionally, some organizations utilize these countries as an intermediate base for their operations.

Temu, a Chinese mail-order company, sends products to Mexico, where they are divided into low-priced shipments (typically under $250) that can be shipped back to the US duty-free. This legislative loophole is now being closed in both the US and Europe.

Ireland, the fifth largest contributor to the US trade deficit, also accounts for a surprisingly high export surplus. This situation results from large American companies, primarily in technology and pharmaceuticals, repatriating their profits to the US after benefiting from lower taxes in Ireland.

Tariffs: Opening a Pandora Box?

Inflation is the primary issue here. Approximately 50% of US imports are provided to American companies. Consumers typically do not purchase steel or aluminum bars directly. However, the companies that utilize these products, such as those producing beverage cans or cars, will likely transfer the cost increase directly to the final consumer.

The same negative impact can be anticipated internationally. A tariff war involves retaliation policies by economic partners. This can affect technology transfers, strategic supplies, and financial flows. As discussed later in this book, it encourages economic partners to consider cooperation and shift their business to other, more favorable nations.

---

[22] *The Wealth of Nations*, 1776, Book IV, Chapter II.

However, the US holds significant advantages in any trade conflict. Foremost among these is the dominant role of the dollar, which constitutes 49% of all international trade transactions and 58% of central bank reserves.

Second, several countries are significant creditors of the United States and hold large amounts of US Treasury bills. These include Japan ($1,060 billion), China ($760 billion), and the UK ($722 billion).[23] If the dollar depreciates, these countries will also experience a reduction in the value of their holdings.

Finally, American companies in the advanced technology sector have reached high valuations. The five largest companies – Apple, NVIDIA, Microsoft, Alphabet, and Amazon – in February 2025 had a combined market capitalization of $14.5 trillion, which is approximately 15% of the total value of the world's 10,000 largest companies.

The US remains a highly attractive market for companies, largely due to the Industrial Policy under the Inflation Reduction Act (IRA). Projections for 2024 indicate a significant rise in foreign investment in the country. This trend is also influenced by the decreasing attractiveness of China and Europe as investment destinations.

Nevertheless, in the long run, a tariff war is always negative for the competitiveness of countries. There are no winners, only losers. The recession of 1929 turned into a deep worldwide depression when countries isolated themselves and erected customs barriers against foreign products. Unfortunately, history is quickly forgotten.

Success Attracts Competition

In 1960, the United States accounted for 40% of the global GDP, and its companies were thriving worldwide. However, by 2023, its share of the global GDP had dropped to 24%, mainly due to rising economies like China. The ascent of China was not foreseen. Instead, the Soviet Union and the Bolshevik movement were considered a more immediate threat with their ideology that workers globally would unite to overthrow capitalism.

Chapter Takeaways

- The US is the only country that excels in practically every factor of competitiveness, from agriculture to advanced technologies, from manufacturing to services.

---

[23] Data for December 2024, source: US Department of the Treasury.

- It was also one of the first countries to establish a global economic presence through foreign direct investments, starting in Europe before expanding worldwide.
- The United States is renowned as the birthplace of management, a discipline that has contributed to the emergence of some of the world's most successful companies and has spread worldwide.

Where Next?

Throughout the 20th century, the greatest challenge to the United States came from the Soviet Union and then Russia. It was the other great empire with material and human resources that could challenge the supremacy of the United States.

Russia was also perceived as attacking the economic and political foundations of the West. Consequently, and for a long time, it monopolized the attention of government and business leaders. Russia was considered the greatest competitive threat. Why?

4 | Countries That Made Their Mark on Competitiveness: Russia

Principle: A country's economy is always shaped by history, for better or worse …

The Legacy of the Past

My first experience with Russia was when I lived in Cannes, the small town in southern France where I grew up. My family ran a haute couture business, catering to English, Belgian, and Russian gentry seeking the Côte d'Azur's sunshine. One of my summer jobs involved deliveries and collections, especially picking up fabric flowers for beautiful dresses. These flowers were crafted by emigrant Russian princesses, who had learned the skill as a pastime in their youth back in Russia.

Then came the revolution.

I took my bicycle, using a shoebox on the luggage rack to carry the flowers. These noble émigrés lived in rundown houses that looked unremarkable. But inside, they were wonderlands: museums filled with samovars, family silver, and many photos of the imperial family and Tsar Nicholas II. For the first time, I realized that another world had once existed and was now lost. I left with my fabric flowers in the shoebox, wondering what had happened.

I decided to learn Russian from one of these noblewomen; but I did not succeed. And when I went to Russia a few years later and tried to put together the few words I had learned, everyone burst out laughing. I was speaking a language that had all but disappeared over 60 years ago. I had a similar experience when I went to learn German in Vienna, Austria, in a small room with an elderly Austrian countess. She, too, had photos from another era all over her old apartment, including those of the Austro-Hungarian imperial court. And one of Emperor Franz Joseph with a little girl with curly blond hair on his lap: it was her.[1]

Nevertheless, I decided to go and see what was happening on the other side of our world, on the other side of the Iron Curtain in Russia. My opportunity arose in July 1968 during a student trip to the former Soviet Union.

Ukraine

Before heading to Moscow, we stopped in Kyiv. Ukraine boasted an abundance of wheat, citrus, and fruit. Additionally, it had significant deep-water ports like Odesa and Sevastopol, facilitating the export of its goods. However, as we discovered later in our research on national competitiveness, wealth in raw materials does not come without risk. To understand the country, we visited a kolkhoz and picked apples. Then, we took part in a session at school with Ukrainian children. It was a math lesson, and I was asked to go to the blackboard to solve a second-degree equation, which, in my opinion, was incredibly complex. I failed. When I sat back down, the teacher told the class that this was evidence that bourgeois countries dislike teaching mathematics. She said math stood for truth, while the bourgeois camp favored falsehoods. I did not know I was part of an international conspiracy. In my opinion, I was just bad at math.

> ### Ukraine and Sicily
>
> Ukraine has been independent, but much of its history has been marked by invasions: the Mongols (the Golden Horde), then the Poles, the Lithuanians, the Ottomans, the Austro-Hungarians, Nazi Germany, and of course the Soviet Union.

---

[1] That world, too, had been turned upside down. As a reminder, outside, on Schwarzenberg Platz, stands the monument to the heroes of the Soviet Union. After World War II, her neighborhood and home were under Russian occupation.

> Wealth is always attractive to neighbors.
>
> The situation is quite similar to that of Sicily. Like the Ukraine, it was once a granary, strategically well placed as the intersection between the western and eastern Mediterranean. The parade of invaders in Sicily is equally impressive: Greeks (and the Athenians lost the Peloponnesian War when they tried to land in Sicily), Romans, Byzantines, Arabs, Normans (with the Dukes of Anjou), and finally Italians, with Garibaldi's landing at Marsala in 1860.

Nevertheless, I was confronted with the politicization of education and political propaganda for the first time. It is impossible to understand, then and probably now, the economic development of certain countries without understanding the impact of the political environment, whatever it may be.

St. Petersburg

Next, we headed for St. Petersburg, the city of Peter the Great. An impressive city built on stilts, it required the requisition of hundreds of thousands of workers (soldiers, peasants, prisoners of war), many of whom died of exhaustion or disease.

What always struck me about Peter the Great was his willingness to go and learn, by himself, in the West, the techniques that were needed to develop his country. His journey to Europe, referred to as the "Great Embassy," occurred between 1697 and 1698.[2] His primary goals were to find allies for Russia against the Ottoman Empire and acquire knowledge of Western technological advancements across multiple disciplines to modernize the Russian military and society. Peter the Great spent some time in the Netherlands, where he worked incognito in the shipyards of Zaandam (near Amsterdam) to learn shipbuilding, a skill he considered essential for his military navy. He also familiarized himself with other Western technologies and recruited experts to work in Russia.[3]

In a way, this was an apprenticeship, a widespread practice in Europe that rarely included a tsar or king. Louis XVI of France enjoyed locksmithing as a pastime, perhaps excessively. One day, a courtier told him: "Sire, when the king does the work of the people, the people will do the work of the king." An insightful premonition …

---

[2] Massie, Robert K. *Peter the Great: His Life and World*. New York: Ballantine Books, 1980.

[3] The following year, in 1698, he went to England, this time out in the open, where he continued his study of shipbuilding and was impressed by the modernity of the Royal Navy. He also visited factories and museums and met with scientists and political leaders. On this occasion, King William III of England signed a treaty of cooperation with Russia. Later, he was to continue his "study" trips to Austria (1698), Germany, and finally France (1717).

Industrial Espionage

In 1712, the French Jesuit priest François-Xavier d'Entrecolles, who lived in Beijing, was instructed by the French court to unravel the mystery of Chinese porcelain manufacture: what gave it an inimitable quality?

He circulated several letters detailing the manufacturing process and even sent samples of Kaolin, the material that explained the transparency and finesse of Chinese porcelain.

On this basis, European porcelain production expanded, with Meissen in German Saxony, the Manufacture de Sèvres in France, Chelsea in Great Britain, and Capodimonte in Italy.

The current fear of industrial espionage in China (and a few years ago in Japan) is deeply rooted in history.

Peter the Great understood that his new empire would remain weak if it did not master the most advanced techniques and spread skills throughout the workforce. He wanted to be an example of this learning process. But he was also undertaking a bit of industrial espionage.

Back to St. Petersburg. On Nevsky Prospect, in front of the Stroganov Palace, I was hit by a bus because, as usual, I crossed the street without looking. However, the driver made me stay on the bus for a while because she wanted to ensure I was OK. This was not just kindness: crashing into a stranger could have cost her job. It seemed excessive to me, because it was my fault.[4]

Moscow

We headed for Moscow on the "Red Arrow," the legendary train that links the two cities. For tourists, Moscow was essentially Red Square, the Goum (the universal state store), Lenin's mausoleum, and, above all, the impeccable changing of the guard. Later, during the Yeltsin era, I was struck by the fact that the changing of the guard was no longer as perfectly timed as it used to be. Sometimes the military can demonstrate the changed mentality of a country.

The plaques honoring the significant battles of World War II at the entrance to Red Square grabbed my attention. They mention Leningrad, Kursk, Stalingrad,

---

[4]A few minutes later, a matron entered the bus, and I decided to give her my seat. She grabbed me violently by the shoulders and made me sit down again. She went on to explain that in the Soviet Union, men and women were equal and that there was no reason to give her privilege.

and major Ukrainian cities like Kyiv, Sevastopol, Kharkiv, and Odesa. This may explain why many Russians still view Ukraine as part of the Russian Empire.

The Complicated Relation Between Two Empires

Peter the Great also turned his attention to the East and Siberia. In 1689, he signed the Treaty of Nertchinsk[5] with Emperor Kangxi of China's Qing dynasty,[6] marking the first border agreement between Tsarist Russia and China. This treaty ended years of conflict over Siberia's Amur region and established an official boundary between the two empires.

Despite occasional cooperation, relations between the two empires have always been tense, even when circumstances have brought them closer together. Russia has always feared that China would invade Siberia to gain access to land and raw materials. Simultaneously, China views Russia as an occupier, especially since the Vladivostok region was ceded to Russia by the Treaties of Aigun (1858) and Peking (1860).[7] China has never forgotten that, in 1960, due to ideological differences and disagreements over the strategies of the international communist movement, the Soviet Union withdrew all its advisors and engineers overnight. This marked the end of the close cooperation that had helped develop China's industrial and technological infrastructure in the first decades after the Chinese revolution of 1949. The result was a deep-seated mistrust between the two empires, which remains to this day.

Regardless of the political regime, attention remained focused on the Western part of White Russia. The rest of the Soviet Union was perceived as existing primarily to supply raw materials and labor. Whether communist or not, the logic of empire still dominated.

Soviet Communism

In 1968, the Soviet Union still appeared strong. No one could have imagined that 20 years later it would collapse. In the streets, slogans from the great Bolshevik revolution decorated every facade. Some were a reminder that the revolution also had economic ambitions: "Communism means all power to the Soviets and the electrification of the whole country."

---

[5] A small town in Russian Transbaikalia near the Shilka River.

[6] Hung, Hing Ming. *The Brilliant Reign of the Kangxi Emperor: China's Qing Dynasty*. New York: Algora Publishing, 2016.

[7] I have also met Russians born in Harbin, the capital of Heilongjiang province in northeast China. Although Chinese, this city received a large Russian population, first to build the end of the Trans-Siberian Railway, then for those who wanted to escape the Bolshevik revolution of 1917. For a time, Harbin was known as the "Moscow of the East."

However, nobody seemed to be fooled. The enthusiasm of the early days and the exploits of Stakhanovism[8] had given way to resignation. Whether on the streets or in private, it was evident that people were adjusting to a world where hope was absent. Nonetheless, it was surprising that intellectuals in Europe and the United States continued to identify with a communist theory that had vanished.[9]

Why Did Soviet Communism Collapse?

I once asked my economics professor[10] at the University of Lausanne who he thought was the greatest economist. He responded that it was undoubtedly Karl Marx. He clarified that, in his opinion, Karl Marx created the most logical and rational system to explain economic mechanisms. However, he noted that its fundamental assumptions were flawed despite the system's coherence. Karl Marx viewed men as altruistic and rational but, in reality, they are selfish and emotional.

Another inspiring insight comes from the research of the most stimulating thinker of the 20th century, Sir Karl Popper (1902–1994).[11] His work on the philosophy of science and his reflections on society and politics have considerably impacted many generations of scientists, politicians, and academics. The "falsification" principle he proposed differentiates science from non-science and is now a cornerstone of epistemology. Popper suggested that knowledge progresses by identifying failures or inconsistencies that challenge an accepted theory. When one part of a theory fails, the entire theory falls apart. By Popper's definition, if a theory is not entirely consistent and contains even a single exception, it should be considered incorrect. The most minor flaw invalidates a theory.

The assertion that "all swans are white" is an example. Popper argues that just because we observe only white swans in our region, no matter how many, it cannot confirm the assertion's validity. The theory is disproven if a black swan is found, as happened near Perth, Australia.[12] Then, it must be supplanted by a new theory that acknowledges the existence of black swans.

---

[8] Alexei Stakhanov (1906–1977) was a Soviet miner famous for his exceptional productivity at work, who became a symbol of Soviet industrial propaganda. The authorities claimed that in a single night's work on August 31, 1935, he extracted 102 tons of coal, 14 times the normal amount of his fellow miners.

[9] Some had left the Communist Party after discovering the Stalinist purges. Conversely, others tried to reconcile with it or overlook the ugly aspects.

[10] François Schaller, 1920–2006.

[11] His two most important books are: *The Logic of Scientific Discovery.* London: Hutchinson & Co., 1959; and *The Open Society and Its Enemies.* London: Routledge, 1945.

[12] Playford, Phillip E. *Voyage of Discovery to Terra Australis by Willem de Vlamingh in 1696–1697.* Perth: Western Australian Museum, 1998.

Karl Popper extends his theory to the democratic system. According to him, its strength lies in its capacity for self-criticism, its acceptance of constant internal attack, and its search for error, enabling it to reform and strengthen itself constantly. In contrast, the weakness of Soviet communism was precisely its refusal to accept internal criticism and its inability to reassess and adapt to changing conditions.

Thus, communism failed because it was static and inward-looking.

Corporate Inertia

The same concept applies to companies. In a market economy, competition is a mechanism that enables all companies to attack the market leader to prove that its business model is weakening and becoming obsolete. When the leader collapses due to the onslaught from other companies, it is replaced by another company — that will ultimately suffer the same fate.

Ignoring internal criticism leads to company failure because they lose the crucial input necessary for reforming or reinventing themselves. No matter how successful or profitable, a company cannot thrive long-term through maintaining the status quo. This also justifies anti-monopoly laws or laws against abuse of a dominant position. A company that blocks this natural adaptation process by stifling market forces inhibits the innovative potential of other companies and a country as a whole.

Two Perils: Complacency and Arrogance

In business, as in government, excessive certainty leads to complacency and arrogance. These two attitudes have led to more failures than any strategic error. In the Soviet model of communism, there was no such thing as uncertainty. The party and its leaders showed the way and had an answer to every question. The system could never be questioned or criticized. Communism declined because it could not reform and adapt to a changing world.

Ultimately, we must question why many individuals in a nation or an organization tolerate false beliefs and indoctrination. Why does reality often give way to illusions? One explanation may be provided by Benjamin Constant (1767–1830) in his book *Principles of Politics*. He wrote: "Men are prone to enthusiasm and to get drunk on certain words. As long as they repeat them often, reality no longer matters to them."[13]

---

[13] Constant, Benjamin. *Principles of Politics Applicable to All Governments.* Translated by Dennis O'Keeffe. Indianapolis, IN: Liberty Fund, 2003. Originally published 1815.

Today, we might call this propaganda or brainwashing. It plagues nations and companies run by authoritarian, self-centered leaders who suppress critical thinking.[14]

War and the Economy

Wars fracture an economy like no other event. In general, also, because they last a long time. They have shaped Russia's history and identity. War also affects the international community, as discussed later in this book, or an individual country, as with the conflict in Ukraine that started in February 2022.

In 2025, Russia's defense and national security spending exceeded 8% of GDP. It represented over 40% of government spending. In a war economy, priority is given to military investments, often reducing funding for other civilian sectors like education, health, or pensions.

The initial impact of a war economy is typically inflation due to increased government expenditure and the scarcity of other goods. In Russia, inflation reached 9.5% in 2024. The population has experienced this primarily through a rapid rise in the cost of living, particularly in essential products. Interest rates also increased, exceeding 20% in December 2024. The risk of corporate insolvencies rises as demand falls and the cost of capital rises. These factors contribute to currency volatility. Between 2022 and early 2025, the ruble depreciated by 22% relative to the dollar.

A war effort also destabilizes the labor market: 43% of Russian companies reported difficulties hiring or retaining staff in 2023. Skilled personnel were attracted by better salaries in the state-owned companies supporting the war effort. Some left the country; others were enrolled in the army.

GDP data overlook the structural changes of a war economy, focusing only on expenditures, not their allocation or relevance. The Russian government predicts 2.5% growth in 2025 (versus the IMF's 1.4%). A war economy creates an illusion of prosperity. It redirects infrastructure investments that are essential for a nation's future development and adversely impacts the well-being of the population.

As Ernest Hemingway pointed out, referring to war and inflation: "Both bring temporary prosperity; both bring permanent ruin."[15]

---

[14] Before leaving, we gave our young Russian guide some balls of wool to knit clothes for her expected child, as we had been told that this kind of gift was very much appreciated in Russia. The next day, the state police came to our hotel and questioned us to find out if this young person was trafficking with us. Such were the times.

[15] Hemingway, Ernest. "Notes on the Next War: A Serious Topical Letter." *Esquire*, September 1935.

Chapter Takeaways

- Throughout history, Russia has been an empire with a torn relationship between Western Europe and Asia. This duality has impacted the development of its economy and trade.
- Russia is immensely rich in natural resources, space, and population. Despite this, it has not been able to transform this wealth into competitiveness and expand its businesses to the rest of the world.
- Centralization has long hindered Russia's potential. Under communism, the impossibility of criticizing policies led to inertia. Competitiveness is based on constantly questioning economic models and the ability to reinvent the future.

Where Next?

We move now from Russia to China, where the competitiveness model was more pragmatic, especially following the open-door policy implemented in 1978.

China's economic development was rapid, formidable, and unparalleled in recent history. In a few decades, it became the world's production workshop and a leader in new technologies, particularly environmental. Success was achieved within the framework of an economy rooted in China's age-old traditions. How was this possible?

5 | Countries That Made Their Mark on Competitiveness: China

Principle: Each nation may have its development strategy, but success relies on coherence and consistency.

Another New World

In October 1981, I landed at Beijing airport for the first time. As managing director of the World Economic Forum (WEF), I led a delegation of business leaders from Europe and the United States.

Looking out of the plane's window, I saw hundreds of peasants on bicycles waiting for our plane to leave the airstrip so they could cross it and return to their fields. Today, things are quite different …

We were accommodated in an army hotel that was surprisingly comfortable. During our initial dinner in the spacious hall where all the guests assembled, we felt somewhat uneasy. Having been portrayed negatively for so long, we wondered how we, as Western capitalists, would be received. Instead we were impressed by how friendly everyone was. Curiosity probably played a role as well.

First Meeting, First Impression

Our first meeting was with CITIC (China International Trade and Investment Company). We were in a miserable, freezing cold room. Underneath the executives' pants, woolen underwear could be seen protruding. Today, CITIC's Beijing skyscraper has 109 floors and stands at 528 m. The one in Hong Kong is smaller, just 126 m high and 33 stories.[1]

There was a strong symbolism in this first visit. CITIC's chairman at the time was Rong Yiren. He was considered a "red millionaire," one of those wealthy industrialists from the Shanghai region whose family had rallied to the Communist Party. The message was one of China's new pragmatism. Henceforth, all skills and contacts were accepted to ensure the development of the open-door policy.

The First Chinese Company

Our first company visit was to a refrigerator manufacturer in the Beijing area. When we arrived, we found ourselves in a foundry. The company managers in the delegation asked me if we had come to the wrong address.

After some investigation, we discovered we were in the correct location. Under the then-dominant economic model of total vertical integration, companies were required to smelt the metal components for their products.

---

[1] Qin, Xiao. *The Theory of the Firm and Chinese Enterprise Reform: The Case of China International Trust and Investment Corporation.* London: Routledge, 2012.

Each company was isolated from others. Moreover, the central authorities determined prices and production quantities aligned with the development plan. The idea that a market and consumers could make their own choices was totally alien.[2]

Military Considerations Were Never Far Away

Two years later, I became a member of the China Enterprise Association (CEMA), one of the first foreigners to do so. At the time, I had 400,000 Chinese colleagues. I was in charge of the WEF symposia in China and always kept a few days at the end of the meetings to educate myself.

The Chinese authorities asked me what I wanted to do, and I replied that I liked visiting factories. I have always been convinced you understand a company or a country better by visiting its factories. But I had unintentionally embarrassed my hosts. After much discussion and reflection, they decided to trust me, and I was able to visit factories all over the country. I then understood their reluctance.

Factories in China during that period had very high ceilings, making it easier to switch to war production, such as tanks and planes. Each company's facilities served both commercial and military needs – hence my hosts' concerns.

The Open-Door Policy

The leap forward for the Chinese economy began in December 1978, when Deng Xiaoping announced the so-called "Open Doors" policy. After ten years of Cultural Revolution (1966–1976), China had radically changed direction and held economic modernization as its primary objective. The plan was to stimulate internal and external competition to increase efficiency, reform agriculture, and balance political control and economic reform to reduce social and economic disparities. To achieve this, the Chinese people had to learn from the advanced economies and integrate their country into the global economy. Deng Xiaoping illustrated this change with the famous phrase: "It does not matter whether the cat is black or white, as long as it catches the mouse."[3]

The development of China's competitiveness was based on several principles that have since inspired many other countries.

---

[2] On the other hand, company directors had immense power over their employees. Later, I visited steel or coal production companies where the manager would explain that he regulated the lives of tens of thousands of employees, to whom he had to provide housing, education for children, and family planning …

[3] We tend to forget that he added – and this is important for understanding what is happening today – that "when you open the window, you let the flies in too."

Pragmatic and Stable

Pragmatic implementation of policies did not exclude a sense of direction. The various development plans clearly described what foreign companies could and could not do. Specific sectors remained closed. However, rules were established and remained relatively constant. Other countries, such as India, have suffered from changing their economic legislation – whether open, closed, or half-open – too quickly. Businesses can adapt to almost any conditions, provided they know what is permissible and can rely on a predictable legislative framework.

In China, investment efforts have primarily targeted infrastructure, especially in the eastern regions near the coast, leveraging the availability of ports for export-ing goods.[4] In contrast, other countries' leaders have often developed strategies to attract foreign companies based solely on favorable taxes. Nonetheless, launching a low-cost operation is pointless if there are no facilities to transport goods to a port or railway station for export.[5] In addition, security is crucial for attracting foreign investment, covering assets, people (especially expatriates), intellectual property, and legal protection.

The Tremendous Impact of Special Economic Zones

China accepted from the outset that it could not develop the whole country at once. It was a considerable mental revolution in a country where absolute equality had been the norm for decades.

In 1980, the government created "Special Economic Zones" to attract foreign investment and encourage interaction with Chinese companies.[6] A Special Economic Zone is more than just a free port, although that is how it often begins. For example, the Jebel Ali Special Economic Zone in Dubai was built around port infrastructure. The same is true of China. Hong Kong is considered one of Asia's oldest Special Economic Zones. However, tax benefits are not the only factors that matter here. Special Economic Zones encompass laws governing business estab-lishment, expedited administrative processes, and the option to employ local or expatriate workers.

---

[4] Infrastructure investments (transport, energy, and housing) have historically represented 30 and 40% of the country's fixed capital expenditure.

[5] This was a problem in Russia during the Yeltsin era. Some companies had to hire private security firms to ensure that products leaving their factories were not hijacked by mafia on the train journey to the border.

[6] Tao, Yitao, and Zhiguo Lu, eds. *Special Economic Zones and China's Development Path.* Singapore: Springer, 2018.

The Miracle of Shenzen

Initially, there were four Special Economic Zones in China: Shenzhen, Zhuhai, Shantou, and Xiamen; 90,000 foreign companies have benefited from this status.

Shenzhen, which was a fishing village 40 years ago, has received almost $300 billion in foreign investment. It has also benefited from its proximity to Hong Kong, now linked by a bridge, and Macau.

Between 1981 and 1993, its growth rate was 40% per year. Today, the metropolitan area has a population of 18 million.

The concept has met with considerable success. According to PwC,[7] there were 845 Special Economic Zones in 1997. Today, there are 5,400 in 147 countries.[8]

Some countries are ready to consider further steps. Dubai, for example, is considering introducing a customary law system (as in England) for its 26 free special zones. The idea is that this type of legislation, as opposed to the civil law found in France with the Napoleonic Code, would be more conducive to business. The economist Friedrich Hayek (1899–1992) proposed the same idea in the last century.

Primarily, Special Economic Zones need effective investment in physical, financial, and legal infrastructure because the goods produced in these areas are typically intended for export. In addition, they must also create an attractive environment for expatriates through housing, tourism infrastructures, or access to culture.[9] In this context, a critical aspect is to integrate the foreign community.

While Special Economic Zones can be very effective in boosting a country's competitiveness, they sometimes come up against political constraints. South Africa is a prime example. I believe Cape Town's development should have followed the model of a Special Economic Zone due to its strategic location, port and airport, advanced financial system, service industry skills, English proficiency, and expatriate-friendly atmosphere. However, and regrettably, Cape Town was also perceived as a "white" city defined by apartheid, making it politically contentious. Otherwise, Cape Town had the potential to develop into another Dubai.

---

[7] PwC. (2021). "Special Economic Zones: Global Best Practices and Emerging Trends." London: PwC. Available at: https://www.pwc.com

[8] Developed economies, like the US with its Foreign Trade Zones, have adopted this strategy. Longstanding zones include New York, Honolulu, Atlanta, Louisville, Dallas, and Puerto Rico. These areas leverage the nation's infrastructure while offering streamlined administrative and customs processes.

[9] For example, there are branches of the Louvre and Guggenheim museums in Abu Dhabi and the Centre Pompidou in Dubai.

In China, the Special Economic Zones capitalized on production, which quickly became a comparative advantage on a global scale. China rapidly established itself as the workshop of the world. It had it all: an abundant workforce, a strong work ethic, available land, a rapidly developing infrastructure, and extremely low wages.[10]

Finally, China decided to put its political ideology to one side. It did not disappear, but was kept in the background. It was invisible to foreign eyes. Chinese authorities and industrialists alike showed great modesty. For the moment, the aim was to learn from more advanced countries.

The Chinese Thinking Underlying the Economy

Understanding China's rise in competitiveness requires appreciating Chinese thinking, which differs significantly from the perspectives of countries where international companies previously operated. China is the only country that can be defined simultaneously as a territory, a prominent ethnic group (the Han), a language, a script, and a political and administrative system that has been functioning for almost 2,500 years.

Therefore, Chinese economic thought and its impact on business management are closely linked to the country's history.[11] Chinese thought values order and harmony with the environment, reflected in its hierarchical system of society. In contrast, Western thought has prioritized individualism and power and has often conflicted with nature since the ancient Greek era.

Between Imagination and Reality

In Western imagination, the famous Silk Road plays a central role in relations with China.[12] Silk has been cultivated in China for over 3,000 years. It reached the Mediterranean at Antioch in Syria, from where it was shipped to Rome and, later, Venice. A little further north, it reached Trebizond on the Black Sea, where it continued by ship to Constantinople and the rest of Europe.[13]

In the Roman Empire, silk held an immense appeal for the wealthy, resulting in considerable expenditure that drained the country's gold reserves. The Roman

---

[10] When China opened up to the rest of the world in 1980, labor costs were on average 20 times lower than in Europe.

[11] During my travels in China, I often spoke with one of my colleagues, Professor Pan Cheng Li. He had spent much of his life studying how ancient Chinese texts impacted business management today.

[12] It began in Xi'an (in fact, from Chang'an, the former imperial capital), where a stele marking its start can still be seen today.

[13] Hansen, Valerie. *The Silk Road: A New History*. Oxford: Oxford University Press, 2012.

Senate tried to ban silk – even then, trade protection measures were fashionable. Finally, the secret leaked out to the West. Legend has it that a Chinese princess hid silkworms in her hair before marrying a prince from Khotan (a small kingdom near Tibet). Another describes how the precious worms were brought back to Constantinople by two monks sent by Emperor Justinian in the 6th century. They put them in their boots (which can't have been very comfortable).[14]

Monks as Adventurers

As early as 1249, the King of France, Saint-Louis, sent a delegation led by the Dominican André de Longjumeau to the court of the Mongol kings who had just founded the Yuan dynasty in China. Other Franciscans would make the same journey a few years later, including Guillaume de Rubrouck,[15] Barthélemy de Crémone, and Jean de Plan Carpin.

The Jesuits made the most notable contributions to the relationship between Europe and China. In 1582, Michele Ruggieri and Matteo Ricci received authorization to reside in China, particularly at the Emperor's court in Peking in 1601. Matteo Ricci, a theologian well-versed in astronomy, physics, and mathematics, has his tombstone preserved in Beijing. He is also the author of a method called "Le Palais de Mémoire" – The Memory Palace[16] – which offers a mnemonic means of remembering the most important passages of the Bible to proselytize.[17] We often overlook the fact that many Jesuit missionaries lost their books during their perilous journeys to China.

The craze for China continued unabated. In 1667, the Jesuit Father Athanase Kircher published a book on China, which included the first dictionary. It was a monumental work, all the more remarkable because Father Kircher had never set foot in China. By the 18th century, virtually every European palace had a Chinese room with lacquered screens, porcelain, and jade trinkets. The fascination was mutual. The palaces that can be visited today in China, such as those in the Forbidden City, show the European gifts appreciated by the emperors, including clocks, automata, and astronomical instruments.

---

[14] Subsequently, silk production began to develop outside China as early as the Middle Ages. In Europe, it started in the 10th century, in Sicily at Catanzaro.

[15] Rubrouck, Guillaume de. *Voyage dans l'Empire Mongol (1253–1255)*. Translated by Claude and René Kappler, with preface and notes. Paris: La Découverte/Poche, 1990.

[16] Ricci, Matteo. (1596). *Method of loci* (as part of his memory techniques). In J. Spence (1984), *The Memory Palace of Matteo Ricci*. New York: Viking Penguin.

[17] Matteo Ricci's method involved arranging his ideas and knowledge in the different palace rooms he could visit according to his needs. Much later, Napoleon used a similar system. He organized his ideas in a large mental secretary and claimed to be able to open and close the drawers at will.

The Influence of Confucianism and Taoism

Confucianism (Kongfuzi, Master Kong, 551–479 BCE) was the first major philosophical influence, suggesting a hierarchical society with the emperor at the top of the nation, the father heading the family, and the manager leading the company. Fundamental principles such as filial piety, education, thrift, discipline, and hard work are also paramount.[18] These values resemble those found in Protestantism and Calvinism, which were important during the Industrial Revolution in Europe. Consequently, Confucianism facilitated China's rapid industrialization during the "Open Doors" policy by emphasizing education, discipline, and hard labor.[19]

Taoism (Lao-Tzu, 6th century BCE) is the other great pillar of Chinese thought. It focuses on the individual and harmony with nature. The goal of Taoism is a mastery of body and mind in tune with the rhythm of the world around us.[20]

From an economic perspective, Confucianism sets hierarchical norms and behaviors within society's framework, whereas Taoism provides insights into individuals' mental attitudes. Characteristics like self-control, politeness, and avoiding immediate confrontation are often observed during negotiations with Chinese businesspeople. However, they should not be mistaken for weakness. Many Western entrepreneurs have been taken aback by the disparity between the polite nature of discussions and the harsh decisions that may follow. Form and substance do not always align.

The Game of Go and Strategic Thinking

The game of Go has significantly influenced strategic thinking in China, Japan, and Korea. In contrast to chess, which focuses on offensive tactics, Go emphasizes strategic positioning and gaining influence.[21] The objective is to encircle and eventually stifle the opponent. Numerous military leaders have adopted Go strategies in their campaigns. Similarly, Chinese entrepreneurs often form alliances and business relationships to enhance their market influence. Historically, these corporate alliances have expanded substantially, resembling large industrial conglomerates.[22]

---

[18]Yao, Xinzhong. *An Introduction to Confucianism.* Cambridge: Cambridge University Press, 2000.

[19] Confucianism's influence is evident in the high savings rate among Chinese households. This pattern is also observed in other Asian nations with Confucian roots, like Singapore.

[20] Kohn, Livia. *Introducing Daoism.* London: Routledge, 2009.

[21] Lozeva, Silvia. "How the Ancient Game of Go Is a Guide to Modern Life." *TED Talks*, November 2017. Available at: https://www.ted.com/talks/silvia_lozeva_how_the_ancient_game_of_go_is_a_guide_to_modern_life

[22] In China, examples include Tencent, Alibaba, China Poly Group, Evergrande, and Country Garden. Similar structures are seen in Japan with the Keiretsus, such as Mitsubishi, Mitsui, and Sumitomo, as well as in South Korea with the Chaebols, such as Samsung, Hyundai, and LG.

Sun Tzu and Clausewitz: Two Opposing Strategic Conceptions

The Art of War by Sun Tzu (sixth century BCE)[23] has significantly shaped Chinese strategy. For centuries, this brief book was essential for military leaders, administrators, and scholars. Rediscovered in Europe and the US in the early 20th century, it became popular among business leaders. The *Art of War* is a concise treatise on military strategy, about 40 pages long, unlike Carl von Clausewitz's[24] nearly 600-page *On War*.

At the heart of Sun Tzu's strategic thinking was the management of influence and psychology, which enabled wars to be won with minimum loss of life or property. It has been suggested, probably mistakenly, that this is a more "humane" way of waging war. Whereas in Clausewitz's text, brutality and attacking force are at the heart of strategy.

Historical context can explain this difference. Sun Tzu's book was written during the "Spring and Autumn" period (771–453 BCE), characterized by constant conflict between the various principalities that coexisted in central China.[25] In this divided environment, winning a war with minimal losses was crucial. A victory that drained the victor's resources (a "Pyrrhic" victory in Europe) could expose them to attacks from another principality. Some authors suggest that this "psychological" dimension of warfare accounts for the importance of military or civilian parades (such as those at sports events) in many Asian countries, as they serve to impress others.

Conversely, Clausewitz's book was composed during and following the significant Napoleonic wars, when human resources were abundant. Innovations in artillery, among other techniques, allowed battles to be won by effectively managing force and movement. In the business world, Sun Tzu's writings suggest a far more nuanced strategic approach for entrepreneurs. Managing influence, even fear, is crucial.

Impressive Technologies

In his book *Science and Civilization in China*[26] published in 1954, Joseph Needham (1900–1995) demonstrated that many of the technologies that have shaped the economic history of various nations originated in the Middle Kingdom. His research uncovered a remarkable array of inventions: the plow, cast iron, compass, steel,

---

[23] Sun Tzu. *The Art of War.* Translated by Lionel Giles. London: Routledge, 2002.

[24] Clausewitz, Carl von. *On War.* Edited and translated by Michael Howard and Peter Paret. Princeton, NJ: Princeton University Press, 1976.

[25] Later, in 221 BCE, Emperor Qin Shi Huangdi unified the country.

[26] "Science and Civilization in China" is a series of books that began in 1954 and continued until 2004, with many contributors. Joseph Needham. *Science and Civilization in China.* Vol. 1. Cambridge: Cambridge University Press, 1954.

parachute, the crank, the suspension bridge, the wheelbarrow, the rudder, locks, the loom, and naturally, paper money, and gunpowder.

All these inventions, and many others, were made by China long before they were "reinvented" by Europe a few centuries later. For example, as early as the 4th century BCE, Chinese peasants were using double-entry bellows to increase the heat of a fire. Consequently, Joseph Needham believed that the transformation of cast iron into steel had already been achieved by the 2nd century BCE.

In 1421, Emperor Zhu Di of China's Ming dynasty commissioned Admiral Zheng He[27] to lead an armada of four fleets to explore the world via the Indian Ocean, Africa, South America, Antarctica, North America, and Australia. This fleet consisted of 100 junks, some 160 m long.[28] The logistics were impressive. The Chinese fleet resembled a floating city, with some ships dedicated to artisans and repair materials, while others transported food, animals, and equipment for growing vegetables and fruit. They had already learned that limes could prevent scurvy. Thus, it would have been reasonable to assume that China had all the necessary elements for rapid development at some point, including technology, a large workforce, agricultural resources, and infrastructure.[29]

Why Was There No Industrial Revolution?

Something was missing. In the section on England's Industrial Revolution, we noted the rise of a new class, the bourgeoisie, and the acceptance of societal change in the rapidly industrializing countries of the 18th and 19th centuries.

A new social class can only thrive in a society that embraces it. For centuries, Chinese thought has been shaped by Confucian ideals of balance and harmony. The social hierarchy, led by the emperor, existed to maintain stability, supported by a highly skilled but restrictive administration. An example is "Keju," the civil service examination system started in 587 CE.[30] Initially focused on mathematics and astronomy, it soon prioritized memorizing Confucian texts, emphasizing respect for fathers, lords, and emperors. Millions of Chinese tried to pass this exam. It was open to everyone (except women) and was seen as a means of social advancement through education.[31]

---

[27] Menzies, Gavin. *1,421: The Year China Discovered America*. New York: William Morrow, 2003.

[28] By comparison, in 1492, when Christopher Columbus set sail for America, he had three ships – La Nina, La Pinta, and La Santa Maria – averaging 22 m in length.

[29] For example, a 1,794-km Grand Canal linked Hangzhou to Beijing.

[30] Elman, Benjamin A. *A Cultural History of Civil Examinations in Late Imperial China*. Berkeley: University of California Press, 2000.

[31] "Keju" was abolished in 1905, but the attraction of entering the civil service has survived. In 2023, 2.6 million candidates applied for the government entrance exam to access 37,000 vacant positions.

Respect for Masters and Tradition

An immense reverence for the "masters" also explains the difficulty in leading an economic or technological revolution. In the Chinese mind, reproducing a work means paying homage to an illustrious predecessor. In the West, imitation is a minor part of art but is considered illegal in business, leading to many misunderstandings.

The Art of Copying

In 353 CE, the famous calligrapher Wang Xizhi invited 42 scholars to a party at his home to celebrate spring. Everyone was asked to sit down by a stream with cups of wine floating in it. When one of the cups approached a scholar, he was asked to drink it and write a poem.

In the early hours of the morning, Wang Xizhi was invited to write a preface in memory of the "Orchid Pavilion Poems" (Lantingji Xu). His handwriting (324 characters) was so magnificent that legend has it that Wang Xizhi tried to copy it over 100 times in his life without achieving the excellence of the original.

Two centuries later, Emperor Li Shimin (Taizong), founder of the illustrious Tang dynasty, expressed his desire to be buried with this perfect calligraphy (and had it stolen for the purpose). His tomb mound can be seen today not far from Xi'an and has not yet been excavated.

Wang Xizhi's preface was copied thousands of times – including by emperors Renzong and Gaozong of the Song dynasty – not only because of the quality of the poem, but also because the calligraphy was admirable. It became a must for every apprentice scholar.

The story of Wang Xizhi, in the inset,[32] illustrates this. This approach might be hard to comprehend in the West. Throughout art history, renowned artists have often felt compelled to innovate or deliberately distance themselves from their

---

[32] Miyasaka, Yūji. Wang Xizhi's "Preface to the Orchid Pavilion." *The Epitome of Chinese Calligraphy.* Translated by Michael R. Schaub. Tokyo: International House of Japan, 2014.

predecessors' influence. In Western economic thinking, progress takes precedence over respect for the past. This is the famous "destructive innovation" theory advocated by Joseph Schumpeter (1883–1850).[33] It lies at the heart of every industrial revolution. However, to work, it must be underpinned by respect for intellectual property, which protects innovation.[34]

Intellectual Property

Even today, intellectual property remains a permanent point of contention between China and the rest of the world. This is reflected in legislation.

In Europe, the first law on monopolies dates back to 1624 in England (Statute of Monopolies). It stipulated the existence of protection of invention patents for 14 years. A second law in 1710 ("Statute of Anne") was probably the first to recognize copyright and formally protect artistic creation. While in France, Pierre-Augustin Caron de Beaumarchais created the Société des Compositeurs et Auteurs Dramatiques in 1777,[35] following a dispute with the Comédie-Française over performance rights to his play "The Barber of Seville."

In the US, Congress passed two pieces of legislation in 1790: the US Copyright Act and the US Patent Act. They aimed to protect creators, not only in the artistic field but also in industry, to support economic innovation. From then on, almost all nations that experienced an industrial revolution, particularly in the 19th century, passed legislation protecting intellectual property.

In contrast, the first law in China concerning intellectual property was the "Trademark Law of the Republic of China," which was not promulgated until 1923. It focused primarily on trademark protection, establishing rules for registering and using trademarks.[36]

This is a recurring theme. Protecting intellectual property is crucial for a nation's economic and technological advancement. Countries that do not embrace

---

[33] Schumpeter, J.A. (1942). *Capitalism, Socialism, and Democracy.* New York: Harper & Brothers.
[34] During one of my trips to China, I remember asking a company director, who was part of our delegation, what his goal was. He replied: "To visit my machines." He explained that he had been selling machines to Chinese companies for years but had never received any feedback on their use. Of course, he suspected that these machines had been dismantled for reproduction.
[35] Beaumarchais, Pierre-Augustin Caron de. *Mémoires.* Paris: Chez Ruault, 1782.
[36] China is not the only country that resisted a Western stance on intellectual property rights. Brazil has historically enforced stringent restrictions on foreign patents and copyrights and protectionist policies that benefit domestic industries, and until the 1990s, Brazil did not grant patents in strategic areas such as pharmaceuticals and agricultural chemicals to promote a policy of autonomous industrial development.

this principle typically face weaker economic growth and reduced appeal to foreign investors. With the advance of globalization, the desire to standardize national intellectual property laws has intensified, culminating in the establishment of the World Intellectual Property Organization (WIPO) in Geneva in 1967.

However, since the 1980s, China has made significant efforts to align its legislation with international standards. The establishment of Special Economic Zones spurred rapid development in key sectors while shielding other areas, particularly agriculture, from sudden liberalization.

Fractured by Rapid Growth?

Between 2009 and 2019, the Chinese economy grew by an average of 7.7%. This was followed by the impact of COVID-19 and a real estate crisis. China provides an example of the transition from rapid expansion to a more sustainable long-term growth rate.

Real estate in China is a key sector of the economy, as it employs many subcontractors. What's more, owning an apartment is the dream of every Chinese household. Even today, 70% of the Chinese population's savings are invested in real estate. Yet by 2023, the combined debt of the two largest real estate groups, Evergrande and Country Garden, had risen to $540 billion. Most other real estate companies were also incurring considerable losses.

The significant increase in housing construction in China is primarily attributed to the migration of individuals from rural areas to urban centers. Between 1980 and 2020, nearly 600 million people in China migrated to urban areas. During this time, the urban population increased from 20% (190 million) to 64% (900 million) of the total population. This migration is considered the largest in modern history.[37] Now, the trend of moving to big cities on China's east and south coasts is slowing due to urban congestion and stressful living conditions; the growth of inland cities is also reducing this movement eastward. This means more Chinese are choosing to return to the countryside or their family origins.

The Diversification of Chinese Companies

The Chinese government has tried to diversify its economy, aiming to reduce the current overreliance on the real estate sector. As part of this strategic initiative, China is focusing on expanding its most productive industries, particularly those with high added value. These sectors include the automotive industry, with an

---

[37] Miller, Tom. *China's Urban Billion: The Story Behind the Biggest Migration in Human History.* London: Zed Books, 2012.

emphasis on electric vehicles, as well as batteries, solar panels, biotechnologies, and semiconductors. Today, China is the world's leading exporter of electric vehicles. In 2022, production was 5.9 million. By 2025, it should exceed 12 million. Moreover, China has also become the world's leading producer of key components, from rare materials to batteries.

However, this strategy is hindered by the low level of household consumption in China, which constitutes only 37% of GDP, in contrast to the 60–70% seen in industrialized countries. Exports are thus critical to prevent overcapacity. However, these exports are generating tensions with China's primary trading partners, who are starting to implement tariff and customs barriers.

Exploring New Markets

To mitigate this, China has entered into over 25 bilateral trade agreements with various nations, primarily within the Global South. These agreements encompass 40% of Chinese exports. Presently, Brazil, Indonesia, and South Korea engage in more trade with China than with the US.

The challenges of exporting have led many Chinese companies to adopt a direct investment strategy. In 2023, they particularly focused on Saudi Arabia, Malaysia, Vietnam, Egypt, and Morocco. For the first time in eight years, Chinese companies are earning more from the Global South than from the US and Europe.

This strategy is consistent with the restructuring of a fragmented global economy, which will be further explored in the chapter on multi-alignment, Chapter 17. Protectionist policies and tariff barriers implemented by several of China's traditional trading partners have encouraged the country to seek opportunities in other markets. This is one of the many unintended consequences for countries that want to shield themselves from competition. In the end, they lose both their attractiveness and competitiveness.

Chapter Takeaways

- China's economic success demonstrates that it is possible to develop competitiveness that is both global in perspective and rooted in a country's history and fundamental values.
- In the early 1980s, China adopted a pragmatic policy of attracting foreign companies, clearly defining which sectors were open and which were not. The proliferation of Special Economic Zones has enabled the development of competitive clusters that have energized the rest of the economy.

■ China's next challenge is to define a greater role for domestic demand in its competitiveness model. Today, it accounts for less than 40% of GDP, as opposed to nearly 70% in other advanced economies.

Where Next?

The remarkable success of China has often overshadowed the significant revolution in competitiveness that Japan achieved during the latter half of the 20th century. Japan was regarded as the major competitor to the United States and Europe for years.

The Japanese model was based on production competitiveness and direct state intervention in the country's major economic decisions. This model led to economic tensions with the rest of the world, somewhat similar to those we see today with China.

6 | Countries That Made Their Mark on Competitiveness: Japan

Principle: Success is not guaranteed for any country or company. Even the best must keep reforming, as complacency can destroy even the leaders.

Success Is Never Guaranteed

I arrived in Japan for the first time in 1972. Discovering Japan at the age of 21 was an enlightening experience. Following that trip, I returned several times – and the wonder never faded.

Japanese society is characterized by hierarchy and order. In this country, even demonstrations are orderly. I remember visiting a factory where the workers all wore red armbands. I asked what it meant. "They are on strike" my host replied. On strike but at work...[1]

---

[1] One day in Tokyo, I saw a street demonstration. As usual, in such circumstances, the leaders are in front, the crowd is behind them, and the signs are behind them. But as they reached the crossroads, the procession stopped at the red light and waited peacefully for it to turn green before continuing its march. I thought of the contrast with the Paris of 1968, with its flying cobblestones and torched cars.

At the time, Kakuei Tanaka (1918–1993) had just been elected Prime Minister. He was known as the "Bulldozer."[2] He did not end well; in 1983, he was sentenced to four years' imprisonment for accepting bribes from the Lockheed Martin Company (a world leader in defense and aerospace). Nevertheless, he left his mark on his era. Japan had demonstrated its revived economic power and resilience for the first time since the conclusion of the war.

Japan is a blend of tradition and modernism. To a Western mind, it is remarkable that the two coexist and do not affect the other. In the streets of Tokyo, flamboyant kimonos mix with the dark suits of businesspeople, and wooden houses stand next to steel skyscrapers.

The Japanese Miracle

In the 1970s, Japan's resurgence on the international economic scene represented a similar global earthquake as China's movement in the 2010s. At my university, professors taught us about the Japanese miracle and how the Japanese economy would conquer the rest of the world, starting with the United States.

Indeed, the US was beginning to worry. In 1986, President Ronald Reagan asked business leaders and researchers to create the US Council on Competitiveness. John Young, CEO of Hewlett-Packard, chaired it.[3] Officially, the objective was to promote the overall improvement of US competitiveness through innovation, multisector collaboration, influencing public policy, and improving the education and skills of the workforce. Unofficially, the main goal was to counter Japan's growing technological power. In the background, it also denounced the Japanese government's support for business, notably by promoting exports while closing the domestic market to foreign companies. Added to this was the complaint of dumping. Japan was alleged to have sold its products below cost price, contrary to multilateral agreements, notably those of the World Trade Organization.[4]

The Ministry of International Trade and Industry (MITI) was the driving force behind Japan's industrial strategy.[5] It directed the country away from light manufacturing (like textiles) towards heavy, advanced-tech industries (such as

---

[2] Hunziker, Steven, and Ikuro Kamimura. *Kakuei Tanaka: A Political Biography of Modern Japan.* New York: Times Books International, 1996.

[3] Council on Competitiveness. "About Us." https://compete.org/ (accessed May 14, 2025).

[4] Indeed, it was more sophisticated than that. Japanese companies used high margins in their domestic market, protected from foreign competition, to subsidize their exports at minimum prices. It was a lateral (or cross) subsidy.

[5] Johnson, Chalmers. *MITI and the Japanese Miracle: The Growth of Industrial Policy, 1925–1975.* Stanford, CA: Stanford University Press, 1982.

electronics, automobiles, and steel). MITI executed targeted industrial strategies, supporting specific sectors with protectionist policies, subsidies, and favorable regulations. Additionally, it promoted the clustering of industries such as mechanics and electronics (mechatronics).

In 2001, MITI was restructured and renamed METI (Ministry of Economy, Trade and Industry). However, it remains a remarkable example of state industrial policy. The experience would later be emulated in China, the Gulf States, and now in the US and Europe.[6]

Inspired by Other Countries

The most significant reform of the Japanese economy took place during the Meiji period (named after the emperor) from 1868 to 1912.[7] During this period, the country's top civil servants traveled to Europe and the United States to draw inspiration from best practices (today, this would be called "benchmarking").[8] One country in particular was studied, and traces of it remain to this day: Germany.

Japan's civil code was inspired by the German civil code, as was the education system, particularly for universities and research. The same applies to medicine and the military system, for which German advisors came to Japan. However, Germany's influence was most profound in economic and banking structures. Both countries based their economic development on large integrated industrial groups: the Konzerns in Germany and the Zaibatsu in Japan.[9]

In their respective countries, however, these groups operated with the same structure: centralized management overlooking legally independent subsidiaries, a synergy between entities to increase efficiency, and harmonized commercial and accounting rules. However, they also had in common that they influenced their countries' politics and supported the war effort.

After 1945, these groups were theoretically dissolved. IG Farben was split up to create BASF, Bayer, and Hoechst. Yet they went on to become the largest in their sector. As for the Japanese groups, they had the same fate: to be dismantled. Or almost. These same conglomerates (Zaibatsus) reconstituted themselves as

---

[6] For more details on industrial policies, see Chapter 16, "A Fractured World."

[7] Keene, Donald. *Emperor of Japan: Meiji and His World, 1852–1912.* New York: Columbia University Press, 2002.

[8] A management technique that involves comparing a function, such as customer service, with the best on the market, even in another sector.

[9] Among the major German groups (Konzerns) of the pre–World War II era were Krupp, Siemens, Vereinigte Stahlwerke, and, of course, IG Farben, which included BASF, Bayer, Hoechst, and Agfa IG. The Japanese equivalents were Mitsui, Mitsubishi, Sumitomo, and Yasuda.

"Keiretsu,"[10] a family of companies which, in principle, were independent. However, it just so happened that the directors met regularly, but informally – just like the salespeople, clerks, or researchers – to coordinate their actions.

Sony: Entrepreneurship In Japan

By the end of the 1960s, Japan was dominated by the power of the government and its administration (MITI) and the large groups (Keiretsus) that tacitly reconstituted themselves. Despite this, new names quickly emerged. Among these, the most famous Japanese company internationally was unquestionably Sony. I first met its chairman, Akio Morita, in his Tokyo office in the late 1970s. He was an atypical Japanese entrepreneur who knew both Western and Asian companies well and spoke perfect English. He was exuberant and curious about new ideas. In short, he was an entrepreneur in a country characterized by managers and administrators.[11]

Sony began by selling an electric rice cooker, which was not particularly exciting. But in 1950, the company started manufacturing tape recorders and transistor radios when Masuro Ibuka obtained a license from Bell Laboratories in the USA. From then on, the company went from strength to strength.

Where Does the Name "Sony" Come From?

The company was founded in 1946 by Masuro Ibuka and Akio Morita with 20 employees. Today, there are almost 110,000.

Its original name was *Tokyo Tsushin Kogyo Kabushiki Kaisha* (Tokyo Telecommunications Engineering Corporation). Needless to say, no one outside Japan could pronounce it.

Thus, they decided to change the name to capture foreign markets.

They took the contraction of *sonus* in Latin for sound and *sonny* for "sonny boys" in American (meaning young boy full of energy).

The "Sony" brand was born!

---

[10] Lincoln, James R., and Michael L. Gerlach. *Japan's Network Economy: Structure, Persistence, and Change.* Cambridge: Cambridge University Press, 2004.

[11] Morita, Akio, Edwin M. Reingold, and Mitsuko Shimomura. *Made in Japan: Akio Morita and Sony.* New York: Dutton, 1986.

The story of Sony and Akio Morita is emblematic of the mechanisms of competitiveness in Japan and elsewhere. In the first place, miniaturization has been central to the success of Japanese companies abroad. Japan manufactured small transistor radios, small televisions, and small cars. In so doing, the industry responded to Japanese consumer demand.

Consumer Demand Triggers Competitiveness

Japan has 125 million inhabitants, most of whom live on the outskirts of the country as mountains occupy the center. Japan's population density is one of the highest in the world: 338 people per km^2, compared with 37 in the US. As a result, the living space is relatively small. The products purchased by Japanese consumers reflect this need for miniaturization.

Conversely, in the US, there is considerably more space. For instance, in the 1950s, Zenith produced television consoles encased in beautifully crafted wooden furniture designed to sit prominently in the center of the living room. Although these units occupied substantial space, it was not an issue in a country where ample room was the norm. Gradually, however, the development of urban areas in the US and Europe led consumers to look not only for smaller devices, such as televisions, radios, microwaves, and even cars, but also cheaper ones. Soon, American homes wanted smaller TVs in every room and transistor radios everywhere.

This move towards smaller products was not easily accepted. I recall talking with the director of a leading car company in Detroit. He told me: "Professor, Americans will never buy small cars. I have been in this industry for 30 years – I know…" In 1997, however, the Toyota Camry became the best-selling car in the US – and remained so for 11 years. I always thought of sending him a Christmas card every year to remind him of his brilliant prediction with the simple words "I know…" – but I never dared.

Natural occurrences can lead companies to create products they might not have initially considered. This is evident in Japan, where construction firms have been compelled to innovate anti-seismic technologies for constructing buildings, especially skyscrapers. For instance, Japan has developed anti-seismic construction technologies that are now sold to countries worldwide where earthquakes threaten urban areas.[12]

---

[12]A highly effective method is basic isolation, where isolators are placed between a building's foundation and its superstructure. Made of rubber, steel, or both, these insulators let the building move separately from its foundation, minimizing seismic force transmission to the structure.

Underestimating Domestic Competition

Another key factor that influences a country's competitiveness is the level of competition within a country. Once, talking with Akio Morita in his office, he pointed out the window to show that major competitors like Panasonic and Toshiba were advertising nearby. He remarked, "When you are at Philips headquarters in Eindhoven, what do you see outside? Philips, Philips, Philips…"

The theory is that, for a company to compete in international markets, it must first learn to compete in its home market. He believed that one major issue for European industry was its prolonged protection in domestic markets, primarily via a national preference system for public contracts. On the other hand, Japanese and American companies had learned to compete in their home markets by being in extreme competition with each other.

Being Overprotected…

An example of overprotection is the computer industry and technology in general.

For years, European IT companies lived in a protected environment at home. Olivetti in Italy, Nixdorf in Germany, Bull in France, ICL in the UK or Norsk Data in Norway.

Today, most of these names belong to the past.

As each country protected its national champions, when they went abroad, they suffered reverse discrimination. The Germans would not buy French precisely because their German companies could not sell freely in France.

The unintended consequence was to choose an American competitor as an alternative.

As a consequence, for many years in Europe, the number two computer manufacturer in each country, after the national champion, was no longer another European company, but an American one.

Akio Morita also showed the impact an entrepreneur can have on a company. One of Sony's iconic products, the Walkman, was inspired by his desire to listen to music while playing golf without lugging around a bulky tape recorder. He instructed his engineers to create a compact, portable device compatible with earphones, ensuring it would not bother other users. This led to the creation of the Walkman, destined to dominate global markets. This approach resembles Bill Hewlett's, who desired a pocket calculator to fit in his shirt pocket.

Processes Under Control

A key factor in Japan's competitiveness is the high quality of its production. Principles such as stringent quality standards, the "just-in-time" method developed at Toyota,[13] and efficient process management have been adopted globally and have thrived in Japanese manufacturing.

After World War II, Western companies traditionally believed that enhancing quality resulted in increased costs for the company and higher prices for consumers. Yet, an American, Edward Deming (1900–1993),[14] demonstrated that the opposite could be true. More quality means fewer defects, fewer repairs, and lower costs and prices. In his words: "We have learned to live in a world of mistakes and defective products as if it were an inevitability of life… It is time for a new approach."

Deming was not a prophet in his own country. He traveled to Japan to find a receptive ear for his theory. Today, the Deming Prize is the most sought-after quality award. In many Asian factories, the slogan "Do it right the first time"[15] is posted on every wall. These principles apply to the manufacturing industry and all sectors of activity, including services. Airlines, for example, have learned to also measure quality in terms of the time it takes for passengers to board or disembark a plane.

Quality theory came back in the USA and Europe in the early 1980s because of the outstanding performance of Japanese companies, particularly in the automotive industry.[16]

Strengthening Industrial Competitiveness

This competitive advantage in production led Japan to focus on industry at a time when Europe and the United States were turning away from it. Today, it still accounts for around 30% of GDP. By contrast, the share of industry in the US, Great Britain, and France has fallen back to 18% of GDP. The deindustrialization of parts of the United States and Europe resulted from globalization. It has enabled many companies to source low-cost products from countries with much lower production costs.

---

[13] Ohno, Taiichi. *Toyota Production System: Beyond Large-Scale Production*. Portland, OR: Productivity Press, 1988.

[14] Deming, W. E. (1986). *Out of the Crisis*. Cambridge, MA: MIT Press.

[15] I have often repeated this principle to my students, asking them to pass their exams the first time – and it hasn't always worked…

[16] Among those who took up the torch in these countries was Josef Juran (1904–2008), who emphasized: "15% of problems in a company are due to people, and 85% to management and processes."

Certain countries have performed more favorably: Switzerland relies on its manufacturing sector for 25% of its GDP, classifying it among the most "production-focused" nations globally. Germany followed a comparable path. China stands out as the overall leader, becoming the world's manufacturing hub in a few short years, with industry contributing nearly 40% to its GDP.

Societal pressures have also contributed to deindustrialization in specific sectors. Many industries, such as aluminum, have relocated to avoid the consequences of pollution in their home countries. Furthermore, the increase in legislation, even when justified by public opinion, has driven many companies to relocate to countries with fewer administrative complexities.[17]

Brands Impact a Country's Image

A country's production power is often associated with its brand image. A country "is" what it makes. A nation's image of dynamism remains closely linked to a product or a company.

Japan's influence emerged with Sony radios and Toyota cars. Germany evokes premium brands like Mercedes, BMW, Audi, and Bayer aspirin. France is synonymous with luxury items from LVMH and glassware from Saint-Gobain. The United States shines with Apple, McDonald's, Amazon, Tesla, and Microsoft.

Japan's competitiveness has long relied on miniaturization, production process excellence, and price performance. But what about innovation? I liked to ask my students to name a fundamental Japanese invention that had changed our lives (and they could not mention the Walkman). After a few unsuccessful attempts, such as the transistor (Bell Laboratories) or the VCR (Ampex), silence set in.

The answer is that Japan's competitiveness stemmed not from original inventions but from its ability to transform these innovations into appealing products that surpassed those of other nations in terms of quality, speed, and cost. China adopted a similar approach subsequently, followed today by Vietnam. However, Japan has caught up again and is also innovating in more fundamental ways. These include LED (light-emitting diode) technologies with companies like Nichia, QR code technology with Denso Wave, and advanced robotics with Honda (Asimo).

---

[17] It's important to distinguish between an industry's size and its sophistication. Europe's and the United States' low figures often mask advanced technologies not seen in other more industrialized nations. However, robust industrial capabilities are crucial for any state; below a certain threshold, vulnerability increases.

There is also the remarkable ability of some Japanese companies to reinvent themselves. Originally, Nintendo, founded in 1889, made traditional Japanese "Hanafuda" playing cards.[18] After many unsuccessful attempts to diversify (including cabs and love hotels…), Nintendo entered the console and video game market with great success.[19] Few companies can pull off such a successful turnaround. The secret undoubtedly lies in the concept of *core competencies,*[20] which enables a company to follow a common thread in its diversification. For Nintendo, it is gaming.

An Aging Japan

The Japanese have one of the longest life expectancies in the world: 87 years for women and 81 years for men. As a result, Japan has an elderly population, with 28% over 65 years old. By 2050, this ratio is set to rise to 40%.

The dependency ratio, that is between people aged 65 and older and those of working age (15–65), is now 48 elderly people for every 100 of working age (48%).

In the United States, the ratio is 25%, in Italy 38%, in Germany 34%, and in France 31%.

The ageing of the population has major implications for health, retirement, and workforce policies. It also has a considerable impact on public finances.

Japan's public debt exceeds 270% of GDP. It is the highest in the industrialized world (even if most of it is domestic debt, which mitigates the risk).

Despite its many strengths, the Japanese economy began to slow down in the 1990s, leading to what has been termed the "lost decade" (which extended beyond 10 years). There were cyclical factors at play, such as the bursting of the real estate bubble, which affected property sales, the banking system, and, ultimately, the stock market.

---

[18] Firestone, Mary. *Nintendo: The Company and Its Founders*. Minneapolis: ABDO Publishing Company, 2008.

[19] The Finnish company Nokia followed a similar path. Founded in 1865, it started in paper, then diversified into rubber and cables, followed by telecommunications and cell phones.

[20] Prahalad, C. K., & Hamel, G. (1990). "The core competence of the corporation." *Harvard Business Review*, 68(3), 79–91.

This situation led Japan into a prolonged period of deflation, causing declines in investment and production. This trend was further intensified by China's rise as it replaced Japan as the "factory of the world."

Is Japan the Future of the Industrialized World?

Japan faces deep-rooted challenges, such as the dominance of large conglomerates, weak start-up activity, overregulation in some industries, and low labor mobility, all compounded by an ageing population.

Japan may represent the future of industrialized countries when they fail to adapt quickly to structural changes in the global economy. Competitiveness is invariably viewed in comparison to others, particularly as emerging economies continuously alter the dynamics, affecting even the most successful players.

Moreover, as the population ages in affluent nations due to increased life expectancy and declining birth rates, three critical issues emerge: national debt, extended retirement periods, and possibly immigration.

I remember visiting the president of a major Japanese bank during the period of glorious growth. Amidst the French Impressionist paintings adorning the walls, he said to me. "We are no longer interested in Europe; it is finished…"

Whether in Japan, the US, Switzerland, or elsewhere, arrogance and complacency have failed more countries and companies than any strategic error.

Chapter Takeaways

- Japan's spectacular rise in competitiveness since the early 1960s challenged the economic dominance of Europe and the US. The country's competitiveness was based on production excellence; that is, delivering products better, cheaper, and faster than the rest of the world.
- This strategy was driven under the direct supervision of the government (more specifically, the Ministry of International Trade and Investment) and implemented by large, vertically integrated industrial groups (the Keiretsu).
- Today, Japan is confronting the emergence of China, whose competitiveness model is relatively similar. However, China has emphasized attracting foreign companies, while the Japanese market remained relatively closed to foreigners.
- This policy may change because of Japan's aging population. It may encourage the country to be more open to attracting an international workforce.

Where Next?

From Asia, we return to Europe, and more specifically to Germany, whose industrial competitiveness has served as a model for continental Europe.

Contrary to popular belief, Germany's industrial success should not be solely attributed to large conglomerates. It also significantly depends upon numerous smaller enterprises. They constitute the so-called "Mittelstand" (enterprises in the middle), mostly family owned. They embody a longstanding tradition of small yet highly competitive enterprises that have formed the foundation of Europe's competitiveness, both in the past and present.

7 | Countries That Made Their Mark on Competitiveness: Germany

Principle: Each nation hosts both large and small enterprises. Yet, competitiveness is often better achieved by mid-sized companies that excel in innovation and globalization. They are the backbone of a nation's long-term prosperity.

The Strength of Companies "In the Middle"

"In medio stat virtus" (in the middle lies virtue – or strength). Aristotle's principle, drawn from Nicomachean Ethics,[1] also applies to economics.

In every part of the world, including the poorest nations, the economic hierarchy places large corporations at the top and small businesses (less than 10 employees), like shopkeepers and artisans, at the bottom.

---

[1] Aristotle. *Nicomachean Ethics*. Translated by Roger Crisp. Cambridge: Cambridge University Press, 2014.

The difference in competitiveness lies in the middle with medium-sized companies. According to the German definition, a company in the middle, or "Mittlestand," employs a maximum of 250 people and has sales not exceeding 50 million euros.[2]

The Heart of Europe's Economic History

Historically, companies in the "Mittlestand" developed in Germany mainly along the Rhine. It has always been a major waterway in Europe. Cities such as Cologne, Strasbourg, and Rotterdam have become major commercial centers thanks to their access to the river. The Rhine is also linked to industrialization, particularly in the Ruhr, a region rich in coal and steel.

The Rhine also provided a link – albeit indirect – between the great commercial and cultural centers of the Renaissance, namely Flanders and Northern Italy. Bruges, Ghent, and Antwerp that were renowned for their fabrics, wool, and cloth products, while Venice was the gateway to spices, silk, and riches imported from the Orient.

Helmut Schmidt, Chancellor of Germany, 1974–1982

"In my government, all my ministers understand monetary theories – that is not the case in other countries…"

Helmut Schmidt was probably the most brilliant politician I have ever met. He excelled at everything, and apart from politics and economics, had a passion for chess, music, and the arts.

He dedicated his book on art in the Chancellery to me when it was in Bonn. The book features numerous pieces of 20th-century German art, with a masterpiece visible in the background of each photo.[3]

Outside, the monumental sculptures of Englishman Henry Moore reigned supreme. Helmut Schmidt, incidentally, spoke perfect English.

In music, he has recorded Johann Sebastian Bach's concerto for four keyboards, BWV 1065 for Deutsche Grammophon.

Later, I met him again several times when we shared the same conference stage. He had become embittered. It was hard for such a talented man to leave the limelight.

---

[2] Institut für Mittelstandsforschung. 2021. The Role of the Mittelstand in Germany's Economic Resilience. Bonn: IfM Bonn.
[3] Helmut Schmidt (1982). *Kunst in Kanzleramt.* Wilhelm Goldmann Verlag: Munich.

Meanwhile, Northern Italy was also an innovator in creating small art businesses. Leonardo da Vinci, Raphael, and Michelangelo ran painting workshops that were veritable micro-businesses to meet the growing demand for their works. Later, Titian and Rubens went even further and developed quasi-industrial production, employing up to 20 people.[4]

Germany Today

All along the Rhine trade route, numerous small businesses sprang up. "Small" because Germany was fragmented into a myriad of free towns (over 100 in 1380, including Hamburg, Lübeck, and Augsburg) and mini-sovereign states. These companies did not have the geographical reach to expand as they did in the unified countries of the day: France and Great Britain.

Today, these companies have spread throughout the country, forming the backbone of Germany's competitiveness. Around 3.5 million small and medium-sized enterprises in Germany are estimated to meet the "Mittelstand" criterion.[5] For example, Baden-Württemberg is famous for its high-tech industries, particularly in mechanical engineering, automotives, electrical engineering, and biotechnology. Its neighbor, Bavaria, is renowned for its automotives, mechanical engineering, electronics, aerospace, and biotech companies.

North Rhine-Westphalia has concentrated on heavy industry, particularly in the Ruhr region, and many small companies have developed as suppliers to the larger ones. In Hesse, with Frankfurt, the focus is on companies specializing in the financial services, IT, and technology sectors. Saxony is home to mechanical engineering, the automotive industry, and technology.

Well-Targeted Strategies

The power of Mittelstand companies lies primarily in the fact that they specialize in well-defined niche markets. Often, they offer only a limited number of products. However, in their field, they have a high level of innovation and technology based on years of experience.

They are oriented towards foreign markets. Exports often account for over 90% of their sales. After the war, Germany even set up "export schools" to help these companies find international markets.

---

[4] Family businesses were also born. For example, the Cosmati were a line of Italian craftsmen and architects famous for their work in mosaics and marble marquetry, a technique known as "Cosmatesque." Their "business" was handed down in the same family for centuries.

[5] Langenscheidt, Florian, and Peter May, eds. *The Best of German Mittelstand: The Family Businesses*. Frankfurt: Deutsche Standards Editionen, 2015.

Family Capital is Key

Mittelstand companies are generally family businesses held by the same shareholders for generations. This family shareholding maintains a long-term perspective and stability in economic development. According to the EY 2023 Family Business Index,[6] the world's 500 largest family businesses collectively generate $8.02 trillion in revenues and employ 24.5 million people;[7] 76% of family businesses surveyed are over 50 years old.

For the record, the world's oldest family-run business is Houshi Ryokan, a hotel located in the village of Awazu, Japan. It was founded in 717 and has been run by the same family for over 46 generations.

The multiplication of family businesses over the generations has created new management structures such as "Family Offices" or "Family Foundations." Their goal is to assist future generations in comprehending and managing the income flow, primarily from the dividends they receive. According to investment company Preqin, the number of family offices increased from 1,285 in 2019 to 4,592 in 2023, reflecting the demand for this type of service.[8]

A New Class of "Rentiers"

According to some estimates, people in advanced economies will in 2025 inherit about $6 trillion, which is roughly twice as much as 60 years ago.[9] Consequently, a new social class is forming, comprising individuals set to inherit family assets but earning little or no current income from them. The traditional rentier emerged from the 19th-century industrial revolution. They thrived in Paris during its peak era of café culture and absinthe drinking, often viewed as idle gamblers and debauchees. The good times did not last long. World War I and the crash of 1929 wiped them out.

However, since World War II, families have been rebuilding their wealth in Europe, the United States, and now Asia. Today, the generations that follow the baby boomers are born into families with more accumulated capital, completely

---

[6] This index is produced in cooperation with the University of St. Gallen: https://family businessindex.com (accessed May 14, 2025).

[7] Europe accounts for $3.05 trillion of these revenues. Germany remains a proportional leader, with 78 companies in the ranking (the largest being the Schwarz Group), compared with 32 in France (LVMH), 20 in Italy (Exor), and 13 in Great Britain (Wittington). The US has 118 (the largest being Walmart). However, new centers of family enterprise are emerging. China (with Hong Kong) now boasts 31 family businesses (Country Garden), India 15 (Reliance), and Mexico 15 (America Movil).

[8] Preqin (2023). Preqin Family Office Report 2023. London: Preqin Ltd. Available at: https://www.preqin.com

[9] "The New Inheritocracy." *The Economist,* March 1, 2025, p. 9.

changing their approach to life. In France, for example, in 1970, inheritance accounted for just 35% of total wealth. Today, it is over 65%. Every year, the equivalent of 15% of GDP is passed on. In the United States, some $84 trillion in wealth will be transferred over the next 20 years; $72.6 trillion will go to heirs, while $11.4 trillion will be donated to charities.[10]

This structural transformation is significantly affecting society. Returns on well-allocated capital are increasing at a much higher rate compared to labor income. Specifically, a capital investment of 100 can yield 10–20% annual returns, whereas, for most wage earners, the increase typically ranges from 2–5%.

These accumulating differences over the years contribute to widening social divides, escalating inequalities, and increasing tensions within modern societies.

Human Capital for the Long Term

Managing human capital presents a significant challenge for family businesses due to its long-term nature. Succession planning, in particular, is a major issue at the ownership level. Not all generations may have the same enthusiasm for managing the family enterprise. Consequently, some firms opt to "skip" a generation and hire a professional manager to oversee the transition.

At the employer level, the challenge is to build lasting relationships without being paternalistic. Paternalism often arises from seeing the company as a family extension, which has benefits. Business owners have long assumed social responsibilities even before laws mandated them. In smaller family businesses, employer-employee ties are strong. Still, in larger family firms, these bonds weaken, leading to more traditional labor disputes.

Companies in the Countryside

Ultimately, mid-sized companies play a vital role in economic diversification. Often situated outside of major urban centers to reduce costs and due to historic factors, these businesses help promote balanced regional development. The dispersion of these Mittelstand companies also gave rise to significant trade fairs like those in Hanover and Frankfurt, which historically provided isolated entrepreneurs with opportunities to convene despite limited communication facilities.

These trade fairs continue to thrive today, even amidst advances such as the Internet, social networking, and artificial intelligence, because face-to-face interactions remain essential. Remarkably, even globalization has not eroded this long-standing model, nor the practices established over centuries. The city of Taicang,

---

[10] Source: https://www.cerulli.com (accessed May 14, 2025).

in China's Jiangsu province, is now home to over 400 medium-sized German companies. There are German-style houses and even an "Octoberfest."

Chapter Takeaways

- Germany's competitiveness is rooted in European culture, influenced by Protestant values like work, savings, and education that bear similarities to Confucian principles.
- In the 19th and 20th centuries, Germany developed large industrial conglomerates that converted the country's natural resources into advanced production technology, a model later adopted by Japan. Like Great Britain, Germany rapidly focused on exports, notably to China, when it opened up and, thus, became one of the leading industrial powers of the 20th century.
- Germany's competitiveness includes the "Mittelstand" – family-run, medium-sized, highly specialized companies focusing on cutting-edge technologies and exports. It differs from many countries where the corporate structure primarily consists of large international corporations at the top and many local micro-businesses at the bottom but fewer enterprises in the middle.

Where Next?

Until now, we have reviewed the competitiveness of large nations because, for many years, economic power was linked to a country's size, economic resources, and population.

One of the significant transformations of competitiveness in recent decades is that advances in modern technologies and communications have allowed relatively small nations to emerge as competitive forces globally. These countries, located in central and northern Europe, the Gulf states, and Southeast Asia, demonstrate that economic success can be achieved through competitiveness strategies regardless of a nation's size.

8 | Economies That Made Their Mark on Competitiveness: Singapore, Hong Kong, Dubai, and the European Nordic Countries

Principle: Size is no longer an obstacle to conquering the world through competitiveness. But success does not necessarily translate into political power.

Small, but Prosperous

Size has long been a condition for success. Russia and France were the most populous nations in Europe in the 19th century.[1] China combined both a large territory

---

[1] 40 million inhabitants for Russia and 29 million for France, in 1800.

and a large population.[2] Finally, the United States has considerable natural and technological resources.

Economic power was also linked to a country's military impact. For that, you needed to have large reserves of men. In the second half of the 20th century, new technologies and a more peaceful environment gave smaller countries a chance. Suddenly, size became less of an obstacle on the road to success.

Singapore, Hong Kong, and Dubai are just a few of the economies that have become exemplars of this revolution. Beginning with very modest resources, they have achieved remarkable success globally. They now serve as a model for other countries looking to enhance their competitiveness. Despite apparent differences, they share several common policies.

Singapore: The Birth of a Nation and a Success Story

It was August 9, 1995, during the era when fax machines were the primary mode of communication, particularly for countries with different alphabets. At IMD, we had recently released our World Competitiveness Yearbook a few weeks prior, and things were relatively calm during that summer. Unexpectedly, faxes started accumulating on the machine as requests for the report surged. The majority of these requests were from Singapore. On the national holiday, August 9, then–Prime Minister Lee Kuan Yew[3] highlighted the nation's top position in world competitiveness in his speech. Naturally, everyone was eager to learn more.

It was something to be proud of. In 1965, when Singapore gained its independence from Malaysia, it was just a tiny tropical port, hot, humid, and infested with mosquitoes. Today,[4] according to the World Bank, GDP per capita is over $82,000, one of the highest revenues in the world.

Hong Kong: A Blend of History and Modernism

I went to Hong Kong for the first time in 1973. It was fascinating to look at entirely different worlds living side by side. Hong Kong Island, with its skyscrapers, was the Manhattan of Asia. In Kowloon, on the other side of the bay, there were the back-streets and small stores run by Chinese emigrants.

Taking the train north, one arrived in the New Territories on the Chinese border. From a distance, one could see peasants working in fields dotted with loud-speakers broadcasting slogans. The Cultural Revolution was still in effect.

---

[2] 300 million inhabitants for China, in 1800.

[3] Lee, Kuan Yew. *The Singapore Story: Memoirs of Lee Kuan Yew.* Singapore: Prentice Hall, 1998.

[4] 2024.

At the center of the city was the Kowloon Cricket Club (I spent a whole afternoon there without understanding what was happening) and the Hong Kong Jockey Club to remind everyone that this was a British colony.

Dubai: Anything Is Possible

Dubai's history is just as dazzling. It gained independence in 1971, and I visited the city for the first time in 1979. Back then, one had to drive from Abu Dhabi, letting the car cool down occasionally and avoiding camels on the road. Today, there is a floodlit highway between the two cities, and vegetation is permanently irrigated.

I was to give a speech at the Dubai Chamber of Commerce in an austere building in the old city. Today, the Chamber of Commerce boasts a futuristic building hosting three parallel chambers specializing in trade, international investment, and digital development. Around the old building, there were only small, rudimentary houses. Today, Dubai has 69 skyscrapers over 200 m high.

Any Similarities?

These three seemingly distinct cities, shaped by their unique histories and cultures, share a surprisingly similar economic strategy.

Port Infrastructure

At the beginning of their expansion, they could rely on a deep-water port along a major trade route. Singapore's port is one of the world's most important for container traffic (currently sixth in terms of size per ton transported). Hong Kong's Victoria Port ranks 16th, and the port of Jebel Ali in Dubai is 26th.[5] Specifically, Hong Kong has experienced setbacks due to the emergence of Chinese ports that are now among the top five globally. Once, Hong Kong's thriving economy was due to its strategic position as a conduit and exporter of Chinese products; however, that is no longer the case.[6]

The ports of these three cities are mainly transit ports in strategic locations: on the Strait of Malacca for Singapore, at the entrance to the China Sea for Hong Kong,

---

[5] World Shipping Council. "Top 50 Ports." https://www.worldshipping.org/top-50-ports (accessed March 2, 2025).

[6] Today, products are exported directly from mainland China via Ningbo, Tangshan, Shanghai, Tsingtao, and Guangzhou ports. For a long time, Hong Kong's prosperity thrived as it was a substitute for Shanghai, which was closed to international trade when the Communists took power in 1949.

and near the Strait of Hormuz between the Persian Gulf and the Gulf of Oman for Dubai. A relative exception is Hong Kong. It has also become the gateway to the Pearl River Delta Region, which extends to Macau, Shenzhen, and Guangzhou. The United Nations Human Settlements Program[7] estimates that 120 million people live in this region and that the GDP generated there (estimated at $2,000 billion) is comparable to Canada's.

The Importance of Tax Advantages

In addition to their efficient port infrastructures, the three cities offer significant tax advantages based on duty-free zones. For example, the Port of Singapore is a tariff-free zone for almost all its tariff lines. US exports to Singapore are duty-free under the US–Singapore Free Trade Agreement. Similarly, Dubai's Jebel Ali Port Free Zone (Jafza) is the largest in the Middle East. Thanks to various tax advantages, it has become a hub for the region's trade.

These three cities also share a customs system that is not only favorable but also highly efficient, thanks to the advanced development of e-customs. The digitization of customs processes, whereby customs declarations and documents are submitted and processed electronically, streamlines the customs clearance process, making it faster and more efficient. In a port context, this reduces waiting times, as all documents can be submitted in advance, even before the ship touches the quay. Digitizing customs processes improves transparency, reduces paperwork, and minimizes the risk of errors and fraud.

Following the initial success of their port areas, these cities have increased the number of free trade zones. Singapore has nine free trade zones, while Dubai boasts 24, specializing in technology, media, e-commerce, jewelry, and healthcare.[8]

A First-Class Infrastructure

These three cities have also invested massively in their infrastructure, particularly land and air communications. Tax advantages alone are not enough to attract foreign investment. Products or services must be able to be efficiently transferred into or out of a country. Otherwise, tax advantages are useless.

---

[7] United Nations Human Settlements Program (UN-Habitat). (2016). "Urbanization and Development: Emerging Futures - World Cities Report 2016." Nairobi: UN-Habitat.

[8] Similar strategies have been developed in Ho-Chi-Minh-Ville in Vietnam and Noida (near New Delhi) in India. The Dominican Republic has over 70 free trade zones, some comparable to China's or Dubai's special economic zones.

Dubai International Airport ranks as the 3rd busiest in the world, while Hong Kong's Chek Lap Kok sits at 13, and Singapore's Changi Airport holds the 16th position. Much like seaports, these facilities function as key transit hubs.[9] These results are impressive considering that Hong Kong's population is 7.4 million, Singapore's 5.4 million, and Dubai's 3.3 million.[10] Other attractive policies include administrative efficiency, 100% foreign ownership of companies, intellectual protection, and security.

Still, one wonders why other cities with similar natural resources didn't adopt the same model. Cape Town in South Africa and Durban have been cited, and one could add Muscat, Aden, Djibouti, Port-Louis (Mauritius), Puerto Rico, Santos (near São Paulo), Valparaiso, etc. These ports are strategically positioned with some infrastructure, yet this has not sufficed. While historical factors play a role, they don't explain everything.

Leadership and Strategic Vision

Stability, vision, and leadership come first. Lee Kuan Yew was Prime Minister of Singapore from 1959 to 1990. He then stayed on as "Minister Mentor" until 2011. Sheikh Mohammed bin Rashid Al Maktoum[11] has led Dubai's destiny since 2006. Such stability is rare, especially compared to Western countries.

Then, there is a vision of economic development: open to the outside world and based on market economy principles. Above all, the strategy is clear. International companies can adapt to almost any local rules, provided they do not always change. There is also the ability to communicate clearly and capture the imagination.[12]

Similarly, Hong Kong and especially Dubai have entered a race to build the world's tallest buildings. Today's record belongs to the Burj Khalifa in Dubai, which reaches an impressive height of 828 m (two and a half times the Eiffel Tower in Paris) and consists of 163 stories.

A Different Model of Social Peace

Social peace is essential. Lee Kuan Yew believed a successful government should share prosperity with the public through infrastructure like hospitals, schools, and housing.

---

[9]Airports Council International (2024). "Preliminary World Airport Traffic Rankings Released." April 14, 2024.

[10]For reference, in my country, Switzerland, with its 9 million inhabitants, Zurich Airport ranks 71st in passenger transport. These 2022 figures may vary slightly depending on the source, or whether they refer to international passengers only or freight.

[11]Wilson, Graeme. *To Be the First: The Authorised Biography of His Highness Sheikh Mohammed bin Rashid Al Maktoum.* Dubai: Motivate Publishing, 2023.

[12]When I first visited Singapore, there were signs everywhere: "It is green, clean and it works."

The economy must reflect everyday life. Singapore has also maintained social harmony by enforcing ethnic diversity in housing to prevent ethnic ghettos, a common issue elsewhere. Singapore's population comprises 53% Chinese, 13% Malay, and 9% Indian.

The significant contribution made by tourism to the economy sets Dubai apart from Hong Kong and Singapore. Tourism accounts for 9% of GDP. More than 14 million people visited Dubai in 2002, attracted by holidays and events. There are almost 800 hotels, with over 150,000 rooms. One of the most famous hotels is the Burj Al-Arab. Built on a small peninsula and opened in late 1999, it is often considered the world's most luxurious hotel. It has become an icon of the city.[13] The hotel's emblem can still be seen on car license plates in Dubai.

I first went there in the early 2000s. On the other side of the peninsula was a sandy beach and nothing else. One evening, I remember seeing a man sitting on the sand beside his two camels. He was watching the sunset over the sea. Those who know Dubai today realize, as I do, how much that image belongs to the past. Freeways crisscross the city these days, and it is almost impossible to cross on foot or walk around.

Switzerland, the Netherlands, and Northern Europe

These achievements should not overshadow other small countries' considerable, long-term success in both competitiveness and social stability.

IMD's World Competitiveness Yearbooks[14] analyze the performance of governments on over 300 criteria each year. The top-ranked regions are Switzerland, the Netherlands, most Northern European countries – Denmark, Sweden, Norway, Finland – and more recently the Baltic States (Estonia, Latvia, and Lithuania).

Sweden and Denmark benefit from a long history of prosperity, also thanks to their political power and the legacy of past kingdoms. The Netherlands drew its initial prosperity from managing one of the largest world trading networks of maritime routes and companies. The same was true of the Baltic States. Their trading activities extended to the Baltic Sea in the west – as part of the Hanseatic League – and to Ukraine and Russia in the south, reaching Constantinople by land and river.

---

[13] Smith, John. 2015. *Burj Al Arab: The Icon of Luxury Hospitality*. Dubai: Gulf Publishing.
[14] IMD World Competitiveness Center (2023). "IMD World Competitiveness Yearbook 2023." Lausanne, Switzerland: IMD.

Switzerland is different. The country is old politically (founded in 1291), but "young" economically. In 1900, estimates (notably Angus Maddison's) put Swiss GDP per capita at around $4,300 (in constant dollars). Today, Switzerland has one of the highest per capita GDPs among developed nations, at $87,000. Moreover, the Credit Suisse Global Wealth Report[15] estimated that, by 2020, the Swiss held an average of almost $700,000 in capital per adult. This would make them the most prosperous people in the world.

Recipe for Success

These countries have, to varying degrees, similar features that explain much of their success.

- They are open market economies with high stability and predictability in economic and political law.
- Economic infrastructures (transport, energy, communications, etc.) and social (education, health, old age) are of good quality and maintained through investment.
- Research and technological development are among the economic priorities that enable the creation of new businesses and support entrepreneurship.
- Apprenticeship is developed in educational institutes and companies to ensure a high employability rate among the population.
- Flexible work structures support high participation in the economy of all parts of the population; for example, through part-time work and greater involvement of women in professional activities.

In the past, there was a wide agreement on societal values. However, controversies have emerged due to an immigration policy that now draws mixed reactions from the public. This issue has sparked significant national debates in countries like Sweden, Denmark, and the Netherlands.

One key difference among these nations is their taxation structures. Scandinavian countries tend to tax individuals heavily while shielding companies, whereas Switzerland offers more protection to individuals. However, these differences are fading due to the OECD's effort to harmonize international corporate taxation.[16]

---

[15] Credit Suisse Research Institute. (2023). "Global Wealth Report 2023." Zurich, Switzerland: Credit Suisse.

[16] This point is further developed in Chapter 15.

A Fractured Europe? Confronting Entropy

Entropy is a concept linked to thermodynamics. It was first introduced by Rudolf Clausius in 1865 to describe energy dissipation.[17] Extending the idea to human affairs, it implies that any system naturally tends to drift towards more disorder, inefficiency, and complexity unless it is constantly managed.

Europe is a good example. Comprising 27 member states, along with the European Commission, the Council of Ministers, a Parliament, and numerous institutions, the European Union consistently seeks to maintain its relevance. Consequently, a certain level of unity is crucial for its survival in an increasingly size-oriented global landscape.

Excessive Fragmentation Stems Weakness

The concept of the nation-state is often associated in Europe with the Treaty of Westphalia, signed in 1648, which marked the end of the Thirty Years' War. It laid the foundations for modern states in Europe and beyond.[18] In particular, it enshrined the principle of the territorial and political sovereignty of states, meaning that each state has the right to govern its territory without outside interference.

In theory, all nations are equal, regardless of their size. However, in today's world, a country's size seems to be more important than its economic performance. Even if small countries are improving their competitiveness, they do not benefit from a similar increase in credibility on the international political stage.

For example, on December 15, 2021, Lithuania hurriedly evacuated its embassy in Beijing. A Taiwanese representative visiting Vilnius had triggered a diplomatic crisis. China's significant power, with its population 600 times greater than Lithuania's, stood in stark contrast to the small European nation. Despite Lithuania's GDP per capita being double that of China, the difference in scale rendered it insignificant.

Size Matters

Within Europe, there is an increasing disparity between the economic performance of countries and their political influence. Geographically, Europe comprises 49 countries,

---

[17] Clausius, Rudolf. *The Mechanical Theory of Heat: With Its Applications to the Steam Engine and to Physical Properties of Bodies.* Translated by John Tyndall. London: John van Voorst, 1867.
[18] Osiander, Andreas. 2001. *The States System of Europe, 1640–1990: Peacemaking and the Conditions of International Stability.* Oxford: Clarendon Press.

40 of which have less than 20 million people. The European Union is similar, where only 4 of its 27 countries – Germany, France, Italy, and Spain – have a population exceeding 45 million.[19]

Since the United Kingdom left the European Union, the imbalance between large and small nations has become even more noticeable. Germany and France alone account for almost 45% of European GDP. The temptation is great to create a France-Germany "duopoly" to rule Europe.

The same situation exists in the US. In 2023, California had a real GDP of $4,100 billion (more than Great Britain…) accounting for 14% of the US GDP. By comparison, Wyoming had a GDP of just $52 billion and Vermont $45 billion.

Alliances as a Solution?

Therefore, we can expect that smaller countries will multiply their economic and political alliances to collectively safeguard their interests in a world increasingly dominated by the "big boys."[20]

Regional agreements such as the European Union, the Mercosur in Latin America, the Association of Southeast Asian Nations (ASEAN), The Gulf Cooperation Council, and the African Continental Free Trade Area (ACFTA), will proliferate. They are considered alternatives to the waning influence of the multi-lateral system, represented by international institutions such as the World Trade Organization (WTO) in Geneva.

The fundamental problem posed by globalization is the representation of smaller nations. As we shall see later in the chapter on the evolution of globalization, the resurgence of powerful political and economic empires threatens multilateral institutions. In a conflict of interests, small nations are almost always marginalized.

The increasing geopolitical uncertainties reinforce the necessity for smaller nations worldwide to strengthen their cooperation and better coordinate their destiny. Benjamin Franklin emphasized this principle during the signing of the US Declaration of Independence in 1776:

We must all hang together, or most assuredly, we shall all hang separately.

---

[19] Next come Poland (38 million), Romania (21 million), and Holland (17 million). All the others – 19 countries – have fewer than 10 million inhabitants. Switzerland is comparable, with 9 million inhabitants.

[20] It should be noted that in a political alliance, such as a federation, size is always offset by an upper assembly (Council of States in Switzerland, Bundesrat in Germany, and Senate in the US and France) where member states are represented irrespective of their population. This is not the case with the European Union, which has only one legislative chamber, the European Parliament.

Chapter Takeaways

- Small nations have often been overlooked in competitiveness analyses. However, the opening of the world economy and the development of new technologies has enabled many smaller countries to benefit from rapid expansion. Examples include Singapore, Dubai, Saudi Arabia, Abu Dhabi, and the Dominican Republic.
- In Central and Northern Europe, similar patterns of competitiveness and success existed but were rooted in a longer history and different cultures. These include the Scandinavian countries, Finland and Switzerland.
- There are similarities between small nations: excellent infrastructure, a skilled workforce, a good education system, access to leading-edge technology, and often an advantageous tax system. However, economic competitiveness does not necessarily lead to political power. It may create vulnerability if large economic blocs want to impose their views on other nations.

Where Next?

We now head back to Asia, to a medium-sized country, Thailand (population of 71 million), whose competitiveness has often been linked to the dynamism of its tourism industry. While this is true, Thailand's economy is also characterized by strong attractiveness to foreign investment and openness to Southeast Asia, Japan, and the United States.

Thailand may be an example of a multi-aligned world, where nations outside the large economic blocs opt to collaborate with numerous partners, irrespective of political considerations or past relationships.

9 | Countries That Have Made Their Mark on Competitiveness: Thailand

Principle: Tourism can aid a nation's development, provided it doesn't hinder diversification into other sectors. Additionally, sectors that employ many people but use low technology should not be disregarded as contributors to a country's development and social stability.

A Country of Hospitality and Employment

Thailand occupies a special place in Southeast Asia. It is the only country in the region never to have been colonized by a Western power.[1] Its economy is highly diversified, from tourism to industry to agriculture. Its entrepreneurs are highly competitive. The job market is dynamic, with one of the lowest unemployment rates in the world. The country's diversity and complex urban-rural mix make governance difficult.[2]

---

[1] Wyatt, David K. *Thailand: A Short History*. 2nd. New Haven, CT: Yale University Press, 2003.
[2] I met several ministers and three prime ministers (Prem Tinsulanonda, Abhisit Vejjajiva, and Prayut-Chan-o-cha), and this issue was always mentioned.

Thailand has a population of 71 million. Its GDP per capita is around $7,000.[3] Thailand's economy is diverse and impressive. It is a top rice exporter and a leader in rubber, palm oil, and tin production. Its companies excel in textiles, distribution, cement, and electronics. The automotive production sector (trucks, cars, and motorcycles) is also very dynamic, with numerous foreign investments, notably from Japan and China.

The Formidable Impact of Tourism

Although Thailand is seen as a tourism-driven economy, with tourism contributing 15% to its GDP and drawing about 35 million visitors annually, it has balanced this with other sectors to avoid dependency on tourism alone. This contrasts with some countries where tourism can distort competitiveness assessments.

According to the World Travel & Tourism Council (WTTC),[4] the total contribution of tourism — including direct, indirect, and induced impacts — is almost 10% of world GDP. Tourism represents 9% of employment worldwide, or about 274 million people.[5] Thus, tourism is one of the world's largest industries, and it is more important than automotive, oil, or food.

A Springboard for Economic Development

Tourism's contribution to a country's prosperity is uneven and proportional to its economic development. The Maldives, for example, derives a third of its GDP from tourism. In Thailand, as we have seen, it is 15%, in Spain 14%, in Italy 13%, and 12% in China, France, and the United States.

Tourism straddles the gap between the local economy and the global economy.[6] Tourism revenues are often recorded in public accounts as an export; by contrast, the social impact is essentially local. A competitive strategy for tourism implies that a country must be able to offer one or more of the following advantages: water (or snow), sun, nature or exotism, culture, and safety.[7]

---

[3] Its main neighbors are Malaysia (33 million inhabitants), with a GDP per capita of $12,000, and Vietnam (97 million) with $4,100.

[4] World Travel & Tourism Council (WTTC). *Travel & Tourism Economic Impact 2023: Country Reports*. London: WTTC, 2023.

[5] "About," because in most countries, many people make their living from tourism, but "informally," that is without being registered.

[6] See Chapter 13.

[7] Paris, Beijing, Orlando, Shanghai, Las Vegas, New York, Tokyo, and Mexico City are the world's most visited cities.

Developing countries often see tourism as a first step towards competitiveness. Initially, infrastructure expenditures can be limited. It can even be a strategy for ecotourism, where the aim is to be part of a preserved environment. This is the case in Africa (for animal life) or Latin America (for tropical forests, mountains, or lost civilizations).

A Deterrent to Economic Diversification?

While the advantages of tourism are apparent, there are also disadvantages. Focusing on rapid financial returns has led some countries to neglect diversification into other infrastructures or investments to develop local industry, exports, or foreign investment.[8] Nations that depend exclusively on tourism often experience a lack of broader economic development. While tourism can give the appearance of economic advancement by capitalizing on natural or cultural resources, it frequently fails to evolve into higher value-added activities.

In addition, tourism growth is often linked to real estate. However, real estate markets can be cyclical and subject to fluctuations. Without regulation, this can result in real estate bubbles and subsequent financial bubbles. State intervention may then be necessary to stabilize the market, which could increase public debt.

Aversion by the Local Population

Tourism can also harm the environment, disrupt territorial planning, and affect local culture. Some countries, like Oman and Botswana, have addressed this by restricting tourism to specific areas. Too much tourist success can also create resentment among the local population. Venice recently decided to ban large cruise ships from docking near the city center. In 1950, Venice attracted 50,000 tourists a year. Today, it is over 30 million![9]

Effectively Managed Tourism Boosts Competitiveness

Thailand demonstrates that tourism can be a vital strategy for enhancing competitiveness, provided it is leveraged to foster the development of other sectors. The objective should be to generate a broad economic impact by transferring technology, skills, and training to a larger populace. As with other regions, competitiveness should drive diversification.[10]

---

[8] World Bank. 2017. Tourism and Competitiveness. Washington, DC: World Bank. https://www.worldbank.org/en/topic/competitiveness/brief/tourism-and-competitiveness.

[9] Anti-tourist protests by local residents seem to be on the increase. This was recently the case in Barcelona (12 million tourists for 1.6 million inhabitants) and in the Canary Islands.

[10] Thailand also faces challenges, mainly the household debt which is worth 92% of the GDP and a slower diversification in traditional sectors such as raw materials, food, and car manufacturing.

Thailand is also remarkable in another way that often goes unnoticed: it has the lowest unemployment rate in the world, usually around 1%, often less. Several factors might explain this. One is the agricultural sector, which employs 32% of the workforce and has relatively low productivity. Another factor is tourism, as previously mentioned, and there are likely many jobs in the undeclared informal sector. Additionally, labor migration occurs to other countries in the region, such as Korea and Japan, as well as to countries in the Middle East. Approximately 113,000 emigrant workers return remittances, amounting to 1.8% of Thailand's GDP annually.[11]

The Contribution to Employment

Thailand's labor laws allow flexibility in hiring and firing. This approach aligns with an economic principle that suggests companies' ability to manage their workforce within the legal framework can result in increased job creation compared to restrictive legislation.

Indeed, companies are more likely to employ new staff if they know that they can quickly adapt their numbers in the event of future problems. In the case of very rigid legislation, they will wait as long as possible, knowing that their decision will be more or less irreversible.[12]

In Thailand, not all jobs are high value-added. However, these jobs have the advantage of involving many people in the workforce. An employee who greets customers at a store entrance or on an escalator has the potential to advance within the company. On the other hand, individuals who are not involved in employment may not experience similar opportunities.

Employment Rate Is Fundamental

The employment rate indicates the number of working-age people involved in a country's wealth creation. Thailand's example shows that it is a key factor not only for a country's economic success but also for its social stability. The official employment rate in Thailand is 68%.

By international comparison,[13] the employment rate in Iceland, the Netherlands, New Zealand, and Switzerland exceeds 80%. In the UK, it is 76%, and in the US, it is 71%. By contrast, in France, the rate is 68%, and in Italy, it is 61%.

---

[11] International Organization for Migration (IOM): *World Migration Report 2024.*

[12] The debate remains open, as some companies have abused this principle. I remember visiting a paper company in the US that had been bought out by a foreign competitor. A large number of employees were laid off within a week, only to be rehired the following week under a new employment contract with different terms and conditions. In Europe, this would have caused a riot…

[13] Organisation for Economic Co-operation and Development (OECD). (2023). "Employment Outlook 2023." Paris: OECD Publishing. https://doi.org/10.1787/empl_outlook-2023-en

A low employment rate is a risk to social stability. It also implies that taxes are focused on a limited number of companies and individuals who work. The result is often a high rate of taxation that demotivates the active part of the population.

Economists often focus too much on productivity. While important, low productivity associated with high employment sectors such as tourism, agriculture, and construction are also essential for balanced economic and social development. A sound economy cannot function solely based on highly qualified people thriving while others remain unemployed or precarious.

Chapter Takeaways

- Thailand's success illustrates two important factors in competitiveness: tourism and employment rates. The former impacts a country's attractiveness, while the latter cements social stability.
- Tourism, which accounts for around 10% of global GDP, is often seen as a catalyst for a country's development, as it capitalizes on existing geographical and cultural assets. However, it creates low value-added jobs and requires significant investment, particularly in real estate. As such, it risks slowing down a country's industrial diversification.
- The employment rate, which is high in Thailand, is often overlooked in terms of competitiveness. An economy that employs many people contributes to the stability of a society, a key factor of competitiveness. Conversely, when the employment rate is low, fewer working individuals must carry a substantial portion of the tax burden. This is the case in France.

Where Next?

Staying in Asia, we now move to another medium-sized country, South Korea (population 52 million), which, contrary to Thailand, once had an image problem. For decades, the country was considered extremely efficient but closed and unattractive to foreign investment and expatriates.

The world's opinion changed in just a few years. This was achieved thanks to a "soft power" strategy that had a considerable impact globally, particularly on young people. Competitiveness is also a matter of perception: how can one change one's image?

10 | Countries That Have Made Their Mark on Competitiveness: South Korea

Principle: Success also means leveraging how to manage an image and the influence it creates.

The Country of the Quiet Morning Is Heard

"Soft power" is a concept first defined by Professor Joseph Nye, former dean of Harvard's Kennedy School of Government.[1] It is the ability to attract and convince rather than coerce. Korea has become a master in this field.

South Korea has a population of 52 million. Despite the war and tensions with North Korea, its economy and competitiveness have developed exceptionally well

---

[1] Nye, J. S. (1990). *"Soft Power." Foreign Policy*, (80), 153–171. https://doi.org/10.2307/1148580

in recent decades. According to the IMF, GDP per capita is just over $33,000 (current prices), placing the country between Japan and Spain.

Korea was once known for its strength in heavy industries like shipbuilding and automobiles. Recently, the focus has shifted to advanced technology sectors such as telecommunications, IT, and consumer goods.

A World Leader in New Technologies

For example, Korea has positioned itself as a world leader in LCD (liquid crystal display) screens for computers, tablets, televisions, and telephones. This was followed by important innovations such as active-matrix displays (TFT-LCD), which offer better image quality, and then OLED (organic light-emitting diodes) and QLED (quantum-dot LED) displays.

Korea is also a world leader in robotics. According to the International Federation of Robotics,[2] Korea has the highest density of robots in the world, with 1,000 industrial robots for every 10,000 employees in production, compared with 399 in Japan, 322 in China, and 274 in the USA.

Korea's image is associated with large, often family-owned industrial groups known as Chaebols.[3] These are comparable to the German Konzerns of the 1930s or the Japanese Keiretsu. Examples include Samsung, Hyundai, SK, LG, Lotte, and Hanwha.

Despite its economic successes, the country's image has been marred by corruption scandals in both the private sector and government. To restore its reputation, the "Land of Morning Calm" employed a soft power strategy.

Pop Music and Gaming

Internationally, Korea's image has improved with the emergence of a new sector in the music industry: K-pop. For example, BTS, Blackpink, Stray Kids, and Seventeen have gained worldwide fame, creating an upbeat, modern, and distinctly different image of the country.[4]

The popularity of K-dramas, illustrated by the international success of films such as "Parasite," has considerably strengthened Korea's cultural presence. These media products often highlight Korean values, traditions, modern life, and cuisine with dishes such as kimchi (a traditional pickled vegetable dish).

---

[2] International Federation of Robotics (IFR). (2023). *World Robotics 2023: Industrial Robots.* Frankfurt.

[3] Chang, Sea-Jin. 2003. *Financial Crisis and Transformation of Korean Business Groups: The Rise and Fall of Chaebols.* Cambridge: Cambridge University Press.

[4] Russell, Mark James. *K-Pop Now!: The Korean Music Revolution.* North Clarendon: Tuttle Publishing, 2014.

South Korea's influence in the gaming industry and the world of e-sports, with games such as "StarCraft" and "League of Legends," has also contributed to its soft power, particularly among young people around the world. In 2023, Seoul hosted the world championship of the "League of Legends" game in front of tens of thousands of people.

The impact of e-sports[5] has become so considerable that the International Olympic Committee is considering including them in its program. However, traditional sports are also hosted in South Korea: the 1988 Olympic Games in Seoul, the 2002 FIFA World Cup, the 2018 Winter Olympics in Pyeong Chang, the 2024 Youth Olympics in Gangwon, etc. The Korean government supports these initiatives to balance tradition with future technologies and youth aspirations.

Celebrity Endorsement

Companies have long acknowledged the influence of soft power and the ability of celebrities to shape their public image.

Such a policy is not exclusive to Korea. Dubai has also used soft power extensively to create its image. The government called on celebrities such as David Beckham and Roger Federer to praise the good life in Dubai. The idea was to show that a society respectful of its traditions could coexist with foreign cultures and new technologies.

Great Britain was probably a forerunner in this field. It was quick to recognize that music and sports, commonly taught in British education, could promote the country's image. The government and monarchy have taken major sports clubs and musical groups seriously. In recognition of services rendered, the monarchy readily awards honorary titles: the Beatles or the Rolling Stones are "Sirs."

Rolex, the watch manufacturer, was a pioneer of celebrity endorsement. In 1953, Sir Edmund Hillary and Tenzing Norgay wore a Rolex Oyster Perpetual on their ascent of Mount Everest. Later, Paul Newman displayed a Rolex Daytona. And today, the list of such affiliations would be long: Michael Jordan with Nike, George Clooney with Nespresso, Beyoncé with Pepsi, Taylor Swift with Diet Coke, Cristiano Ronaldo with Herbalife, Leonardo DiCaprio with TAG Heuer, or David Beckham with Adidas.[6]

Social Networks

Soft power, from the point of view of both governments and companies, is taking on a particular dimension today with the emergence of "influencers"

---

[5] Such as football or car racing.
[6] Pringle, Hamish. *Celebrity Sells*. Chichester: John Wiley & Sons, 2004.

(or "YouTubers"):[7] 22% of Internet users worldwide admit to assiduously following the advice of influencers. Social media is their market of choice, with 4.2 billion users spending an average of 2.25 hours daily.[8]

The smartphone is a widely used medium. On average, individuals spend 6 hours and 54 minutes daily on the Internet, with two-thirds spent on mobile devices. During mobile usage, 44% of the time is devoted to social media. Social media platforms are now used not only for messaging and photo sharing but also as sources of information, tools for brand and product comparisons, and platforms for shopping.

A Good Deal for Everyone

In China, livestreams and influencers generated over $400 billion in sales in 2022, accounting for 15% of online business, up from 3.5% three years earlier. TikTok and Douyin are the top platforms there. At the same time, Instagram and YouTube lead in the US and Europe, with influencers responsible for 5% of online sales. Social media is increasingly taking over from traditional search engines like Google, particularly among younger generations.[9]

Influencing can be quite profitable, with average commissions of 2% for video games, 4.5% for books on Amazon, and up to 10% for beauty products. The new generation has understood this. In 2018, the Lego company commissioned a survey of 3,000 8–12-year-olds to ask them what profession they would like to be in when they grow up.[10]

In the US and Great Britain, 30% said they wanted to be YouTubers, and only 11% wanted to be astronauts (compared to 56% in China). Gone are the days when children wanted to be firefighters, nurses, or police officers. In Brazil, for example, 45% of the population report following influencers.[11]

Soft power has thus entered a new dimension, shaped by new technologies and celebrities, both established and up-and-coming. Nevertheless, the basic concept remains very powerful.

---

[7] In six months in 2022, Kendall Jenner, an American actress, generated $3.7 million worth of advertising for Prada on her Instagram site. In China, Li Jiaqi sold over $1.7 billion worth of lipstick in a 12-hour livestream in 2021.

[8] This varies by country: Filipinos spend 4 hours 15 minutes, Americans and Chinese just over 2 hours, Swiss 1 hour 25 minutes, and the Japanese less than an hour.

[9] Lorenz, Taylor. *Extremely Online: The Untold Story of Fame, Influence, and Power on the Internet.* New York: Simon & Schuster, 2023.

[10] LEGO Group. 2018. LEGO Play Well Report 2018. Billund, Denmark: LEGO Group.

[11] During his presidential campaign in 2022, Luis Inacio Lula da Silva received support from pop star Anitta who has a following of 63 million, which benefited the visibility of both parties.

Chapter Takeaways

- South Korea is a prime example of a country that has successfully transformed its image. Initially, it was labeled as an extremely efficient but relatively closed economy dominated by large conglomerates (the Chaebols), which were highly innovative but not particularly exciting.
- A "soft power" strategy has increased Korea's international visibility, particularly among young people. It was achieved by promoting sporting events such as the Olympic Games, pop music groups, and even its cuisine and maintaining a strong presence on social networks.
- Consequently, South Korea has boosted its image of attractiveness and openness, increasing its economic and political prestige. A good international reputation is always an invaluable asset for competitiveness.

Where Next?

We remain in Asia with two countries illustrating different approaches to transforming natural resources into competitiveness.

Within just a few years, Malaysia transformed its natural resources wealth into revenues invested in cutting-edge technologies. Such a policy has also attracted significant foreign direct investment.

Conversely, Mongolia, which also has considerable natural resources, has focused more on raw extraction and distributing income to the population. This has led to increased vulnerability in competitiveness, as the country sometimes relies heavily on variations in international commodity prices and decisions made by significant foreign investors.

11 | Secure Access to Raw Materials and Energy

Principle: natural resource wealth is a double-edged sword. Well or poorly managed, it can determine a country's future.

Malaysia: A Rich and Diverse Country

Upon arriving in Kuala Lumpur, the Petronas Towers are one of the first sights to catch your eye, representing both the national oil company and the country's economic strength. Malaysia stands out as one of the rare nations that has effectively transitioned from a commodity-based economy to one with higher value-added industries.[1]

Malaysia has abundant reserves of oil, natural gas, tin, and iron. Its agricultural sector is particularly renowned for producing palm oil, rubber, and timber, primarily concentrated on the island of Borneo. However, the nation has progressed beyond being a mere exporter of raw materials. It has developed a strong manufacturing industry, emerging as an exporter of electronic goods, electrical components, and automotive assemblies.

---

[1] Malaysia, a federation of 13 states, is a constitutional monarchy headed by a king elected for five years. The country comprises the Malay Peninsula, where most of the population lives, and East Malaysia, i.e., northern Borneo, comprising the states of Sarawak and Sabah.

Following the 1969 riots, the government implemented the "Bumiputra" policy[2] to support ethnic Malays in economic, political, and social areas. Initially seen as too restrictive for foreign investment, the policy was gradually relaxed. Now, Malaysia is open to foreign investment, with some limitations on ownership and employment in specific sectors like finance and real estate.

New Technologies

A striking example of Malaysia's move towards technological activities is the development of Cyberjaya. Created in 2003 at the instigation of then Prime Minister Mahathir Mohamed, this new city is 25 km south of Kuala Lumpur.

It aims to attract high value-added research and development activities. Microsoft, BMW, and Nokia have all decided to set up regional headquarters here. This is especially symbolic since the land used to be covered with palm plantations.

In 2025, Malaysia and Singapore signed the Johor–Singapore Special Economic Zone to attract high-end technology investments in sectors like artificial intelligence, semiconductors, quantum computing, and manufacturing equipment.[3]

Johor has already developed into a global hub for data centers, receiving investments from companies such as Nvidia, Microsoft, and ByteDance, and generating approximately 35,000 jobs.

Mongolia: A Bumpy Road to Wealth

When you leave Ulaanbaatar airport, do not take the wrong road: to the left, you're heading for the capital; to the right, you're heading for the country's vast, arid steppes. At the very end is the famous Gobi Desert. Marco Polo described it thus: "It is a very vast desert … where nothing is to be seen, no birds, no trees, no stones, only sand."

Today, Mongolia is attracting significant interest for the first time since its independence from China in 1911.[4] In 2023, Mongolia's mining industry accounted for

---

[2] Mason, Richard, and Ariffin S. M. Omar, eds. *The "Bumiputera Policy": Dynamics and Dilemmas*. Penang: Universiti Sains Malaysia Press, 2004.

[3] "Johor-Singapore Special Economic Zone." PricewaterhouseCoopers (PwC), January 2025.

[4] The country is vast: 1,564,000 km^2 with just 3,200,000 inhabitants. It has the lowest population density in the world: 2 people per km^2! Mongolians believe that almost the entire population is descended from Genghis Khan. His gigantic statue stands in the center of Ulaanbaatar. But the country is opening up to the rest of the world: a Louis-Vuitton store was opened not far away.

28% of GDP and 92% of exports.[5] According to World Bank estimates, Mongolia's GDP per capita in 2023 exceeds $5,000. This compares with $463 in 2000!

Natural Resources: A Double-Edged Sword

In 2000, the Canadian company Ivanhoe estimated that there were probably the largest copper and gold deposits discovered in recent decades in an area called Oyu Tolgoi (Mongolian for "turquoise hill"), near the Chinese border.[6] Today, the mine is thought to contain 12.7 million tonnes of copper reserves, 966 tonnes of gold, and 2,400 tonnes of silver.[7]

This discovery was the starting point for an extensive raw materials policy approved by the Mongolian government. In 2015, it opened up 31 million hectares, or 20% of its territory, to exploration and mining.[8]

Malaysia and Mongolia illustrate how a sudden influx of raw material wealth can affect a country, both positively and negatively. Economists have even called this the "curse of raw materials," acknowledging the possible detrimental effects. Professors Richard Auty of Lancaster University and Jeffrey Sachs of Harvard and Columbia Universities,[9] among others, have developed this thesis.

Poor Management: A Danger for Long-Term Competitiveness

There is frequently a negative link between a nation's long-term growth and a high volume of raw materials exports. Nations like Russia, Kazakhstan, Brazil, South Africa, Nigeria, and the Democratic Republic of Congo (DRC), to name a few, are abundant in raw materials but do not always experience robust economic growth.

These economies often depend on volatile commodity prices, making it hard to forecast revenues and plan investments due to a lack of pricing control.

---

[5] East Asia Forum. "The Hidden Cost of Mongolia's Mining Boom." February 7, 2025. https://eastasiaforum.org/2025/02/07/the-hidden-cost-of-mongolias-mining-boom/ (accessed May 14, 2052).

[6] Hancock, Tom. *The Mongolian Mining Revolution: Oyu Tolgoi and Beyond.* London: Routledge, 2015.

[7] Rio Tinto. "Oyu Tolgoi." December 2024. https://www.riotinto.com/en/operations/mongolia/oyu-tolgoi (accessed May 14, 2025).

[8] To date, 30% of Mongolia's soil has been analyzed, leading to the discovery of 6,000 vast deposits of 80 different metals. In January 2019, 32% of the country's 1,670 mining licenses were for gold veins (Switzerland is the biggest buyer) and 18% for coal. Mongolia's most important customer is China, which absorbs 86% of its exports, including copper, coal, molybdenum, zinc, and iron.

[9] Sachs, Jeffrey D., and Andrew M. Warner. *Natural Resource Abundance and Economic Growth.* Cambridge, MA: National Bureau of Economic Research, 1995.

Major exchanges, like the London Metal Exchange in industrialized nations, handle most non-ferrous metal trades. In the US, the Chicago Mercantile Exchange, which developed the futures system for agricultural commodities, acquired the Chicago Board of Trade in 2007, solidifying its market dominance.

The Next Challenge: New Rare Materials

It is difficult for countries to resist the temptation to focus their economic development on exporting raw materials. New raw materials like the coveted rare earths are often found in developing countries.

The Democratic Republic of Congo accounts for two-thirds of the world's cobalt production. It is mined by large foreign companies (Glencore of Switzerland and CMOC of China). However, there are also cases where private individuals work under dire conditions in small wells. Chile has the largest copper and lithium reserves in Latin America. However, Chile is in danger of being dethroned by Bolivia, which appears to have even more significant lithium resources in the "Solar of Uyuni."

The 17 rare earth elements crucial to the new "green" economy are primarily sourced from impoverished areas globally.[10] At present, China is virtually monopolizing the processing of rare earths. Today, for example, it produces most of the components used to manufacture solar panels, wind turbines, and car batteries.

Mali's Ephemeral Wealth

In the 14th century, Mali was Africa's richest empire, trading gold (and slaves) with the Arab world and Europe.

At the time, Mansa Musa, who ruled Mali, was considered the richest man in the world. His pilgrimage to Mecca in 1324 remains famous for its opulence and pomp.

Then, sea routes to the Americas were discovered. Europe and China sourced gold and silver from across the Atlantic, and Mali lost its wealth.

Today, according to the International Monetary Fund, Mali's GDP per capita is just over \$900, putting it in 167th place worldwide (2022 figures). Mali has become one of the poorest countries in the world.

---

[10] They are also present in regions like the US and Europe, including Sweden, Portugal, and Finland. The environmental impact of mining these elements and the opposition from local communities have frequently hindered their development.

Historical evidence suggests that excelling in producing a raw material does not necessarily secure future success (see the Mali insert). In some instances, technological advances have made natural resources outdated. For example, rubber tapped from rubber trees was supplanted by synthetic rubber derived from petroleum. Natural fibers like cotton, wool, and silk, traditionally used in textiles, have frequently been substituted with synthetic fibers like polyester, nylon, and acrylic. Similarly, vegetable oils were substituted with synthetic oils and wood with plywood or plastic. These technological changes repeatedly devastated entire nations. This happened in Egypt, where a significant portion of wealth came from cotton farming. Another instance is the Amazonian city of Manáos, which once amassed great wealth from natural rubber.[11]

A Circular Economy?

Certain industrialized nations are now shifting their focus from procurement to recycling. Northvolt in Sweden exemplifies this strategy by advancing new lithium-ion and sodium-ion battery technologies. Their goal is to produce "batteries made from batteries," meaning they plan to recycle materials from old batteries to reduce the need for importing new resources.[12]

This is the idea of a circular economy.[13] Companies like Ikea apply it by allowing customers to return used furniture for recycling and use in new products. This method could also be extended to electronics, requiring products to be designed for easy disassembly and component reuse.

This transition will not occur overnight. For many years, traditional and new materials will coexist. In 2024, the world had 440 nuclear reactors, with 50 more under construction. Additionally, there are still 6,000 power plants using oil and gas, and 2,400 relying on coal.

Turning Raw Materials into Added Value

The world will continue to need raw materials, even the most traditional ones. Copper, for example, will be used in both the conventional economy and the modern, electrified one.

Occasionally, fate steps in. During the 1980s, Dubai recognized that its oil resources were depleting faster than its neighbor, Abu Dhabi. In response, its leader,

---

[11] Its prominence was so great that it drew Sarah Bernhard, who performed "La Dame aux Camélias" at the Teatro Amazonas in 1905.

[12] Despite the promising concept, the company filed for bankruptcy in March 2025, highlighting that effective implementation is critical for competitiveness.

[13] Lacy, Peter, Jessica Long, and Wesley Spindler. *The Circular Economy Handbook: Realizing the Circular Advantage*. London: Palgrave Macmillan, 2020.

Sheikh Mohammed Al Maktoum, implemented a robust strategy to diversify the economy into sectors like trade, finance, technology, and tourism, paving the way for its present-day prosperity.

Like tourism, raw materials should be leveraged to shift an economy towards higher value-added activities. Historically, nations like Japan, Switzerland, Singapore, and Denmark, which had few natural resources, thrived by diversifying their economies early, focusing on exports and foreign investments. Switzerland is well-known for its chocolate companies. It is the top producer and consumer of chocolate globally, with each person eating 8.8 kg annually. However, the country is not growing a single gram of cocoa beans.[14]

Therefore, there is no commodity curse — just bad strategy.

Chapter Takeaways

- Malaysia exemplifies a nation that has transitioned rapidly from extracting raw materials to fostering competitiveness through the high added value of new technologies. This policy has significantly enhanced the country's attractiveness to foreign investors, further strengthened by establishing Special Economic Zones.
- Conversely, Mongolia has encountered challenges in leveraging its natural resource wealth to enhance its competitiveness, which would have facilitated the diversification of its economy and the transition towards higher value-added industries.
- This last example illustrates the concept of the commodity curse, which has been used to explain why countries rich in material resources sometimes have more difficulty developing their competitiveness than other countries lacking such wealth.

Where Next?

In the next chapter, we look at how countries ensure long-term competitiveness by investing regularly in their economic and social infrastructure and maintenance.

Investments of this nature typically involve substantial costs and long durations, presenting challenges for governments that tend to prioritize initiatives with immediate benefits for the population. Nevertheless, they provide a stable framework for a country's economy and intergenerational wealth. Finally, they provide jobs for a wide range of skills, from the least skilled blue-collar workers to engineers.

---

[14] Chocosuisse. *Chocology: The Swiss Chocolate Industry, Past and Present*. Bern: Chocosuisse, 2000.

12 | Efficient Economic and Social Infrastructure

Principle: It is generally accepted that infrastructure is the fundamental investment determining a country's economic future. In general, this is true.

The Nordic European Countries

Upon exiting Copenhagen airport, travelers will notice two groups of taxis: one with Danish plates and another with Swedish plates. This is due to the Øresund bridge, which has connected Denmark and Sweden (specifically Copenhagen and Malmö) since July 2000. The only indication of crossing a country's border is when the name of the telecommunication network changes on your cell phone.[1]

Right next door is the Middelgrunden offshore wind farm complex. When it was launched in 2000, it was the world's largest wind farm. Today, wind power covers over 50% of the country's electricity needs. Two Danish companies, Vestas and Oersted, are among the world leaders in this sector.

---

[1] The Øresund Bridge is 7.8 km long and comprises a road, rail tunnel, and bridge over the strait. The bridge has an air draught of 57 m, allowing large ships to pass underneath.

As for Copenhagen's Kastrup airport, mentioned earlier, it is the 17th largest in Europe.[2] Still, it is often considered one of the best in terms of user-friendliness. All these investments are remarkable for a country of 6 million inhabitants. However, it is not the only example of outstanding infrastructure investment in the Nordic countries.

Norway: Wealth at Work

Norway, for example, has over 1,800 road and rail tunnels linking a country divided by geography. The Laerdal road tunnel, at 24.5 km, connects Oslo and Bergen by road and is the world's longest.[3] A little further on is the world's longest underwater tunnel, the Ryfylke, which is 14.4 km long and reaches a depth of 292 m.[4]

With a population of 5.4 million, Norway finances many investments through its sovereign wealth fund, which is partly fueled by oil and gas revenues. This fund, the largest in the world, manages over $1,400 billion. A country's investment in its infrastructure is often expensive (because it also has to be maintained). Still, economists believe it is one of the few more or less safe bets a nation can make on its future.

Investing for the Future

Intelligent infrastructure investment is essential for a nation's competitiveness and development. "Intelligent" is the key word. Many poorly designed infrastructures do not meet any needs. For example, there is an impressive list of bridges that lead nowhere in Oregon and Mongolia and China.

Some investments, like some construction of Olympic sports facilities, have a shorter lifespan than the effort involved. After the event, these buildings often become underutilized or neglected. The International Olympic Committee now mandates that cities which want to host the Olympic Games present in their candidature project how they will maximize the reuse of infrastructure post-event. The Paris Olympics were the first to follow this formal requirement.

Overdoing It

Countries can also err on the side of excess. Dubai and China have sometimes invested excessively, particularly in real estate. The original strategy was not necessarily wrong.

---

[2] Airports Council International. *Top 10 Busiest Airports in the World Shift with the Rise of International Air Travel Demand*. Montreal: Airports Council International, April 14, 2024.

[3] Switzerland is also said to have 1,800 tunnels, including the Gothard, which is the longest in the world for trains: 57.1 km.

[4] One is struck by the technology behind every detail when driving through these tunnels. Sometimes, the lighting changes color to keep drivers alert during the journey. At other times, there is a traffic roundabout, deep underwater, to direct the circulation to another tunnel, to another island…

In the case of China, it was to attract farmers to the industrial cities, where they would find employment.[5] For Dubai, it was to attract foreign firms[6] and tourism.

Supply-side economics means that investment precedes and, theoretically, creates demand. However, there may be too great a mismatch between investment and demand, or the market may be saturated. In this case, a price correction on assets can destabilize companies and individuals. In such a case, debt is exploding, and the government has to intervene, as it did in Dubai in 2009. In China, by 2023, the two major real estate groups, Evergrande and Country Garden, had a combined debt of over $500 billion.

Not Doing Enough

The World Bank and Oxford Economics estimate that $94 trillion needs to be invested by 2040 to meet the various infrastructure requirements of the population.[7] China currently absorbs around 30% of global infrastructure investment. Worldwide, the most significant deficit is in roads, which account for around 50% of the investment shortfall, particularly in developing countries.

The United States faces the largest infrastructure investment gap at around $3.8 trillion. This has led to measures like the Infrastructure Act, which allocates $1,200 billion, plus $280 billion for science and semiconductors. In Europe, cross-border infrastructure connections require $600 billion in investments.

In addition, it can be estimated that 2–4% of the replacement value of infrastructure assets should be devoted to maintenance. Unfortunately, this is often not the case. Governments tend to economize on maintenance costs when public finances are weak.

Megacities: A New Infrastructure Challenge

Of the world's 20 largest agglomerations, only Tokyo, New York, Los Angeles, and Osaka are in industrialized countries. The other largest cities – Mumbai, Delhi, Dhaka, Mexico City, São Paulo, Lagos, and Jakarta – are in developing countries. All have more than 20 million inhabitants.[8]

---

[5] It is estimated that around 300 million people have migrated from rural to urban areas in China over the past 40 years. The share of the urban population has risen from less than 20% in 1980 to over 60% in 2020.

[6] According to the Chamber of Commerce, there will be more than 3,200 foreign firms in Dubai by 2023.

[7] World Bank, & Oxford Economics (2017). "Global Infrastructure Outlook: Infrastructure Investment Needs 50 Countries, 7 Sectors to 2040." Washington, DC: World Bank Group.

[8] Encyclopedia Britannica. *List of the World's Largest Cities by Population*. https://www.britannica .com/topic/list-of-the-worlds-largest-cities-by-population (accessed March 2, 2025).

The Wealth of Big Cities

According to McKinsey, the 600 largest cities in the world already generate almost 60% of its GDP.

Thus, and this time according to Price Waterhouse, Tokyo hosts 26.8% of the Japanese population but creates 34% of the GDP, London 20.3% of the population and 25.4% of the GDP, Paris 16.2% of the population and 26.5% of the GDP.

In the United States, 90% of GDP is generated by 10% of its counties (administrative divisions of the states – there are 3,142 of them); essentially, in cities.

The concentration of wealth is even more marked in developing countries. Buenos Aires, for example, is home to 32.5% of Argentina's population and generates 63.2% of the country's wealth. Bangkok is home to over 11 million people, a 7th of the country's population, but accounts for almost 40% of GDP.

The United Nations[9] estimates that Africa's population will double by 2050 to over 2.2 billion. By the same date, for example, Nigeria will have become the third largest country in the world (440 million inhabitants), surpassing the United States. One of the reasons is that Nigeria has the highest fertility rate in the world, over 6%, compared to 1.5% in China.

While megacities may concentrate a country's wealth (see insert), they can also be places of hardship in many nations. Poverty and security issues are often a problem.[10] Additionally, statistical data can be hard to collect.

Megacities also face challenges related to the coexistence of diverse value systems with those of the surrounding areas. Major urban centers often host a cosmopolitan population highly educated and skilled in economic matters. On the other hand, surrounding regions, particularly agricultural ones, remain attached to traditional, local values. This has led to a widening gap in mentality between the urban elite and the rest of the country.[11]

---

[9] United Nations, Department of Economic and Social Affairs, Population Division (2022). "World Population Prospects 2022: Summary of Results." New York: United Nations.

[10] For instance, Brazil and Mexico account for 29 out of the 50 cities with the highest homicide rates per capita.

[11] Thailand has experienced this cultural split on several occasions, with far-reaching political consequences that have affected social peace in the country.

In addition to megacities, a new development is the emergence of mega-regions that cluster cities. By 2030, forty mega-regions will account for two-thirds of the world's GDP and develop 80% of its technologies. For example, the new bridge linking Hong Kong and Macau (55 km long) is consolidating the economic development of the Pearl River Delta region, home to 120 million people and a GDP comparable to that of South Korea.[12]

In wealthy countries, technology can help solve many problems affecting the management of cities and their infrastructures. This is the concept of "smart cities."[13] Among the experiences most frequently mentioned in international studies are those of Zurich, Oslo, Singapore, Dubai, Vancouver, Los Angeles, Beijing, Seoul, Hong Kong, Canberra, Montreal, Denver, Bilbao, Bengaluru, Brisbane, Busan, Sydney, and Shanghai.

Artificial intelligence can also support city management in areas such as transport flows, energy consumption, and security.

New Capitals

To address urban congestion, many countries have relocated their political capitals. Brazil moved its capital from Rio de Janeiro to Brasilia in 1960, Pakistan from Karachi to Islamabad in 1967, Nigeria from Lagos to Abuja in 1991, and Kazakhstan from Almaty to Astana (now Nur-Sultan) in 1997. Egypt[14] and Indonesia[15] are working on similar projects. Malaysia has already transferred part of its administration to a new city, Putrajaya, located 20 km from the official capital, Kuala Lumpur. It may one day become the country's capital.

The Age of Electricity

According to the International Energy Agency, the world is entering the age of electricity, following the age of coal and oil. In Europe, the power demand will increase by 40% until 2033.[16]

---

[12] New cities are also being built from scratch. In Saudi Arabia, the construction of the city of "Neom" and its surrounding area in the north of the kingdom is estimated at over $500 billion dollars.

[13] IMD Smart City Observatory (2023). "IMD Smart City Index 2023". Lausanne: International Institute for Management Development.

[14] The "New Administrative Capital" 45 km east of Cairo.

[15] Called "Nusantara," it is located on the island of Borneo, in the province of East Kalimantan, and the first stage of construction was inaugurated in 2024.

[16] International Energy Agency. World Energy Outlook 2024. Paris: International Energy Agency, 2024. https://www.iea.org/reports/world-energy-outlook-2024

The Energy Transition Commission estimates that achieving zero carbon emissions by 2050 will require annual investments of $2,500 billion. About 55% should go into energy production, while the remaining 45% should be invested in the grid for electricity storage, transmission, and distribution. It will also require more "traditional" infrastructures, such as dams and pylons, which are not necessarily very popular with the population.[17]

Cities have a considerable environmental impact. They consume two-thirds of all energy and are responsible for 70% of greenhouse gas emissions. New technologies are also boosting demand. Goldman Sachs predicts data centers will see a 160% rise in energy use by 2030. In Dublin, Ireland, 80 data centers consume as much electricity as 20% of households.[18] A query on an artificial intelligence platform consumes up to 10 times the energy of a standard Google search.[19]

Intergenerational Impact

There are many reasons why investment in infrastructure considerably impacts a country's competitiveness. The first is an intergenerational impact. These investments benefit not only the current population but also the future. In the long term, they remain the property of a country and cannot be removed.

Turgut Özal, President of Turkey (1989–1993), Prime Minister (1983–1989)

In Davos, a meeting was organized between Turgut Özal and the Greek Prime Minister Andreas Papandreou, when relations between the two countries were verging on war.

Özal's political commitment had made him many enemies, and he had narrowly escaped an assassination attempt in 1988. He was surrounded by maximum security.

On the way back, it was snowing. On the mountain road between Davos and Landquart, a tire burst, and the driver had to stop to change it. The security guards were worried. A small farm was nearby.

---

[17] Source: https://www.energy-transitions.org (accessed May 14, 2025).

[18] Research and Markets. *Ireland Data Center Colocation Market - Supply & Demand Analysis 2024-2029.* Dublin: Research and Markets, 2024.

[19] As an unexpected consequence, the debate on nuclear energy is resurfacing. Amazon and Google have agreed to buy energy from companies operating small modular reactors, and Microsoft concluded a 20-year power purchasing deal with a unit of the Three Mile Island plant.

> They asked if their "boss" and his wife could stay a few moments. The farmer and his wife agreed. They had just sat down to dinner and offered this unknown guest some soup. He gladly accepted.
>
> The next day, there was a turmoil in the international press: the Turkish Prime Minister ate with a Swiss farmer. The astonished farmer was surrounded by journalists who ask him a thousand questions. Then his wife blurts out: "I told you he was someone important: he had clean hands…"

However, ownership can be shared between the public and private sectors in the short term during the construction and initial operation phases. This principle is behind public–private partnerships or BOT (Build, Operate, Transfer) operations, a concept pioneered by President Turgut Özal of Turkey.[20] In this case, a company, often a foreign one, assumes the initial investment and benefits from the right to operate for several years.

Ownership is then transferred to the host country. This is how many dams were built in Turkey and many hotels when China opened up. Today, these are part of a country's long-term infrastructure.

Impact Analysis

Infrastructure investments and cultural or sporting events have wide-ranging economic and social impacts. These effects are analyzed through impact assessments, which are becoming increasingly important.[21] These analyses began in the United States in the 1930s in the wake of the many "New Deal" projects, particularly the construction of large dams. They were formalized by the work of John Maynard Keynes.

The aim is to identify the short- and long-term economic and human impacts of a project (a large factory) or event (the Olympic Games) on the rest of the economy. These effects can be direct, indirect, or induced. They involve supplier contracts, job creation, skill development, increased consumption, environmental impact, and taxes. Infrastructure investments are essential for job diversification, supporting high-level skills like engineers and manual labor in construction.

---

[20] Walker, Chris, and Charles Smith. *Privatized Infrastructure: The Build-Operate-Transfer Approach*. London: Thomas Telford, 1995.

[21] H. Craig Davis (1990). "Methodologies of economic impact analysis: an overview." In *Regional Economic Impact Analysis and Project Evaluation*, edited by H. Craig Davis, 13–30. Vancouver: University of British Columbia Press.

A country's success depends on skills at all qualification levels, not just university graduates. This ensures competitiveness and social stability, which are essential for long-term prosperity. Thus, infrastructure is a fundamental sector, as it affects all sectors of activity, and its economic and human impact extends over several generations.[22]

Chapter Takeaways

- Investment in advanced infrastructure is not the exclusive domain of rich countries such as Northern Europe, which excel in this area. Today, every developing country can boost its competitiveness by investing in cutting-edge infrastructure that is sometimes far more efficient than that of industrialized countries.

- Infrastructure development also creates urban planning problems, particularly with the proliferation of megacities worldwide and issues related to congestion and energy consumption. As a consequence, for example, new capital cities are being constructed in various parts of the world to address these challenges.

- Impact studies are conducted to evaluate the effects of new infrastructure on the economy and human environment, including projects like dams, communications, and major events like the Olympic Games.

Where Next?

In the next chapter, we will examine the decision-making and strategic aspects of national competitiveness. Each country can manage its competitiveness in very different ways, depending on whether it prioritizes exports or investment attractiveness, proximity or global reach, or openness to the world.

There are no right or wrong answers to these dilemmas, only strategic choices that must be made and consequences that should be accepted.

---

[22] As Margaret Thatcher humorously put it: "You and I come by road or rail, but economists travel by infrastructure."

PART

II

13 | Competitiveness Dilemmas for Nations

Strategies for competitiveness are always a matter of choice. Nations may lean in different directions based on their history and economic and social priorities. However, addressing the following questions cannot be avoided.

Is It Better to Be Aggressive or Attractive?
How to Balance Proximity and Globality?
How Far Should an Economy Open Up?
Is a Diversified Economy the Ultimate Goal?

Is It Better to Be Aggressive or Attractive?

Principle: Does success depend on exports, foreign investment, or attracting business?

Taiwan and Ireland

Everything seems different between Taiwan and Ireland.

Taiwan has 24 million inhabitants on a territory of 35,000 km². This creates one of the highest population densities in the world: 676 people per km². Per capita (nominal) GDP is around $34,000. [1] In 2001, it was $13,300. Ireland has 5 million inhabitants on a territory twice as large, i.e. 70,000 km^2. The population density is 71 people per km^2. GDP (nominal) per capita is around $102,000. It was $42,000 in 2000. [2]

When it comes to competitiveness, these two nations exemplify fundamentally different strategies for economic growth. Taiwan has embraced a vigorous, export-driven economy, whereas Ireland has concentrated on luring foreign investment. Despite their differing approaches, both countries share a commitment to new technologies. This focus has paid off for both, frequently highlighting their competitiveness as exemplary.

Taiwan: A Leader in New Technologies

Taiwan's presence in international markets is illustrated by the success of its companies, which have often become benchmarks in their field. Taiwan Semiconductor Manufacturing Company (TSMC) is the world's largest semiconductor manufacturer, with a 55% market share. The company is now building a gigantic factory in Arizona to serve the American market. An investment of $60 billion is planned!

Hon Hai Precision Industry (Foxconn Technology Group) is the world's largest manufacturer of electronic components and assembler of products such as the iPhone at its Shenzhen plant in China. Acer, Asus, and Quanta have established worldwide reputations in computer hardware and services, cell phones, and components. HTC specializes in smartphones, like MediaTek, and virtual reality. [3]

Well-Educated and Export-Oriented   This success is underpinned by a government policy encouraging investment in technology and a highly science-oriented education system. In the latest PISA rankings, [4] Taiwan is in third position, just behind Singapore and Macau. It is also worth mentioning the strong work ethic of the Taiwanese population.

The government policy resulted in Taiwan's current account surplus of 12.9% of GDP in 2023, one of the highest in the world. This remarkable figure results

---

[1] International Monetary Fund. World Economic Outlook Database, October 2021. Washington, DC: International Monetary Fund, 2021.

[2] IMF statistics for 2021. In the case of Ireland, these figures are probably overestimated due to the strong presence of large foreign companies in a small economy. The same applies to Luxembourg, with a nominal GDP of $132,000, one of the highest in the world.

[3] In addition to electronics, one could mention the Giant group, the world's largest manufacturer of bicycles!

[4] Organisation for Economic Co-operation and Development (OECD). (2024). *PISA 2023 Results: What Students Know and Can Do.* Paris: OECD.

from national production in high value-added technologies like electronics. Other countries with similar surpluses, such as Singapore (18.8% of GDP), derive much of their wealth from transit trade and finance, or Norway (17.2% of GDP) from energy exports.

Ireland: The Champion of Attractiveness

Ireland has chosen another path, attracting foreign investment with great success.

When I teach my university students, I like to ask them the name of a major Irish company that is competitive in international markets. Without mentioning Guinness and its legendary beer, the room falls silent. It is a bit of a challenge. They could mention Kerry Gold (dairy products and butter), Waterford Glass, or Smurfit Kappa, one of the world leaders in paper and cardboard packaging.

Yet everyone agrees that Ireland has made a remarkable transition to international competitiveness. It has become the "Celtic Tiger."[5] This was partly due to the policy of the Irish government, which, as early as 1986, accelerated a policy of attracting foreign investment. This led, in particular, to the creation of the IDA (Industrial Development Authority), which is considered one of the most dynamic investment agencies in the world.[6]

Taxation and Infrastructure Ireland's attractiveness has developed according to a few well-established principles. At 12.5%, the corporate tax rate has long been one of the lowest in the OECD. With new international standards coming into force, it will be 15%. In addition, Ireland has an extensive network of tax treaties with numerous countries to reduce double taxation for multinational companies.

As a member of the European Union, Ireland has unfettered access to the European market. This is an advantage, especially since Great Britain left the Union. However, many agreements between the two countries remain in place.

Ireland has also invested heavily in its infrastructure – transport, communications, IT, and energy so that even traditionally decentralized regions such as the south coast (Cork) or west coast (Limerick, Galway) are accessible. Nevertheless, 40% of the population still lives around Dublin. Subsidies from European regional policy have enabled Ireland to develop its infrastructure rapidly.[7]

---

[5] MacSharry, Ray, and Pádraic A. White. *The Making of the Celtic Tiger: The Inside Story of Ireland's Boom Economy*. Dublin: Mercier Press, 2000.

[6] IDA Ireland. Annual Report 2023. Dublin: IDA Ireland, 2024. https://www.idaireland.com/annual-reports/ida-ireland-annual-report-2024

[7] For example, between 2014 and 2020, Ireland received 1.2 billion euros from the European Regional Development Fund and the European Social Fund.

Saints and Scholars   Ireland has invested heavily in its education system and higher education. In the PISA study, Ireland ranked ninth, second in Europe after Estonia and just ahead of Switzerland.[8]

There is undoubtedly a historical dimension to this. Ireland was known as "The Island of Saints and Scholars" for centuries. Irish monks preserved Christian texts in their monasteries during the barbarian invasions that ravaged Europe following the fall of the Roman Empire.[9]

Then, they set off to evangelize Europe; like Saint Columbanus, who founded several monasteries in France, Switzerland, and Italy in the 6th century. Saint Brendan is said to have sailed far into the North Atlantic. Saint Gall gave his name to the Swiss town of the same name. Saint Killian preached in German Franconia. Of course, there is Saint Patrick, who evangelized Ireland and, according to tradition, freed it of its snakes.[10]

However, history has made Ireland not only a Celtic-speaking country (Irish is a national language still taught in schools) but also an English-speaking one. This linguistic (and geographical) proximity originally made it an attractive location for Anglo-Saxon investment.

Attractiveness Success   Ireland has enjoyed considerable success in attracting major foreign multinationals. Some of the biggest investors include Apple, which has had its European operations headquarters in Cork since the 1980s. Google also has its European, Middle Eastern, and African (EMEA) headquarters in Dublin, as do Microsoft (since 1985) and Meta Platforms (Facebook).

The Jeanie Johnston Adventure

The Jeanie Johnston is perhaps the most famous sailing ship to carry Irish immigrants to the US. Between 1848 and 1855, she made 16 voyages from the Irish west coast (Tralee) to Quebec, Baltimore, and New York.

However, the ship's renown stems from the fact that not a single passenger or crew member lost his or her life during the numerous Atlantic crossings,

---

[8] OECD. *PISA 2022 Results (Volume I and II): What Students Know and Can Do*. Paris: OECD Publishing, 2023.

[9] Cahill, Thomas. *How the Irish Saved Civilization: The Untold Story of Ireland's Heroic Role from the Fall of Rome to the Rise of Medieval Europe*. New York: Nan A. Talese, 1995.

[10] It is probably a myth and a symbol of evil (the snake), as the country's climate does not lend itself to a native reptile population.

> which lasted an average of 45 days. The credit goes to Captain James Attridge, who never overloaded the ship, and to an unusual innovation for this kind of expedition: a ship's doctor, Richard Blennerhassett, who prevented illness.
>
> The Jeanie Johnston sank in a storm in 1858, and a replica was rebuilt in 2002. I visited it in Fenit, near Tralee. At 47 m long, the boat seemed very small to carry 250 people…

Intel accounts for the largest foreign investment in Ireland in semiconductor manufacturing in County Kildare, followed by Dell and Hewlett-Packard. Ireland is also well positioned in the pharmaceutical industry, with Pfizer, Johnson & Johnson, or Boston Scientific in the Galway region.

Capitalizing on the Irish Diaspora   Ireland's attractiveness to the US also stems from emigration. Some 32 million Americans have Irish ancestry, representing almost 10% of the country's population and 13% of that of New York. Nearly all American presidents, including Barack Obama, boast of their Irish ancestry, and visiting a pub in Ireland is a respected ritual.

Emigration has long been a feature of Ireland. The 1844 census showed a population of 8.4 million, 70% more than today. Then came the great potato famine of 1845 and mass emigration to the US.

Despite Ireland's newly acquired wealth, emigration has continued. According to the Irish Office of Statistics, 29,300 people emigrated in 1912, a ratio of 6.7 per thousand. In 2013, 89,000 people emigrated, a ratio almost three times higher at 19.4. More than 500,000 Irish emigrated between 1945 and 1960.[11]

This can be explained by the ease of travel today. Traveling and emigrating to the other side of the world is more accessible, from the US to Australia. And then, if the opportunity arises, one can return home. Skilled migration's "coming and going" has become a modern-day reality. The importance of the foreign diaspora[12] in a country's attractiveness policy is often underestimated. When China or Estonia opened up to the world, both countries called on their diaspora to help them. They even offered a way back home for the most competent.

---

[11] Central Statistics Office (CSO). (2023). "Population and Migration Estimates." Dublin: Central Statistics Office.

[12] Cohen, Robin. *Global Diasporas: An Introduction*. Seattle: University of Washington Press, 1997.

The Limits of "Aggressiveness"

An aggressive policy based on exports or investments abroad generates foreign exchange earnings in the country of origin or dividends when foreign profits are repatriated. Regarding exports, the impact is positive on the labor market in the country of origin, as jobs and expertise are developed locally. It also has a positive effect on the balance of trade.

On the other hand, companies cannot serve every market with exports. If the country is too big, like China, or if the product is too bulky, like cars, they must make a direct investment abroad. In this case, the country of origin loses jobs (transferred to the host country) and loses income in its trade balance since exports disappear and are replaced by an outflow of the capital needed for investment.

Some critics, however, claim that this money could have been invested in the domestic market rather than benefiting the development of a market abroad. Furthermore, they argue that those nations receiving investment in technology and skills may one day be formidable competitors. Take China as an example. However, it can be assumed that, in the long term, these disadvantages are offset by dividends or royalties or that the market would have been lost had the investment not been made.

Nevertheless, this long term can be particularly "long." Companies often reinvest their earnings within the host market to establish a robust local presence. This practice also leads to reduced tax revenues for the home country.

The most adverse scenario for a home country occurs when a company invests in a low-cost nation to re-import products, components, or services back into its domestic market. This includes clothing manufacturing in Vietnam or outsourcing corporate services such as accounting and back-office operations to India, Poland, or Slovakia.

"Attractiveness" Remains Attractive

Governments, therefore, prefer attractiveness policies, as these create jobs and transfer technology and skills to the domestic market. They enable a country to retain or attract capital and reduce imports, as products are produced locally. This is known as import substitution.

However, there are challenges. Large foreign groups can disrupt the local market by attracting top talent with higher salaries and leveraging their international sourcing of supplies to secure cost advantages. This is why some countries, like China, limit foreign investment to particular sectors, activities like exports, or specific regions.

The Appeal of Luxembourg

Luxembourg's population was estimated at around 660,809 in 2023. However, the number of employees in the labor market was around 469,973.

This meant that the number of active employees represented around 71% of the country's total population.

This is obviously impossible for a country when considering the usual structure of a population, which includes the elderly, the disabled, and young children. In neighboring France, the ratio is 47%.

It can be explained as follows: Luxembourg attracts many employees from neighboring countries (France, Belgium, Germany), who return to their home countries in the evening.

Similarly, in some Swiss border towns, for the same reasons, there are more employees than inhabitants.

However, the success of investment attractiveness policies can create statistical distortions that disrupt an objective assessment of an economy's performance. In 2016, Ireland announced a 26% GDP growth! Later, it was revealed that this was due to a change in Apple's tax practice. The presence of foreign companies in Ireland is so significant that it sometimes masks the reality of the local economy. To this end, Ireland has developed a statistical system that brackets the impact of foreign multinationals.

An Adjusted Gross National Product was introduced in 2017. This indicator adapts GDP by excluding the effects of repatriated profits of large foreign companies or capital movements associated with intellectual property.[13]

In the end, whether it is excess employment or tax revenues, the "super-attractiveness" of some countries creates problems that many other nations worldwide would love to have…

How to Balance Proximity and Globality?

Principle: An economy cannot be entirely globalized; a nation needs to find the right balance between local strategies, which offer stability, and global strategies, which drive growth.

Several factors determine whether a country will adopt one or another of these strategies. The first is politics. A country may wish to develop self-sufficiency, especially if its political regime faces international criticism or sanctions. North Korea is an

---

[13] FitzGerald, John (2018). "Problems Interpreting National Accounts in a Globalised Economy – Ireland." *Quarterly Economic Commentary*, Economic and Social Research Institute (ESRI), Autumn 2018.

extreme case. Other countries are under intense pressure from part of the population to preserve a national, traditional lifestyle. This is the case with so-called sovereigntist or populist governments.

In most countries, agricultural production and the population that depends on it are subjects of debate that go beyond mere economic considerations. Food security is an age-old and deeply emotional priority. Another consideration is the preservation of natural resources. For example, since 2020, Indonesia, which produces 7% and 22% of world demand, has banned the export of bauxite and nickel,[14] respectively, to encourage refiners to invest locally.

Ultimately, the dimensions and population of a nation play a crucial role. Nations with significant populations usually prioritize their internal markets. The US and China have consistently shown an inclination toward self-sufficiency.

India

India is an excellent example of this dilemma. For decades, the country has oscillated between the temptation to open up to the rest of the world and the preservation of its domestic market. From a geopolitical point of view, India has always sought a position of balance between its cultural and historical heritage and the great powers surrounding it: China, which it fears on its northern border, and Russia, with which it has a long tradition of cooperation, particularly militarily.[15]

Against this backdrop, India prioritized developing its domestic market, which is now the largest in the world with 1,450,000,000 inhabitants.

India is often identified with poverty, which indeed exists. However, a growing middle class is estimated to contain between 300 and 350 million people.[16] In major cities such as Mumbai, Delhi, and Bengaluru,[17] part of the population enjoys a standard of living comparable to that of advanced economies. This can also be seen in the power and wealth of the large families who control mighty economic conglomerates.

---

[14] International Trade Commission. Indonesia's Export Ban of Nickel. Washington, DC: International Trade Commission, 2023. Available at: https://www.usitc.gov/publications/332/working_papers/ermm_indonesia_export_ban_of_nickel.pdf.

[15] With joint projects such as the BrahMos and Sukhoi Su-30MK fighter aircraft program, or nuclear reactor construction, as at the Kudankulam power plant.

[16] "How the Middle Class Will Play the Hero in India's Rise as World Power." *The Economic Times*, July 8, 2023.

[17] Previously known as "Bangalore."

> ## Indira Gandhi, Prime Minister of India (1966–1977 and 1980–1984)
>
> "Come, I'll show you how a great democracy works," said Indira Gandhi.
>
> We were in New Delhi, on the lawn in front of the Prime Minister's residence. There were two groups of people sitting on the grass. Anyone could come. Indira Gandhi said a few words to the first group, wandered through the ranks, took a bow and came back to me.
>
> Then she visited the second group. Same ceremony. Meanwhile, her assistants quickly changed the people in the first group, and when she had finished with the second, she could continue, and so on.
>
> At noon, everything stopped. Her helper whispered in my ear, "She's going to eat with her children – she never misses that."
>
> She was succeeded by her son Rajiv Gandhi, who became prime minister when she was assassinated in 1984. I also met him. Rajiv Gandhi was an airline pilot who reluctantly entered politics because his brother Sanjai had died in a plane crash.
>
> He, too, was assassinated in 1990.

Efficient Conglomerates Efficient conglomerates are clusters of businesses operating in various economic sectors, including oil production, vehicles, telecommunications, and retailing. They include Ambani, Tata, Birla, Godrej, Hinduja, Mahindra, and Mittal. They are not unlike the South Korean Chaebols or Japanese Keiretsus we have encountered before, with perhaps the difference that they continue to be run by an entrepreneurial class of owners.

India is home to some of the world's most dynamic entrepreneurs. Ironically, some say the abundance of regulations and restrictions that characterize the local market can only allow the best to survive. Given their local presence and, for the most part, their history, these groups have tried to maintain strong control over the domestic market and prevent access by international companies.

Opening to the World However, when Manmohan Singh[18] (1932–2024) became prime minister from 2004 to 2014,[19] India underwent a period of liberalization of its economy and opening up to world markets. In particular, Singh abolished the

---

[18] Singh, Manmohan. *Changing India*. New Delhi: Oxford University Press, 2018.
[19] He was succeeded by Narendra Modi.

so-called "License Raj," which allowed the government to control the domestic market through company licenses. This system had constrained economic growth for decades and led to corruption that plagued the economy.

Following these reforms, the Indian economy experienced significant expansion, achieving a peak growth rate of 9% in 2007. Singh also rebalanced the long-standing relationship between India and Russia, developing closer ties with the US and providing Indian companies with new markets abroad.

Several Indian companies utilized this opportunity to develop global strategies, particularly in advanced technologies, and successfully entered international markets. Recent examples include Tata, the Mittal group in the steel industry, and Infosys and Wipro in new technologies.[20]

India perfectly illustrates the interaction between local and global economies, each with its benefits and drawbacks. Each nation is confronted with balancing these two types of economies. The challenge is even bigger when politics steps in: voters typically focus on proximity issues and not the global perspective.

How Far Should an Economy Open Up?

Principle: Globalization has been a source of prosperity for countries, but it has also destabilized domestic economies and created employment vulnerability.

The example of India shows that every country faces the same dilemma. Large countries with large local markets are more likely to turn to their local economies. Smaller countries often have no choice but to adopt a globalization strategy. Local and global economies are complementary. However, they respond to different logic.

The Local Economy Is Valuable

The *local economy* comprises all conventional activities close to the end consumer. Examples include personal services such as doctors, social workers, hairdressers, and small shops. At the state level, these responsibilities include administrative, security, or judicial tasks. Various regulations have typically safeguarded the local economy, such as in agriculture. Such policies have historically been aimed at protecting employment because small local businesses employ most of the workforce.

The Global Economy Has Often Taken the Upper Hand

The *global economy*, on the other hand, is exposed to international competition and has to be competitive, especially in terms of price. In general, it is made up of more

---

[20] Davies, Paul. *What's This India Business?: Offshoring, Outsourcing and the Global Services Revolution*. London: Nicholas Brealey Publishing, 2004.

prominent companies than the local economy. Its productivity is higher, as is the intensity of its technological innovation.

The initial era of globalization was characterized by conflict between these two economies. With the liberalization of markets, the global economy gradually intruded on the local economy. By mastering their global logistics and sources of supply, the major international groups could offer local markets products that were more efficient and less expensive than those of the local economy. The success of online retailers such as Amazon and Alibaba is a case in point.

Social Tensions

The resulting relocations and unemployment in industrialized countries created social tensions. The impact quickly took on an emotional and political dimension, as most of the population works or is in contact with the local economy.

Government leaders know that they will be judged, among other things, on their ability to maintain employment or eliminate unemployment. As most voters or the population live in a local economy, leaders will be tempted to react to a crisis by multiplying financial subsidies or customs protection. The tension between proximity and globality stems from the local economy directly impacting consumers' daily lives. A loss of purchasing power, price inflation, factory relocations, or redundancies are events everyone can understand and feel.[21]

On the other hand, the positive impact of the global economy on people's lives is more difficult to explain. A surplus on the trade or current account balance (or even on a budget) often remains an abstract concept with an elusive link to everyday life.

The Consequences of Opening Up

The current account balance is a good indicator of a country's ability to generate international wealth. It represents what a country earns from its activities abroad, whether through trade, industry, or financial investment. For Singapore, Norway, Taiwan, Denmark, and Switzerland, the current account surplus has generally been over 10% of GDP for most of the last few decades.[22]

However, a country's openness to the rest of the world also implies a principle of reciprocity. This applies not only to foreign investment in the country but also to the foreign workforce. According to a study by Mercer, a world leader in labor consultancy, 243 multinational companies had some 94,000 expatriates in their ranks in 2022[23] This must be added to the families of employees transferred to a position abroad.

---

[21] Stiglitz, Joseph E. *Globalization and Its Discontents*. New York: W.W. Norton & Company, 2002.

[22] Organisation for Economic Co-operation and Development (OECD). Current Account Balance Data. Paris: OECD, 2024.

[23] Mercer (2023). Global Talent Trends 2023: Mobility and Expatriate Management. New York.

Considering all expatriates working in a foreign country, including individual workers (71% of the total), researchers, and students, the research company Finaccord reaches a considerable figure of 87 million for 2021.[24] Therefore, the relationship between immigration and competitiveness arises on two levels: the skills of incoming immigrants and their integration. Many countries try to target immigrants with exceptional skills.[25]

So-called "high-level" immigration poses fewer problems than less-skilled workers, who are also needed by the economy. They will be a prerequisite in many economies facing demographic decline, such as Europe and Japan. Integration measures are essential and, sometimes, can be successful. In Switzerland, the 10th most common surname is Portuguese: Da Silva. The first nine most common surnames are all German. The first French surname, "Martin," only comes in the 62nd position.

The Local Economy Should Never Be Neglected

For too long, the heads of some large international companies have been condescending towards the local economy. Unfortunately, they failed to pay particular attention to explaining their business and maintaining close contact with local politicians. I remember a CEO telling me: "We are a global company; we are not interested in local issues." It's even worse in smaller countries, where the domestic market represents only a tiny fraction of a large company's overall sales.

With the emergence of civil society, the backlash has become more evident. Today, large global companies face ever-greater political and societal activism at the local level, independently of the size of the country concerned. Issues include diversity, climate change, energy transition, and governance.

More recently, the fragmentation of the global economy has reset this balance of power. To secure sources of supply, particularly in the aftermath of the COVID crisis, companies have decided to diversify their economic partnerships and bring them closer to the local economy.[26] In English, this is called "nearshoring." In rarer cases, some companies return home altogether, especially if tax incentives exist, as in the US with the Inflation Reduction Act.

---

[24] Finaccord (2022). Global Expatriates: Size, Segmentation and Forecast for the Worldwide Market. London: Finaccord.

[25] In the US, the O-1 non-immigrant visa is intended for people with extraordinary abilities in the sciences, arts, education, business, or athletics. Germany, and almost all European countries, have fast-track visa procedures for "highly skilled" labor. The Gulf States follow the same approach.

[26] Manners-Bell, John. The Death of Globalization: How Supply Chains Have Become Politicized and the Implications for the Global Economy. London: The Foundation for Future Supply Chain, 2023.

Furthermore, consumers often prefer local products that are perceived as more transparent and trustworthy. In the food sector, local products, which sometimes bear the name of the local supplier, are experiencing significant growth rates, even if they are more expensive. Organic products are a case in point.

Therefore, the gap between the local and global economies is narrowing. Meanwhile, many small and medium-sized local companies have taken advantage of the internationalization of logistics and transport to develop global businesses. Conversely, major retail groups have pursued a policy of getting closer to the end consumer to fulfill their new expectations.[27]

As a result of this new piece, some prices will rise. Products that benefited from low-cost global production were cheaper due to cost differences worldwide. This will likely continue for generic technologies like smartphones and computers. However, products closer to end consumers, especially in advanced economies, will become more expensive due to higher production costs and standards.

It is a societal choice that will mostly happen in the wealthiest countries, those whose consumers have some leeway over the price of their purchases and who may be sensitive to emotional considerations.

Is a Diversified Economy the Ultimate Goal?

Principle: The strategic dimensions involving policies of attractiveness or aggressiveness on the one hand, and proximity and globality on the other, underline the importance of having a diversified economy.

One of a competitive economy's principal objectives is to increase its diversification.[28] While business cycles are a more or less inevitable fact of economic life, the best way to mitigate their consequences is to diversify the economy. If one sector does poorly, its underperformance can be offset by the resilience of another. Furthermore, a diversified economy means that the wealth created in a country is better distributed, either by sector or geographically, and social stability is preserved.

Switzerland and Saudi Arabia

Large countries find it easier to diversify their economies if only because of their geographical size. The best example is probably the US, which has the most diversified economy globally, with areas of excellence in almost every sector. Nevertheless, small nations can also develop a high level of diversity. Switzerland is a good example.

---

[27] Strizhakova, Yuliya, and Robin A. Coulter. "Drivers of local relative to global brand purchases: a contingency approach." *Journal of International Marketing* 23, 1 (2015): 1–22.

[28] Porter, Michael E. *The Competitive Advantage of Nations*. New York: Free Press, 1990.

Switzerland: A Long Tradition of Diversification   On my travels, I am often told that Switzerland is the land of chocolate and watches. It is true, but there is more to it than that. Switzerland has leading companies in food (Nestlé), pharmaceuticals (Roche or Novartis), banking (UBS and the so-called private banks), electronics (Logitech), watches (Rolex), and many others. It is also home to numerous "clusters," such as finance in Zurich and Geneva, healthcare in the Lake Geneva region, watchmaking in the Vallée de Joux and Jura, and pharmaceuticals in Basel.

There are also activities such as tourism (in the Alps, for example), education (polytechnic institutes in Zurich and Lausanne, business schools such as IMD, and private schools), international organizations (the United Nations and its affiliated organizations or the World Trade Organization), and non-governmental institutions such as the International Olympic Committee, the Red Cross, the World Economic Forum, or the World Wildlife Fund.

There is also diversification in terms of companies. Regarding the largest, Switzerland has 14 companies on Fortune's list of the world's 500 largest corporations.[29] By comparison, Germany had twice as many (28) for a population 10 times larger (83 million and 9 million respectively). Like Germany, Switzerland has many medium-sized companies (the "Mittlestand"), often family-owned and export-oriented.

Such a close-knit economy has a positive impact on territorial development. Some Swiss "cantons" are more prosperous than others, but there are no poor cantons. In other words, each region benefits from competitive economic activity that ensures minimal prosperity for every citizen. It is the case for tourism in Valais, Biel's watchmaking industry, and Jura's industrial components.

Diversification as an Insurance   Switzerland is not a perfect example – no country is. However, it underlines the long-term importance of not depending on a single source of wealth, however successful. Industry sectors evolve, natural resources can be depleted, and technologies become obsolete. The critical advantage of diversification is that it cushions cyclical shocks. When one industry is in crisis, another can compensate for the growth deficit.

But, above all, a diversity of economic resources enables the cross-fertilization of technologies and skills. It means that the success of one sector can emulate the creation and development of another. For example, the textile industry in the St. Gallen region led to the creation of a dyeing industry in Basel, which in turn led to chemicals and pharmaceuticals. Similarly, watchmaking in the Jura region led to the development of precision mechanics.

---

[29] Fortune (2023). Fortune Global 500: The World's Largest Corporations. New York: Fortune Media IP Limited. Available at: https://fortune.com/global500/.

Other countries, such as Denmark and Sweden, and Singapore and the United Arab Emirates, are also quickly diversifying their economies. However, the Kingdom of Saudi Arabia has probably devoted today the largest amount of investment and energy to implement such a diversification strategy.

Saudi Arabia: When Ambition Drives Diversification   While Switzerland has already largely achieved diversification, the Kingdom of Saudi Arabia started its implementation only a few years ago. The objectives are outlined in "Vision 2030,"[30] an initiative launched in 2016 by Crown Prince Mohammed bin Salman, which now constitutes the country's strategic direction.[31] The diversification strategy aims to decrease the country's reliance on hydrocarbon revenues. Currently, approximately 50% of the country's GDP and 62% of budget revenues are derived from these activities.

However, the Saudi economy is undergoing significant transformation, driven by the expansion of alternative energy sources such as solar, wind, and nuclear power. Saudi Arabia also invests significantly in new industries, including logistics, e-commerce, advanced technologies and research, corporate headquarters, finance, tourism, and events.[32]

A Wealth of Comparative Advantages   The diversification strategy of the Kingdom is worth noticing because it enjoys significant comparative advantages that are increasingly rare in the global economy.

The primary factor is that the Kingdom possesses substantial developable land. Saudi Arabia is a vast country that is essentially flat. With an area of 2.149 million square kilometers and 38 million inhabitants, it has one of the lowest population densities in the world: 15 people per km^2.

In comparison, Saudi Arabia is six and a half times larger than Germany (357,000 km^2) but has only 45% of Germany's population (84 million). Even the US, the largest industrialized nation, has a population density twice as high at 34 people per km^2.

Thus, Saudi Arabia has extensive uninhabited land areas to develop infrastructure requiring large spaces, such as logistics facilities.

---

[30] Kingdom of Saudi Arabia. Vision 2030. Riyadh: Council of Economic and Development Affairs, 2016. https://www.vision2030.gov.sa/media/rc0b5oy1/saudi_vision203.pdf

[31] Some of the key objectives are: diversification of the economy, increasing the weight of the private sector from 40% to 65% of the GDP, privatization of some government companies (e.g., Aramco), 50% of renewable energy by 2030, mega infrastructure projects (e.g., Neom City), attractivity for foreign direct investments and decision centers, more female participation in the workforce, etc.

[32] Such as the AFC Asian football tournament in 2027, the 10th Asian Winter games in 2029, the World Exposition in 2030, and the FIFA World Cup in 2034.

The population is young: 50% are under 25 and are largely well educated. It creates a dynamism in the economy reflected not only in a good command of advanced technologies but also in a positive attitude towards progress and the future.

Decisions are made quickly, and projects are implemented faster than in many other countries. The country also has substantial financial resources to support its projects.

Finally, Saudi Arabia's strategic location between the Middle East, Gulf countries, and Africa boosts its regional business cooperation opportunities and geopolitical influence.

Few countries objectively enjoy such advantages: open spaces, constructability, access to advanced technologies, considerable energy and financial resources, quick decisions, geopolitical influence, and a young, qualified, and motivated population. Most of today's so-called advanced economies had such advantages at one stage of their development but no longer have them today.

Chapter Takeaways

- A nation's competitiveness is often the result of strategic choices that determine whether a country wants to be aggressive rather than attractive, or whether it wants to prioritize the local over the global. Historical factors and value systems influence these choices. Various strategies can be combined, with countries differing in the emphasis they place on each strategic priority.

- Each country must also determine, accordingly, how much it wants to open its economy to the rest of the world and thus to the competitiveness of other nations. Such choices ultimately impact the diversification of the economy, which is one of the ultimate goals for ensuring long-term competitiveness.

- Thus, a fundamental dilemma exists between rapid improvements for the immediate benefit of the population and long-term competitiveness strategies for future prosperity. Putting the important before the urgent is often perilous; however, it defines a true leader.

Where Next?

A country's decisions are deeply influenced by the value systems that define a national mindset, which guides major political and economic decisions. The value system shapes how a country manages its competitiveness and sets its ultimate goals.

Value systems vary from country to country, and they also evolve over time. However, this evolution seems to be moving in the same direction, from a community-based value system to an individual-based value system, and at an ever-increasing pace.

14 | The Importance of Value Systems

The impact of value systems on the economy has been underestimated for too long. The competitiveness of a nation or a company cannot be reduced to a few sophisticated mathematical formulas. Strategies are always influenced by values and mindsets, which result from a long history.

The Historical Context of Value Systems.
How Values Systems Evolve Over Time?
How Values Impact Economic and Social Structures?

The Historical Context of Value Systems

The new global divide is not just a consequence of economic change. It also originates in the evolution of value systems, which are increasingly competing – within countries and internationally – and influencing each other. The rapid succession of new generations – millennials, X, Y, and Z – profoundly impacts people's attitudes and expectations. It is no longer possible for governments and companies to ignore these social debates, which sometimes puzzle them but always concern them.

Competence alone is not enough for competitiveness; a unique set of values and attitudes is required to stand out as an individual or nation. In the words of President Thomas Jefferson: "Nothing can stop the one with the right mental attitude, and nothing can help the one with the wrong mental attitude."

The Origins of the Mindset Inquiry

In the 18th century, the philosophers of the Age of Enlightenment[1] began a lengthy debate on the relationship between the economy and a nation's value system and its impact on society. The most famous is probably Jean-Jacques Rousseau (1712–1758). The agricultural revolution is said to have led to the emergence of inequality and social violence (see insert).[2]

Jean-Jacques Rousseau's Visit

In 1749, Rousseau visited his friend, writer Denis Diderot (1713–1784), confined in the Donjon de Vincennes. It was excessively hot. He sat down under an oak tree, read the Mercure de France and came across the question posed by the Académie de Dijon: "If the progress of science and the arts has contributed to corrupting or purifying morals."

In his Confessions, he would later declare that he had suddenly had "a mind dazzled by a thousand lights." Man is naturally good, and it is through institutions that men become evil…

In 1753, the same academy came back with another essay: "Discourse on the origin of the foundations of inequality among men." In this essay, Rousseau famously asserted that progress does not come without adverse consequences for humanity.

Later, many thinkers of 19th-century Europe also focused on studying value systems and their impact on society. This led, among other things, to the creation of a new field of knowledge, sociology, one of whose founders was Émile Durkheim (1858–1917). For example, in his book, *On the Division of Social Labor* (1893),[3] he put forward the theory of anomie. He used this concept to describe a state of social disintegration or disorder resulting from the absence or breakdown of shared societal norms and values.

---

[1] Dupré, Louis. *The Enlightenment and the Intellectual Foundations of Modern Culture*. New Haven: Yale University Press, 2004.

[2] Recent excavations in Neolithic tombs in Sudan, eastern France, and central Europe indicate violent massacres between large numbers of individuals, long before the advent of agriculture. What's more, according to primatologist Jane Goodall, even chimpanzees can wage war against each other and engage in raiding parties.

[3] Durkheim, Émile. *The Division of Labor in Society*. Translated by W.D. Halls. Introduction by Lewis A. Coser. New York: Free Press, 1984.

Catholicism and Reformation

The values shared in a society often find their origin in religion.

In Europe, a great schism in the value system occurred when Christianity split between the reforms of Martin Luther (1483–1546) and John Calvin (1509–1564), and the reaction of the traditional papal church, a process known as the Counter-Reformation.[4] It triggered a considerable split in mentality in Europe and impacted not only religion but also culture and the economy. For example, in 1685, King Louis XIV's revocation of France's Edict of Nantes (which in 1598 had guaranteed the rights of Protestants in France) was one of the country's most disastrous economic decisions.[5]

The influence of religion on the economy was particularly highlighted by Max Weber (1864–1920) in his book *The Ethics of Protestantism and the Spirit of Capitalism,*[6] published in 1905. Comparing the development of German regions with their religion, Protestant or Catholic, he argued that there was a correlation between economic success and the ethics that flowed from a religious choice.

He suggests that Protestantism in its various forms, notably Calvinism (found in Switzerland), encouraged traits and behaviors that contributed to the emergence of modern capitalism. These include emphasizing hard work, discipline, thrift, and rational investment. In Protestantism, the notion of "vocation" ("Beruf" in German, which also means "mission") is central. Weber believes this has led to the valorization of professional work to express religious faith, fostering a rigorous work ethic. In Latin nations, on the other hand, the word "work" comes from the Latin "tripaliare," meaning torture. The word's etymology suggests that work is sometimes perceived as punishment in these societies. This is in contrast to Protestant and Confucian cultures, where work is seen as a means to gain freedom from poverty or achieve a better life.

How Value Systems Evolve Over Time

Value systems evolve in each country and over time. The relationship to work is essential, but other life goals are added as a country's prosperity increases.

In our studies on the competitiveness of nations, we have aggregated many statistical results to form the basis of the following theory, which identifies four phases in the evolution of value systems.

---

[4] Bireley, Robert. *The Refashioning of Catholicism, 1,450–1700: A Reassessment of the Counter Reformation.* Washington, DC: Catholic University of America Press, 1999.

[5] An estimated 200,000 to 300,000 Protestants emigrated to the Netherlands, England, and the British colonies. Most of them were highly skilled, and it was one of the greatest "brain hemorrhages" in history.

[6] Weber, Max. *The Protestant Ethic and the Spirit of Capitalism.* Translated by Talcott Parsons. London: Routledge, 1992.

The "Hard Work" Phase

A country and its citizens identify with the same value system at work, which should lead to prosperity. The number of hours worked is a good indicator. In this respect, Mexico is in first place, with 2,257 hours per year.[7] Yet, on the other hand, working hard does not necessarily mean working well. Productivity does not necessarily follow.

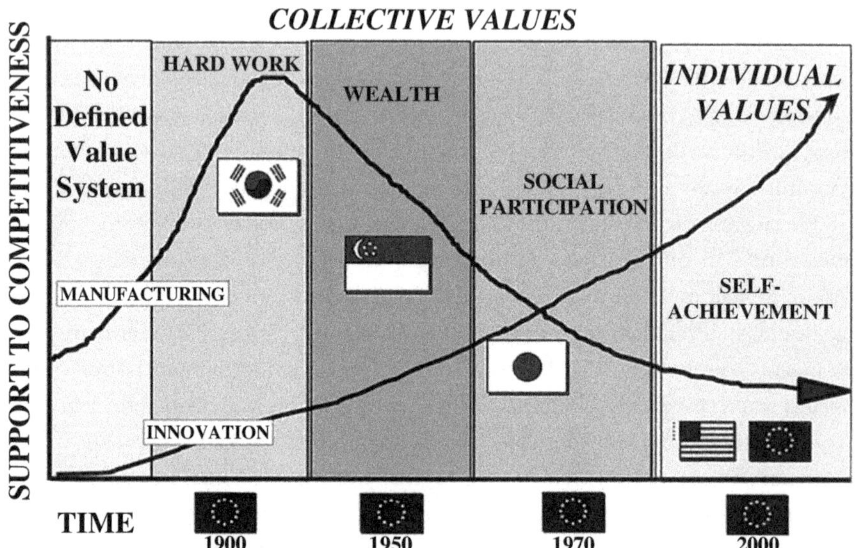

The Koreans, who have long been in the lead, are easing off a little with 2,024 hours a year. I have often been told that, in the past, Korean factory employees got into the habit of sleeping on the company site so as not to waste time traveling.

Many companies, especially in Asia, are building dormitories, or even towns, around their production sites to boost the productivity of those who work there. Foxconn, a Taiwanese company and a world leader in semiconductor assembly, has created a production site in the Longhua district (Shenzhen) that employs, houses, and feeds 200,000 people. The concept of the "company town" is not new. In 1880, George Pullman, president of Pullman Palace,[8] founded such a town in Illinois. There have been over 2,000 such towns in American industrial history.

---

[7] Data for 2022.

[8] Leyendecker, Liston E. *Palace Car Prince: A Biography of George Mortimer Pullman*. Niwot, CO: University Press of Colorado, 1992.

In Europe, company towns have flourished in Germany: Leverkusen for Bayer, Wolfsburg for Volkswagen, and Sindelfingen for Mercedes-Benz. They illustrate a "paternalism" dominant culture in the nascent industrial society. This value system is based on the notion of productivity. The more you work, the better.

The "Wealth" Phase

In this second stage, persistence and hard work evolve from mere ethical values to essential tools for generating personal wealth. This is the situation in Singapore today (with 2,200 hours worked annually): most people continue to work hard while seeking substantial earnings to enhance their quality of life.

A similar trend exists in the US, though it impacts only a portion of the population. On average, the country logs 1,780 working hours annually, with relatively limited vacation days. Despite this, numerous Americans consider business success and income significant social indicators and work harder. Sometimes, achieving business success becomes an obsession or, in the best case, a national pastime.

The "Social Participation" Phase

In this phase, work and income are not enough. People also want to be consulted about their work, aspirations, and way of life. This is what Japan, many Eastern European countries, and, to a certain extent, China experience today.

These three phases characterize a *collective value* system in which a person's identity is closely linked to the success of the community in which they live. However, at a particular stage in a country's development, these collective values gradually give way to more *individual* values. Collective values do not disappear entirely but become less of a priority.

The "Self-Fulfillment" Phase

In this fourth phase, individuals prioritize themselves over their country or workplace. Some call this trend "meism," indicative of ego dominance. Most people in Europe and parts of the US are currently experiencing this phase.

On average, the French work 1,500 hours yearly, whereas the Germans put in about 1,340 hours annually. Germany ranks lowest internationally in terms of hours worked, trailing Denmark, Norway, the Netherlands, Sweden, Iceland, and Austria. These countries work fewer hours than France, except Switzerland, which averages 1,570 hours a year.[9]

---

[9] Organisation for Economic Co-operation and Development (OECD). (2023). *OECD Employment Outlook 2023: Working Hours and Labor Market Dynamics.* Paris: OECD Publishing. https://doi.org/10.1787/empl_outlook-2023-en

It is crucial to emphasize that the hours worked are not always aligned with productivity levels. Reducing working hours below a specific point may not be balanced by an equivalent rise in a nation's overall competitiveness.

France is one of the world's most productive countries when considering GDP per hour worked. However, because the employment rate is below the average for industrialized nations, the government must tax those employed heavily to fund public spending.[10]

Accelerating Phases

Historically, collective values have bolstered the competitiveness of the manufacturing industry by promoting diligent employees. In contrast, individual values thrive in innovative societies that encourage challenging the status quo for better solutions or opportunities.

Each country goes through the four value phases at a different pace. Europe was in a phase of hard work in the early 1900s. In 1950, after the war, it was a phase of reconstruction and wealth. From 1968 onwards, priority was given to social participation. Today, it is individualism.

Moreover, the process accelerates today as each country goes through the same phases of evolution. In Europe, it took around 70 years to evolve from the phase of hard work to that of individualism. In China, on the other hand, it only took 30 years or so.

Before these four phases, some countries struggled to identify a unifying value system, especially those in the early development stages of Africa and Central Asia.

What Happens Next?

Reverting to past norms, particularly with a revival of collective values, is challenging but not impossible. This shift can occur during times of conflict, as seen in Ukraine, or through the efforts of political leaders who argue that individualism ultimately erodes the social fabric of a state.

Additionally, future generations might anchor their identity in value systems that transcend their national borders, such as environmental sustainability, renewable energy, diversity, or good governance. They will likely share these ideals through the Internet and social media, forming new virtual communities.

Nations find it challenging to resist the natural evolution of value systems. It is vital to manage this process through changes in law and shifts in public and

---

[10] For more details on these figures, see Chapter 19.

private attitudes. Civil society often drives governments and companies to adapt their perspectives quickly, as seen with post-pandemic work structures and gender diversity recognition.

How Values Impact Economic and Social Structures

Impact on Savings

Value systems directly impact attitudes to work and influence fundamental economic criteria such as savings.

Protestant asceticism encouraged savings and investment rather than conspicuous consumption. Capital accumulation is essential to the development of capitalism since savings, in theory, enable investment. Saving would, therefore, be a sign of economic virtue. However, this is not always the case when differentiating between a household's attitudes and those of a nation.

John Maynard Keynes (1883–1946) demonstrated that the state can sometimes bend the rule of virtuous saving. In times of recession, it is permissible to create money, "ex nihilo," and thus artificial savings, to invest them in major projects.

Nevertheless, there is still a specific correlation between household savings rates and value systems. In Germany (Lutheran), the savings rate is 15% of GDP, in Switzerland (Calvinist) 22%, and in China (Confucian) 35%. The European average is 10%. The US is at 5%.[11]

Max Weber does not claim that the Protestant ethic is the sole cause of capitalism. Still, he maintains that it played an essential role in forming capitalist culture and institutions in Western Europe.[12] In contrast, Catholicism views earthly occupations as temporary steps towards a better afterlife, downplaying economic development and personal success as they are not seen as signs of predestined grace.

Competitiveness of the Group

In *The Descent of Man* (1871),[13] Charles Darwin questions the origin of civilization's "high moral values" like compassion and pity, which theoretically should

---

[11] World Bank. (2023). "World Development Indicators: Gross Savings (% of GDP)". Washington, DC: The World Bank. Available at: https://databank.worldbank.org/source/world-development-indicators

[12] These rules are not set in stone. Today, Bavaria, a predominantly Catholic state, accounts for 18.5% of Germany's GDP and is the second-richest Länder after Rhineland-Westphalia.

[13] Darwin, Charles. *The Descent of Man, and Selection in Relation to Sex*. London: John Murray, 1871.

hinder survival. He suggests that "group competitiveness" might be the answer; a cohesive group without a strong leader could outlast one dependent on a leader who might eventually vanish, leaving the group an orphan.

This ability to cooperate, which anthropologically explains the success of our human species, lies at the heart of the competitiveness of nations. Switzerland, for example, has been prosperous because, as a group, it functions as a tightly knit society based on a multitude of associations, interactions, and checks and balances. States, like groups, survive in the long term when they have a solid internal capacity to cooperate. Others break down…

In some countries, the intelligence of group members is too often dispersed and subject to antagonistic forces. Reaching a common goal and decision is impossible despite everyone's skills. Exceptional leaders can sometimes restore order to a nation whose social system is disintegrating and whose collective norms are weakening. Unfortunately, this usually does not last long, and in time entropy returns.

What Is the Moral Value Of Success?

The Great Philanthropists

This tradition lives on in the US today through the many entrepreneurs who have made fortunes and contributed to philanthropic causes.

These include Bill Gates (donations: $76 billion), Warren Buffet ($32 billion), Georges Soros ($32 billion), Michael Bloomberg ($13 billion), and Elon Musk ($8 billion).

This attitude is also found in other countries, notably India, with Jamsetji Tata (donations: $102 billion), Azim Premji ($21 billion), or Hong Kong with Li Ka-Shing ($11 billion).

Others have followed suit. Elton John has donated over $600 million to charity.[14]

Protestantism and Calvinism teach predestination, where only a select few are saved. This uncertainty drives people to find assurance of salvation through success in their careers and economic endeavors, viewed as signs of divine favor. If success is seen as a unique connection with God, it involves accepting responsibility by giving back to society, such as through philanthropy.

---

[14] www.peakng.com/top-philanthropists-in-the-world/ (accessed May 15, 2025).

Andrew Carnegie (1835–1919) exemplified the tradition of donating part of one's wealth.[15] After earning his fortune in steel, he devoted much of his life to charity and cultural support. He felt there was no shame in making money, but that:

Any man who dies rich dies dishonored.

Alain Peyrefitte (1925–1999), a former French minister and Académie Française member, claims in his book *Le Mal Français*[16] that countries of the "Counter-Reformation" (mainly Southern Europe) tend to be overly hierarchical, resistant to reform, and face challenges in maintaining social cohesion. Another Frenchman, Michel Albert, former French Commissaire au Plan, in his book *Capitalism Against Capitalism* published in 1991,[17] proposes a similar theory. The economic world would be split into two value systems. "Rhenish capitalism," seen in Germany, Japan, and northern Europe, features significant state economic involvement, long-term company perspective, strong social protection, and robust union–company–state dialogue. Conversely, "Neo-American Capitalism" in the US and UK focuses on short-term profit, high capital mobility, advanced financial markets, and minimal government regulation.

Can Extremes Be Reconciled?

The ideal scenario would merge the benefits of these two contrasting models.

In Asia, the same values found in European Protestantism are also emphasized by Confucianism. For instance, China often refers to a socialist market economy with Chinese characteristics. In Europe, Sweden has exemplified the Rhenish model, or social democracy, theorized by Nobel laureate Gunnar Myrdal.[18]

Myrdal emphasized the interconnection between economic and social issues. He argued that policies should not simply aim for economic growth but also tackle inequalities and social problems. He supported state intervention in the economy to address market imbalances, redistribute income, and provide a social safety net. The focus is on reducing income inequality.[19]

However, this implied high taxes, especially for the wealthy, which conflicted with the Arthur Laffer curve showing the relationship between tax rates

---

[15] Nasaw, David. *Andrew Carnegie.* New York: Penguin Press, 2006.

[16] Peyrefitte, Alain. *The French Disease (Le Mal Français).* Paris: Plon, 1976.

[17] Albert, Michel. *Capitalism Against Capitalism.* New York: Wiley, 1993.

[18] Myrdal, Gunnar. *Beyond the Welfare State: Economic Planning and Its International Implications.* New Haven: Yale University Press, 1960.

[19] For the record, his wife, Alva Reimer Myrdal, also received the Nobel Peace Prize in 1982 – they are probably the only couple to have combined this honor…

and tax revenue.[20] According to Laffer, if tax rates are gradually increased from a low level, tax revenues follow a similar curve until they reach a peak. From this point onwards, any further increase in rates reduces tax revenues. In effect, the incentive to work or invest disappears.

The problem is that every country probably has a different peak rate. People will react differently according to their economic interests and value systems of the society they live in or desire. The challenge for every government is to find the right balance.[21]

Chapter Takeaways

- Competitiveness relies on rational economic decisions but is also deeply influenced by the cultural context and value system. It is known as the "soft side" of competitiveness and defines a country's priorities and strategies.
- Consequently, the value system fundamentally shapes a country's competitiveness profile. While values differ from country to country, they evolve over time in similar directions, notably shifting from collective systems to a much more individualistic mindset ("meism").
- The evolution of value systems is difficult to influence. However, managing the consequences by adapting strategies to the population's changing economic and social priorities is essential. A competitive nation or company always aligns with the aspirations of society at home while being sensitive to the cultural differences of the countries where it operates abroad.

Where Next?

Value systems and how they evolve have consequences that reverberate throughout society and the economy. They impact first and foremost education, apprenticeships, and, ultimately, employability.

In addition, they also shape important economic issues such as debt management and tax systems. All of these are influenced by historical context and the evolution of value systems through the ages.

Finally, it is the fundamental responsibility of national administrations to integrate these different value systems and economic structures into a coherent system that is effective and accepted by the entire population.

---

[20] Laffer, Arthur B. "The Laffer Curve: Past, Present, and Future." *The Heritage Foundation*, June 1, 2004.

[21] From the 1980s onwards, this balance seems to have been upset in Sweden. The result was a major exodus of wealthy entrepreneurs and their companies, such as Ikea and Tetra Pak.

15 | Competitiveness Challenges for Nations

Each nation's future competitiveness faces fundamental challenges that require long-term strategies. These are the following.

Education, Apprenticeship, and Employability
Confronting the Rise of Debt
Managing Taxes Effectively
Fostering a Competent Administration

Let's look at the principles behind each of these challenges in turn and examine the solutions different countries have evolved to tackle them.

Education, Apprenticeship, and Employability

Principle: Dual education is fundamental to success: higher education must be coupled with apprenticeship.

Education Beyond Universities: Germany, France, Northern Europe, and Switzerland

The key to success in education lies in a dual system of university and apprenticeship, which has its roots in the European Middle Ages.

Universities in the Middle Ages were prestigious institutions, but their economic impact was limited. They were aimed at the elite, and teaching focused mainly on theology, rhetoric, and law.[1] However, most of the population had no access to education. Skills were acquired by working and following the training given by elders, the "masters."

This was the "companionship" that would lead to the apprenticeship system we know today.[2] The objective was not only to be educated but also to be "employable." This role was also served by the construction of the great cathedrals, which flourished and provided a unique training ground for artisans.

European Cathedrals: The First Incubators

The construction of cathedrals in Europe in the Middle Ages was a major factor in developing apprenticeships and encouraging the mobility and internationalization of a workforce.

Cathedrals: Feats of Engineering

In France alone, over 80 cathedrals were built between 1,130 and 1,250, and dozens more throughout the rest of Europe. They were true feats of engineering and management.

In 1195, for example, the nave of Notre-Dame de Chartres was already 36.50 m high, slightly higher than that of Notre-Dame de Paris. In 1211, the vault of the Reims church reached 38 m, that of Amiens 42 m in 1220, and the choir of the Beauvais church exceeded 48 m.

The size of these buildings was sometimes considerable: Amiens Cathedral measures 8,000 m^2 on the ground, or one and a half times the size of Notre-Dame de Paris. It could accommodate 10,000 people!

---

[1] Among the oldest are the universities of Bologna (founded in 1088), Oxford (1096), Salamanca (1134), Paris (1150), Cambridge (1209), Padua (1222), Naples (1224), Coimbra (1290), Prague (1348), and Basel (1460).

[2] Perrin, Christopher. *The Apprenticeship Model: A Journey Toward Mastery*. ClassicalU, 2022.

The know-how of the artisans and master builders was impressive. It led to the development of architectural inventions (such as buttresses to neutralize the pressure of the vaults) and technological inventions such as the "squirrel," a device enabling a single man to lift a 600 kg weight to the top of a building.[3]

There was also an organizational (or managerial) challenge. The many trades represented had to be trained, coordinated, and integrated into a final plan, just like a business. Indeed, building a cathedral could require the employment of hundreds of people over decades.

Mobility as an Aid to Training

As with the employees of modern companies, craftsmen could come from very different regions. In the Middle Ages they were highly mobile, traveling Europe from one building site to another.[4]

The Gothic cathedrals had an important economic function beyond their religious vocation. If bishops insisted on having such a monument in their diocese, it was because they knew it was a source of prestige, income, and wealth. The cathedrals also served as commercial and cultural centers for an entire region and, in the case of the most famous, even beyond.[5] In addition to its religious significance, the cathedral was also a meeting place. One could do business in and around its precincts, attend theater plays, and even eat. Indeed, cathedrals were very lively and even noisy places.

The Emergence of Guilds

The training spirit of the Middle Ages was perpetuated through guilds and apprenticeships. The apprentice learned a trade from his master and often lived under his roof. Parents paid for their children's apprenticeship, culminating in an examination. The apprentice then received a certificate, making him a journeyman and allowing him to be admitted to the trade.

---

[3] Fitchen, John. *The Construction of Gothic Cathedrals: A Study of Medieval Vault Erection.* Chicago: University of Chicago Press, 1961.

[4] Villard de Honnecourt was such a craftman. He was born around 1200 and left a "Carnet" tracing his travels in Europe according to the sites he worked on, from Cambrai Abbey to the cathedrals of Reims, Laon, Chartres, and Lausanne, and even as far as Hungary around 1235: *A facsimile of the Sketchbook of Villard de Honnecourt. Paris: Édition d'Albert Lenoir.*

[5] The presence of saints' relics and the faithful's pilgrimages could also provide the diocese with additional income.

Later, journeymen were organized into guilds, brotherhoods, or corporations, which enjoyed privileges of location, production, or taxation from the state. However, this system was not without its abuses, leading to monopolistic attitudes that hampered economic growth. Jacques Turgot,[6] the French Comptroller of Finance under King Louis XVI, tried to mend such excessive power (see insert) but was not listened to.

A Missed Opportunity…

In 1776, Anne-Robert-Jacques Turgot (1727–1781), Controller General of Finances under King Louis XVI in France, published an edict abolishing almost all guilds. Article I is surprisingly topical:

> It will be free for all persons, of whatever quality and condition, even foreigners…to embrace and exercise throughout our kingdom…any kind of trade and any profession of arts and crafts that they may see fit… Let us abolish all privileges… for which no one of our subjects may be disturbed in the exercise of his trade and profession, for any cause and under any pretext whatsoever.

Freedom of trade and individuals prevailed over the shackles of guilds.

Later, Edgar Faure (1908–1988), who was a French Prime Minister, declared that if the French monarchy had followed this policy, the revolution could have been avoided. Well, perhaps…

The Significance of Apprenticeship

These days, apprenticeship remains at the heart of a country's competitiveness. It is a system that combines education and vocational training, public and private, and aims to develop a population's basic skills. The aim is to learn a trade and thus become "employable."

Apprenticeships provide a structured approach to combining practical experience with theoretical education. Typically, these programs are conducted within both corporate environments and specialized educational institutions. Switzerland is

---

[6] Poirier, Jean-Pierre. *Turgot: Laissez-Faire et Progrès Social*. Paris: Perrin, 1999.

often considered an example of an apprenticeship system and its impact on a country's competitiveness.[7]

The long-term success of this approach is indisputable. In countries with well-developed apprenticeship systems, youth unemployment is at an all-time low: 6.4% in Switzerland and 6.9% in Germany, almost half the OECD average.[8]

The first principle of achieving success involves integrating companies, trainers, and apprentices through a "public-private" partnership. The dual education system should facilitate transitions between apprenticeship and higher education, such as university programs, ensuring that no irreversible decisions are made at an early stage. Additionally, companies need help to receive apprentices. Hosting a young professional demands time, availability, and specific skills to ensure it constitutes a beneficial investment for the company, the apprentice, and the state.

Prestige And Recognition　　In addition, prestige should be given to those with a certificate of apprenticeship (e.g., a master's degree). Today, an education is not generally regarded as complete unless it ends with a university degree, but this has not always been the case. For a long time, particularly in Switzerland and Germany, the heads of large companies were not necessarily university graduates but could have been apprentices who had climbed the corporate hierarchy.

Today, MBAs (Masters in Business Administration) are popular. But in the past, master's degrees existed for other professions. One could be a master carpenter or a master baker. My grandfather was a master dyer. The prestige was the same, and pride in belonging to a trade was reinforced.

Apprenticeship[9] should be combined with continuous professional training throughout a person's career. Professions evolve with techniques and company changes. Individuals are likely to have multiple jobs in their lifetime. Even within one profession, various sub-trades are continuously changing.

Education in Transition　　An economy's employment structure cannot focus exclusively on the excellence of higher education, however prestigious it may be. A state cannot function solely with university graduates. Plumbers and electricians

---

[7] In Switzerland, 4.5% of jobs are filled by apprentices. Two-thirds of young people between 15 and 20 choose the apprenticeship route upon completing their compulsory schooling and 230 trades are recognized. Training lasts 3–4 years.

[8] Organisation for Economic Co-operation and Development (OECD). (Annual). *OECD Employment Outlook 2023*. Paris: OECD Publishing.

[9] Ryan, Paul. *Apprenticeship: Past and Present*. New York: Berghahn Books, 2023.

will always be needed. On the other hand, emerging technologies and business models, such as energy transition or artificial intelligence, imply a profound change in many traditional jobs. They will never be the same again.

In automotive plants, workers must be trained to assemble vehicles whose main components are electrical and computerized. Roofers must learn how to install solar panels, their colleagues wind turbines, and so on. Apprenticeships enable a country to make this transition gradually and maintain the skills that guarantee employment in a changing economy.

Promoting Employability   Every individual will encounter a variety of responsibilities throughout their career. Furthermore, multiple skills are required to address all aspects of the role within a single job. Governments are, therefore, responsible for creating an environment that enables the transition from one skill to another.

In a country receiving foreign investment, clauses requiring the company to create a training institution next to its location can be a powerful policy. It is what Dubai has done, for example, with its healthcare investments.[10] This creates a network of skills and research around foreign and local companies. Even if a company "loses" employees it has trained, it also finds itself in a competitive, high-quality environment where it can hire others trained by other companies.

Universities: A Legitimate Ambition?

Every country has a legitimate ambition to host prestigious universities. Every year, the Shanghai Institute[11] ranks the world's top universities.[12] There is no doubt that top-level education is essential for the future of a country and its elite. As Oscar Wilde said: "You can never be overdressed or overeducated!"

Like infrastructure, education is rightly seen as an essential investment for a country. However, this must be qualified: education, especially higher education, can also miss its mark. South Korea is a case in point. This country regularly tops the rankings of the best-educated countries. Education has become a national obsession. Many students risk their health and their parents' savings on private tuition. Yet every year in Korea, over 50,000 university graduates cannot find work.

---

[10] These include Mediclinic Middle East, Moorfields Eye Hospital Dubai, and the Harvard Medical School Center for Global Health Delivery.

[11] Shanghai Ranking Consultancy (2023). "Academic Ranking of World Universities 2023." Shanghai: Shanghai Jiao Tong University. Available at: https://www.shanghairanking.com/rankings/arwu/2023.

[12] In 2023, Harvard University and Stanford University will be ahead of MIT. Of the top 14, 12 are American institutions and 2 British (Oxford and Cambridge). Paris Saclay is 15th and ETH Zurich 20th.

On the other hand, more than 30,000 jobs open to high school graduates have no applicants. The prestigious Samsung Economic Research Institute estimates that over 40% of Korean university graduates are "overeducated."[13]

Can People Be Overeducated? In Europe, the top prize for education has often gone to Finland. One delegation after another has come to understand the Finnish "miracle." No doubt, the system is excellent. However, the unemployment rate for young Finns aged 16–24 is 18.4%[14]! (Three times higher than in Germany or Switzerland.) As in Korea, Finland "overeducates" its young people, who ultimately cannot or do not want to find a job that matches their skills.

An obsession with university education is at the root of this problem. In the OECD, 56% of 18-year-olds leave secondary school to attend university. In Finland, Korea, and France, the figure is over 90%. Of course, the question of prestige is ultimately legitimate: what parents would not want to have university-educated children?[15]

The Dangerous Obsession with Mathematics High-level education also suffers from an obsession with mathematics. If it can be calculated, it must be correct... Perhaps, but this also creates a false sense of security, particularly in economics. Many Nobel Prize winners in economics were also brilliant mathematicians: Kenneth Arrow and John Nash were first and foremost remarkable scientists whose work was of interest to economics almost by chance.

However, in 1997, Myron Scholes and Robert Merton were awarded the Nobel Prize in economics for a new method of calculating the price of a derivative.[16] They joined the board of the hedge fund Long-Term Capital Management. In 1998, the company lost $4.6 billion and went bankrupt two years later.

Modern business is more about choices than calculations. Emotional intelligence is just as important as rational intelligence in running a business. The "animal instinct" dear to Keynes sometimes explains economic phenomena better than pure logic. It has also led to a more psychological and behaviorist approach to economics, thanks to the work of professors Daniel Kahneman (Princeton University) and Richard Thaler (Chicago Booth School of Business), both Nobel Prize winners in economics.

---

[13] Samsung Economic Research Institute (SERI) (2022). "Employment Trends of Graduates in South Korea."

[14] Figures for 2023.

[15] There is also a material impact: in Great Britain, a university master's degree earns, on average, 66% more than a bachelor's degree.

[16] Scholes, Myron S. *Derivatives in a Dynamic Environment.* World Scientific Publishing Company, 2000.

Even in science, mathematics has its limits. The great industrial revolution of the 19th century was that of electricity, following on from that of steam. Michael Faraday laid its foundations, or rather those of electromagnetism, in his 1839 book *Experimental Investigations in Electricity*: 332 pages and not a single mathematical equation![17]

Why is this obsession with mathematics in our education systems destroying the lives of so many otherwise perfectly intelligent young people? First, for reasons of selection: when hundreds of students are jostling to get into economics faculties, we must rank them. How?

Through exams where there is only one answer to a single question – essentially mathematics – which can be marked en masse.[18] Economics questions with several possible answers for the same problem are too complicated to manage. However, in doing this, we often demotivate brilliant students who thrive more on emotional intelligence. What's more, to my knowledge, I have never met a business or government leader who referred to an economics textbook or a mathematical equation before making a decision.

Multifaceted Education

Education must remain dual. Alongside academic education to master "knowledge," a parallel training system must teach people to master a "trade."

Some courses combine this approach. For example, theoretical medical studies must be complemented by hospital-based assistant training before students can practice as qualified doctors. The same applies to law, where the title of a lawyer is only granted after an internship. In economics, more university degrees, especially post-graduate ones, require an internship in a company before being finalized.

Both theoretical and formative paths are prestigious and must lead to the same respect and success. Otherwise, many young academics will continue to be "underemployed,"[19] and young apprentices will continue to be "underappreciated." In all cases, education must preserve the pleasure of learning, curiosity, and the ability to think outside the box.

With logic, we often reproduce the past. With imagination, we can create the future. The role of education is to stimulate both.

---

[17] Faraday, Michael. *Experimental Researches in Electricity*. Vol. 1. London: Richard and John Edward Taylor, 1839.

[18] And maybe soon by a virtual assistant using Artificial Intelligence…

[19] Dooley, David, and JoAnn Prause. *The Social Costs of Underemployment: Inadequate Employment as Disguised Unemployment*. Cambridge: Cambridge University Press, 2004.

Confronting the Rise of Debt

*Principle: Taking on debt is not necessarily bad if it allows a country to invest in the future –
but not everyone sees it that way…*

Debt Is Also a Philosophy: Germany, Switzerland, and the Scandinavian countries

A country's debt is like a double-edged sword; it offers quick relief but can choke
its future, especially with rising interest rates. Indebted nations face difficulties borrowing further or must do so at higher rates. Debt histories are often bleak and tied
to past economic and political trends.

The OECD reports[20] that the debt-to-GDP ratios in 2023 was 136% for the US,
116% for France, 93% for Great Britain, 64% for Germany, and 39% for Switzerland.
Japan tops the list with a ratio of 240%, although most of its debt is domestic.

By contrast, 47% of French debt and 41% of German debt is owned by non-
residents. The European Central Bank has recently boosted its lending to member
states, particularly following the COVID crisis, nearing an average of 30% of their
debt. Consequently, Europe seems to be moving towards a "Japanese-style" scenario, which aims to protect the debt from non-resident owners.

On the other hand, Argentina is 99% dependent on foreign financing for its debt.
Its precarious economic situation in the past has led it to systematically reschedule its
debt payments (through the Paris Club)[21] or to borrow massively from the IMF. Therefore, a country's vulnerability to its debt depends on the nature of its creditors, whether
national or international. In the same way, for an individual, there is a fundamental
difference between owing money to one's banker or one's family.

Curbing Debt

Some so-called "frugal" countries have tried to fix the progression of their indebt-
edness in provisions of their constitution or law. Examples include Switzerland[22]
and Germany.[23]

---

[20] OECD. *Global Debt Report 2024*. Paris: OECD Publishing, 2024.

[21] Paris Club (2021) "Annual Report 2021: Paris Club Activities and Debt Restructuring." Paris:
Paris Club Secretariat. Available at: https://www.clubdeparis.org/en/communications/page/
annual-report

[22] Lueber, Benjamin. *The Swiss Debt Brake as a Model for Sustainable Fiscal Policy*. Munich:
GRIN Verlag, 2017.

[23] German Council of Economic Experts. "The debt brake: sustainable, stabilising, flexible."
In *Annual Report 2019/20*, 175–200. Wiesbaden: German Council of Economic Experts,
2019.

The "debt brake" is a fiscal tool to maintain balanced public finances and avoid excessive state debt. Essentially, it ensures that spending is covered by current revenue rather than borrowing. If spending surpasses revenue, steps must be taken to cut costs or boost income to achieve budget balance.

Exceptions are tolerated during economic downturns or crises. At the time that this book is being written, Germany is considering moving emergency defense investments outside the debt brake. This would require a change in the constitution.

This mechanism has benefited states that have adopted the strategy. For example, by 2024, all major industrial economies had debts over 100% of GDP, except Germany, which used this system.[24]

The Philosophical Dimension

There is also an ideological conception of debt that considerably impacts fiscal policies. During the peak of the Greek crisis in 2017,[25] Angela Merkel stated: "Do not spend more than you get – it is amazing that something so simple leads to so much debate." At that time, the nations opposing the European recovery plan, mainly the Netherlands and Finland, labeled themselves "frugal" or "virtuous." Economic policies have always had a moral aspect.

Austerity, perceived as a fundamental value in Protestant societies, derives from the Greek word "austêros," meaning bitter. Thus, austerity measures adopted by governments can be perceived very differently in various countries. In German, the term for austerity is "Austerität," but they also use "Sparsamkeit," which translates to frugality or the inclination to save.

The Moral Aspect

The former Italian Prime Minister Mario Monti highlighted the challenge of aligning an Anglo-Saxon approach to economic recovery through expenditure with Germany's strong aversion to it. He remarked that in Germany, economics is considered "a branch of moral philosophy, and growth as the reward for good behavior." In simpler terms, while Americans view spending or saving as mere tools of economic policy, Germans impose a moral aspect on these actions.

Adam Smith's first book, published in 1759, was titled *The Theory of Moral Sentiments*, emphasizing the deep connection between morality and economics.

---

[24] Under the European Union's budgetary rules, the maximum debt limit for a member country should not exceed 60% of its GDP. A standard that seems a long way off today…

[25] I recall passing by a travel agency window in Berlin with a sign that read: "Spend your vacations in Greece and visit your taxes…"

Historically, Lutheranism and Calvinism significantly influenced Europe's industrialization process, fostering a strong inclination to save, as noted by Max Weber. This inclination to save is also advocated by Confucianism in Asia.

All this once led to economics being classified as a moral science. Economic decisions implied a value system. For example, virtue would be to save and vice to spend. However, governments shifted towards more flexibility after the 2020 COVID crisis, the energy supply breakdowns, and inflation. Yet some still oppose this, comparing a country's economy to that of a household — which is not always accurate.

The Limits of Excessive Thrift

Adam Smith highlighted this ambiguity: "What is prudence in the conduct of any private family may be close to folly in that of a great Kingdom."[26]

While seen as virtues during economic growth, savings and austerity can hinder economic recovery. In his *General Theory*[27] published in 1936, John Maynard Keynes underlined this paradox: "Any attempt to save more by reducing consumption will affect incomes so much that the attempt will necessarily fail."

Printing money was not popular in the past, but now it can be seen to temporarily help overcome crises. Yet flooding the market with liquidity and subsidies can lead to inflation. Choosing between recession, inflation, and debt is difficult. In economics, vice and virtue are often two sides of the same coin, making them hard to distinguish.

Managing Taxes Efficiently

Principle: Taxes are frequently unpopular. Yet, they are the foundation of a country's economy and more…

Georges Clémenceau, President of the French government from 1917 to 1920, summed up the bad reputation of taxes: "France is an extremely fertile country. Civil servants are planted, and taxes grow." Nobody likes paying taxes. And there is nothing more sensitive than tax issues because they are at the center of the relationship between citizens and state power.

Taxation dates back to ancient civilizations like Egypt and Mesopotamia, around 3000 to 2800 BCE. In these societies, taxes were often paid in kind, in the form of agricultural produce or taxed labor such as chores. The tax system primarily relied on agricultural land. Progress in mathematics and geometry allowed states

---

[26] Adam Smith, *The Theory of Moral Sentiments*. London: Andrew Millar, 1759.
[27] Keynes, John Maynard. *The General Theory of Employment, Interest, and Money*. London: Macmillan, 1936.

to develop more advanced methods for assessing and taxing arable land, livestock, inheritances, and sales.

By the Middle Ages, taxation had largely shifted to a monetary system, assessed and paid in cash, particularly among the wealthier classes. The development of a banking system further facilitated this change.[28] The modern income tax emerged in the early 20th century, mainly due to countries needing funds for military expenses during the World War I.

The Tax Burden

The tax burden encompasses all mandatory financial charges within an economy. It includes direct taxes levied on the income, profits, or assets of individuals and businesses and indirect taxes like value-added taxes (VAT) and social contributions made by employers and employees.

France leads the OECD with a nearly 47% tax burden on GDP, while Ireland has the lowest at just over 21%. Scandinavian countries, the Benelux, and Germany all exceed 40%, whereas the US and Switzerland are around 27%.

Tax revenue collection varies internationally. Norway imposes the highest taxes on corporations, with their profits making up nearly a quarter of total tax revenue. In contrast, corporate taxes comprise only 6% of the total in the US and 5.6% in France. The OECD average is about 9%.[29]

In Denmark, personal income tax constitutes the largest part of government revenue at 52%. Following this are the US, Iceland, and New Zealand, each with over 40%, while Switzerland stands at 31%. At the lower end is the Czech Republic, where only 9% of its tax revenues come from personal income tax.

These figures indicate that countries like the US and Switzerland favor taxing individuals over companies to stay competitive. This trend has been evident in Sweden, where 29% of tax revenue is from personal income and 7% from corporate profits.

Why Tax Structure Differs Widely

These tax figures must be seen in the context of two essential factors.

Social security contributions primarily act as an indirect tax burden on businesses and individuals. In Germany, they make up 38% of tax revenues, while in France, they represent 32%. This figure is 24% in the US and 20% in the UK. In Denmark, however, these contributions account for only 13% of tax revenue because most income is gathered through direct taxation.

---

[28] Blankson, Samuel. *A Brief History of Taxation*. London: Lulu Press, 2007.
[29] OECD. *Revenue Statistics 2024*. Paris: OECD Publishing, 2024.

Second, the employment rate[30] measures the proportion of working-age people participating in a country's economy. This rate is over 80% in Iceland, the Netherlands, New Zealand, and Switzerland. It stands at 76% in the UK, and in the US it is 71%. In contrast, France has an employment rate of 68%, and Italy's rate is 61%.

A low employment rate focuses tax pressure on specific companies and high-income individuals. Consequently, countries with decreasing employment rates struggle to reduce tax pressure due to a limited tax base. Additionally, part-time work is rising. In Holland, the average annual work hours are 1,442, with part-time jobs comprising 37% of employment, compared to 14% in France. Also, 17% of Dutch workers are self-employed.

In advanced economies, the job market is adapting to include new work arrangements, such as part-time roles, self-employment, and greater flexibility between the office, clients, and home. This shift not only reduces the average working hours but also entices more people to join the workforce, especially women. In the Netherlands, over 50% of female employees work part-time.[31]

International Tax Harmonization

The OECD has initiated a two-pillar reform to maintain fair competition among companies and countries. The first pillar requires multinational companies with over €20 billion in sales and more than 10% profit to pay taxes where their income is generated instead of in a tax haven. The second pillar, effective immediately, mandates that multinational corporations with revenues exceeding 750 million euros are subject to a minimum tax rate of 15%.[32]

This should not present a significant issue, as a country's appeal relies on more than just its tax regime. Additionally, the intricate systems employed by large companies for tax optimization have reached such complexity that many now agree that a simplified system with harmonized rules may be beneficial.

Taxes as the Price for Social Peace

Tax data shows how the state's role has changed over time. Historically, tribal chiefs or monarchs provided protection, earning their authority. Today, the state is expected to provide not only security via police and military but also to invest in economic and social infrastructure for national prosperity and social peace.

---

[30] OECD. *Labour Force Statistics 2024*. Paris: OECD Publishing, 2024.

[31] Organisation for Economic Co-operation and Development (OECD). *Part-Time and Partly Equal: Gender and Work in the Netherlands*. Paris: OECD Publishing, 2019.

[32] It implies that nations like Ireland, which has a corporate tax rate of approximately 12.5%, and Switzerland will need to increase their corporate tax rates.

As a consequence, people do not just expect investment in economic or social infrastructure. At the same time, they want a redistributive tax policy to alleviate social inequalities and crises. A recent study by the British magazine *The Economist* shows that in rich countries, spending on public services and infrastructure was about 25% of GDP in the early 1950s. Social transfer spending represented just 3% of GDP.[33]

In 2023, infrastructure spending fell to 15% of GDP, while transfer spending rose to 15%. In many countries, states spend less on infrastructure because they have to pay more for transfers. That is the price of social peace.

France illustrates this well, with public spending at 58% of GDP.[34] Over half of this (31% of GDP) goes to redistributive social spending, double what it was in 1960. This has helped lift around 5 million people from absolute poverty and made the country less unequal.

In addition, post-COVID, it is widely accepted that the state's role should also include protecting citizens from life hazards, acting like an insurer of last resort. The state is now considered responsible for citizens' safety, focusing on mitigating crises' impacts rather than avoiding them. Consequently, additional expenses can lead to debt if prosperity doesn't rise accordingly.[35]

Fostering a Competent Administration

Principle: Effective governance fosters national unity and enhances state efficiency. However, this doesn't always hold…

Switzerland epitomizes diversity with 4 national languages, 26 cantons, 2 main churches (Catholic and Protestant), and valley and mountain inhabitants. Urban areas now host 85% of the 9 million people. Its 5.2 million workforce includes one-third of foreign nationals, mainly from the EU, UK, and EFTA. Additionally, 380,000 cross-border commuters work in Switzerland, with 60% in Geneva, Ticino, and Vaud.[36]

---

[33] "Governments Are Bigger Than Ever. They Are Also More Useless." The Economist, September 23, 2024.

[34] International Monetary Fund. 2023. *Spending Efficiency and Reforms: France*. Washington, DC: International Monetary Fund.

[35] Frédéric Bastiat, the 19th-century French writer, summed it up: "The State is the great fiction through which everyone strives to live at the expense of everyone else."

[36] Federal Statistical Office (FSO). *Population Size and Change in Switzerland in 2023: Definitive Figures*. Neuchâtel: FSO, 2024.

In 2021, 39% of the permanent resident population aged 15 and above had a migration background (2,890,000 people). Over a third of this group (1,090,000) has obtained Swiss nationality. In Geneva, foreigners make up 41% of the population. In Switzerland, only 38% of those over 15 years old are considered "pure Swiss," meaning they have a Swiss passport, were born in Switzerland, and have at least one parent also born in the country.

Thus, what prevents such a diverse country from falling apart under the strain of numerous forces? Administration!

Strengthening Society

What ties a mountain farmer in the Grisons and a private banker in Geneva to the same country? While shared landscape, history, and values are factors, they do not entirely explain the sense of belonging. Many nations have taller mountains, deeper lakes, or longer histories. Values also evolve and vary in interpretation. A more straightforward explanation lies in the strength of a country's administration.

This administrative quality holds the social fabric together and ensures consistent development. Both farmers and bankers encounter similar administrative processes and operate within a similar political framework across the nation. There is a notable advantage for any country that achieves such cohesion. In Switzerland, for instance, 69% of citizens have high trust in the police, 60% in the judicial system, and 53% in the political system.[37] In a direct democracy where grievances can quickly surface, maintaining such high levels of trust is remarkable.

Administration and Bureaucracy

These two terms are frequently confused. Typically, administration encompasses all tasks related to managing an organization or system. Bureaucracy, however, is a specific type of organization defined by its formal rules and procedures.

Etymologically, bureaucracy is made up of the word "bureau" and the Greek "Kratos," meaning "power." The term often has a negative connotation. It was first used by the Frenchman Vincent de Gournay (1712–1759) to denounce the excessive administrative control imposed by the state on the economy and society of his country.[38]

---

[37] OECD. *OECD Survey on Drivers of Trust in Public Institutions - 2024 Results: Country Notes - Switzerland*. Paris: OECD Publishing, 2024.

[38] Hont, I. (1983). "Vincent de Gournay and the origins of political economy." *History of Political Economy*, 15(4), 595-609. 10.1215/00182702-15-4-595

The Law of Unexpected Consequences...

The economy reflects Jean Paul Sartre's famous phrase. "Hell is paved with good intentions."

Even the best of ideas can backfire.

At the beginning of the 20th century, the city of Dehli in India suffered from an invasion of cobra snakes in the streets. They were a curiosity for tourists, but a little dangerous in everyday life.

The municipality decided to eradicate them in the following way: anyone who could capture a cobra snake and bring its head to the administration would receive a financial reward. But this was decided without factoring in the inventiveness of the town's inhabitants. They began to raise snakes in their backyards and cut off their heads to claim their money.

Faced with the influx of snakeheads and the cost of the operation, the municipality was forced to cease the policy.

The disgruntled locals put the snakes back on the streets. The result was more cobras in Delhi and less money in the municipal coffers.

Its bad reputation stems from the fact that public opinion believes that they are administered by people who never leave their desks and ignore the reality of their lives. Administration wields substantial influence due to its authority and power. Max Weber first theorized bureaucracy in the early 20th century, viewing it as the most efficient way to manage public administration through formal hierarchy, written regulations, specialization, competence, and long-term career prospects. He claimed that ideal bureaucracies operate neutrally without personal biases or emotions, implying they resist corruption since they follow rules rather than individuals. Weber nevertheless admitted that a bureaucracy can also have a bad reputation. It can be subject to dysfunctions such as excessive formalism, rigidity, resistance to change, or arrogance towards citizens.[39]

Efficiency and Interference

From health pandemics to economic reforms, governments and their administrations are judged on their effectiveness, perhaps even more than on their principles.

---

[39] Weber, M. (1947). "*The Theory of Social and Economic Organization.*" New York: Oxford University Press.

For some countries, efficiency is often approached from a dirigisme angle. A strong, centralized, authoritarian government is sometimes seen as the answer to the population's need for efficiency. China, Russia, Brazil, and Turkey are following this path. In Europe, some are tempted.

For companies, administrative efficiency is fundamental. Globalization has been a way of circumventing the inefficiencies of certain countries. Having the choice of where to invest enables companies to put pressure on governments not to invest or to move and go elsewhere. Yet administrations often continue to enjoy a bad reputation. This sentiment was well expressed by Frederich Hayek:[40]

> The greatest danger to liberty today comes from the men who are most necessary and most powerful in modern government, namely the expert and efficient administrators exclusively concerned with what they regard as the public good.

Inertia

In developed nations, government inefficiency is mainly down to scale. Numerous government officials have created artificial jobs in the public sector to conceal the decline in private-sector employment, especially during the 2000s. On average, the public sector accounts for 18% of the workforce in OECD countries.[41]

In some developing countries, corruption in the administration often stems from inadequate pay and training for civil servants. Bribery can sometimes be the only way to boost a meager salary. Though not justifiable, it is a reality many companies face. Economic corruption often aims to expedite lengthy bureaucratic processes rather than making unlawful decisions. This is not an excuse, merely an explanation.

How Administrations Operate

In many countries, the biggest risk is that the administration often manages itself without proper oversight. This criticism, though sometimes unfounded, is common among the public. It can be explained by Max Weber's view of an impersonal, rational bureaucracy as a significant improvement over past practices.

---

[40] Hayek, F. A. *The Road to Serfdom.* Chicago: University of Chicago Press, (1944).

[41] In Europe, all Scandinavian countries, as well as France, have a public sector accounting for over 20% of total employment. In Switzerland, 24% of the workforce is in the public sector, up from 15% 30 years ago. Norway leads with 31%. There are 160 public sector workers per 1,000 residents. In India, it's only 16.

After him, many researchers have studied the world of public administration. One of the most cynical and entertaining was Cyril Northcote Parkinson, an Englishman whose theories have influenced generations based on three timeless principles:

- "Work expands to fill the time available for its completion."
- "Leaders create subordinates, not rivals."
- "Leaders create work for each other."

As a result, and according to him, bureaucracy would increase by 5–7% a year, regardless of the work to be done.[42]

That was written in 1955. Since then, many administrations have changed; they have modernized, digitized, and adopted a customer-service approach. In several countries, it is now common for all government correspondence to include the name of the responsible person, their direct phone number, and an email address for contact.

In summary, efficient administration is crucial for a country's prosperity and stability. While some view it as an intrusive control or a bureaucratic nightmare, history has shown that no state has survived without a solid and efficient administration.[43]

Chapter Takeaways

- Political and economic leaders consider the domains mentioned in this chapter the most important for a country's competitiveness, albeit the most difficult to manage.
- A problem identified in education, debt infrastructure, or administration can be quickly acknowledged but can take years to remedy. This always frustrates the population.
- A fundamental dilemma exists between rapid improvements for the immediate benefit of the population and long-term competitiveness strategies for future prosperity. Thus, putting the important before the urgent is often perilous; however, it defines a true leader.

---

[42] Parkinson, C. N. *Parkinson's Law: The Pursuit of Progress*. London: John Murray, (1957).

[43] Egypt, Assyria, Rome, Persia, the Baghdad Caliphate, Chinese, Ottoman, and British empires thrived with efficient administrations, while those lacking it quickly fell apart. Alexander the Great's empire disintegrated upon his death due to a lack of a central administration.

Where Next?

In the first part of this book, we described the origin of world competitiveness, its characteristics, and how it developed. We also highlighted how nations formed new strategies to benefit from this new economic and business opportunity.

Nevertheless, a global and open world has been relatively short-lived. From 2018 onwards, globalization began to fracture after the COVID pandemic and with a multiplication of geopolitical conflicts. The world that has emerged is less global and no longer as unified as in the past. What are the consequences?

We shall find out in the next chapter.

PART

III

16 | A Fractured World

Since the late 1960s, the world has been opening up. The trend appeared unstoppable. Gradually, even the most isolated countries began joining an international community where free trade, the exchange of ideas, and unrestricted travel had become the norm.

However, everything changed in 2018 and then with the onset of the COVID crisis. A series of health, economic, and geopolitical crises ended what some considered a great ambition — and what others perceived as an illusion.

Direct Investments as a Marker of Globalization
The Three Ages of Globalization
National Security Defines a New Protectionism
The Return of Industrial Policies

Direct Investments as a Marker of Globalization

A Shift in Globalization

As of 1978, China's "Open Door" policy initiated a process of integration of those economies that were once closed to globalization into a global, open, multilateral system. The collapse of the Berlin Wall in 1989 further accelerated the transition towards market economies, encompassing Russia, former Soviet republics, and Central European countries.

This shift transformed the world economy and facilitated the exchange of ideas, technologies, and mobility while also bringing several challenges. The primary objective was to fulfill the ambitions of countries keen on gaining economic power. At the same time, their populations aspired to elevate their living standards quickly.

During the early 1980s, wage disparities between China and Europe or the US were approximately 1–25. The gap between Western and Central Europe was 1–15 (with nations like Poland, the Czech Republic, or Slovakia).[1] This significant disparity became attractive for Western companies, considering the proximity of these nations.

From Exports to Investments

When companies are remote from large markets, an export strategy is inefficient in addressing demand. For example, it became clear that supplying China with machinery or automobiles necessitated local investment. Moreover, low wages and favorable taxes allowed production of goods that could be re-exported to the company's home or other global markets.

It was a win-win situation for a host country: companies became more competitive, and investment-receiving countries attracted capital and developed their exports and know-how. The shift to direct investment has also significantly impacted the workforce. The number of corporate expatriates has surged over the past four decades of intense globalization. Conversely, some workers in industrialized nations did not share the same enthusiasm as they saw their jobs outsourced.

Foreign Direct Investment Defines Globalization

It is necessary to distinguish between market-serving investments, like those directed to sell products directly to the Chinese domestic market, and sourcing investments, such as those that aim to have products manufactured in one place and then re-exported to supply other markets, including the company's home market. Globalization is thus the transition from an export-driven economy to one focused on direct investments, such as building, acquiring, developing, and managing physical assets overseas.

Today, according to the OECD,[2] the European Union holds $13,117 million in direct investment abroad, and the US $8,240 million. China holds $2,413 million. As for smaller countries, they have been prompted to invest abroad because their domestic markets are limited.[3]

---

[1] Organisation for Economic Co-operation and Development (OECD). *Income Disparities in China*. Paris: OECD Publishing, 2004.

[2] Organization for Economic Co-operation and Development (OECD). (2023). "International Direct Investment Statistics." Paris: OECD Publishing. https://doi.org/10.1787/idis-2023-en

[3] Switzerland, for instance, has $1,552 million in foreign direct investment and receives $3,179 billion in investments from the rest of the world.

During the "pure" globalization era, the preferred model was complete ownership of assets. This allows a company to implement its policies globally with the same products, branding, and corporate culture. Moreover, full ownership helps protect intellectual property since patents and proprietary knowledge remain within the company's ecosystem.

However, direct investment exposes the company to political risks that are sometimes significant in its operating countries. These are mainly related to issues such as nationalization or expropriation.[4] A decline in one export market can be mitigated by redirecting products to another. However, exiting a country's direct investment can result in a significant loss for the company, whether by choice or imposition. This risk of political interference by the host country can hardly be alleviated by the host country, especially when it lacks international influence, as is often the case for smaller nations.

The Three Ages of Globalization

Globalization developed in phases over the past five decades.

The Golden Age   The era from 1978 to 2018 could be considered a golden age. States embraced open markets and international cooperation, while companies focused on investment and efficiency through global management. This period of globalization, characterized, among other things, by a "just in time" attitude, benefited companies by increasing competitiveness and offering consumers cheaper products. However, it had its limitations.

The Age of Vulnerability   The COVID crisis from 2020 onwards underscored the production chain's vulnerability owing to its extreme specialization. There had been a few warning signs that destabilized supplies: earthquakes affecting semiconductor production, the closure of the Suez Canal by a stalled ship, the closure of shipping traffic in the Red Sea destabilized by Houthi rebels, and the impact of drought on the water level of the Panama Canal.

Lorenz's well-known theory about the beat of a butterfly's wings creating a hurricane on the other side of the planet proves repeatedly accurate.[5] For example, I remember that a major German car company could no longer sell its top-of-the-range

---

[4] Nationalization implies a total takeover of a company by the state, which then manages it. Expropriation is a partial takeover of assets. In both cases, the question arises of compensation for the former owners.

[5] Gleick, James. *Chaos: Making a New Science.* New York: Viking, 1987.

models because the semiconductor for the electric driver's seat (worth less than 100 euros) was in short supply.

But the big shock came with the pandemic. The global economy halted when China, the world's factory, adopted a "Zero COVID" policy and went into total shutdown in 2019. Supermarkets were empty of products for the first time since World War II. The COVID pandemic affected 773 million people globally.[6] Despite the rapid development and approval of the mRNA vaccine within a year, vulnerability became a major concern for governments, businesses, and individuals.

Government and business leaders began to focus on "decoupling" or "de-risking"[7] strategies for markets and supplies to provide firewalls during crises. In this second phase of globalization, priority is given to the security of supply and business reliability. It is the transition from "just in time" to "just in case."

The Age of the Fractured Economy   In today's phase of globalization, supply chain uncertainties are pushing governments towards more interventionist policies. This takes the form of increased protectionist measures and more industrial policies. The growing interference of politics in economic decision-making is a characteristic of this new phase of globalization.

A fractured economy is defined by the transition to parallel markets and operating platforms (financial operations, payment systems, or logistics). The global economy remains interconnected but is becoming increasingly restricted and regulated. Government intervention is on the rise, and multilateralism is losing importance.

National Security Defines a New Protectionism

Protectionism has always been present in our economies. Nevertheless, in recent decades, governments have resisted the temptation to do "too much." Many economists have pointed out that an excess of protectionist measures turned the stock market crash of 1929 into a long period of global depression.[8] Today, however, protectionist measures are once again becoming a preferred instrument of political

---

[6]World Health Organization. What the COVID-19 Pandemic Has Exposed: The Findings of Five Global Commissions on Health. Geneva: World Health Organization, 2023.

[7]"Decoupling" means a complete break with a market, such as Russia, for certain industries. "De-risking" implies a reduction in risk through the multiplication of parallel strategies, but not a total break; this is the case with China.

[8]It is important to recall the influence of Ben Bernanke, chairman of the US Federal Reserve from 2006 to 2014, who studied the causes and consequences of the 1929 Depression at length.

decision-making. According to Global Trade Alert, the number of such measures worldwide has risen from 9,000 to almost 35,000 in 10 years.[9]

In the past, most protectionist measures were designed to protect the labor market. They were implemented when a country suffered from unfair trade practices, such as dumping or subsidies. The World Trade Organization accepts such protective measures, provided they are documented, transparent, and temporary.[10] Protectionist tensions between the US, Europe, and Japan marked much of the trade dispute between the 1980s and 1990s.

National Security as A Priority

In the post-COVID era, a new kind of protectionism focuses on national security rather than just job protection. Actions against Chinese companies like Huawei and TikTok exemplify this shift. The problem is that the notion of national security can quickly become a "catch-all" that leaves the door open to all sorts of interpretations: what does *not* concern national security?

For example, what about the steel industry? Today, China produces over 50% of the world's steel, 12 times more than the United States and 25 times more than Germany.[11] Every army in the world needs steel. Should every country protect its national steel production, regardless of the cost, especially in environmental terms?

Moreover, national security is an eminently political concept, defined differently according to the sensitivities of different countries and their governments. In this field, when there is a conflict of interpretation, the states concerned do not want to refer to international arbitration or a third-party organization such as the World Trade Organization.

This inevitably calls into question the concept of multilateralism. This development is disturbing for small nations like the Nordic countries, Singapore, the Gulf States, and Switzerland. Without a multilateral system, they lack a platform to voice their concerns during conflicts with larger nations.

The second new dimension to protectionism is the proliferation of industrial policies.

The Return of Industrial Policies

These policies are not new. As far back as the 1960s, Japan planned and led the country's economic recovery through industrial policies managed by the all-powerful

---

[9] Figures for 2022.

[10] Initially article XIX of GATT, then adopted again by the World Trade Organization.

[11] World Steel Association. World Steel in Figures 2024. Brussels: World Steel Association, 2024.

Ministry of International Trade and Industry (MITI). Japan was not unique in this regard. In France, the "Plan Calcul" similarly aimed to foster the growth of the nation's computer industry.[12] France was among the few Western industrial nations that maintained a Commissariat au Plan to steer its economic policies.

The original dirigisme of "plans" – akin to the so-called "planned economies" of Communist countries – was abandoned in the 1980s. It became clear that the speed of technological innovation and its impact on the economy and the world of work meant that bureaucrats could no longer plan what would happen.

Today, industrial policies have taken a different turn. They focus on investment aid and subsidies in so-called "strategic" sectors. They aim to regain control over developing and manufacturing new technologies, such as semiconductors, artificial intelligence, biotechnologies, the energy transition, and climate change.

The problem is that when a major country starts to support its economy with industrial policies, it inevitably elicits a similar response from other trading partners. An often-ignored aspect of industrial policies is the need for new skills in national administrations. Government goals must be implemented and monitored by those with industrial and managerial expertise, which isn't always the case.

Proliferation

At the federal level, the US has earmarked over $2,000 billion in grants and subsidies for infrastructure, semiconductors, and clean energy investments.[13] In addition to this support, the various states are also helping to attract not only American companies but foreign ones. For example, the Taiwanese semiconductor company TSMC is currently the largest investor in Arizona.

The problem with such policies is that they generate similar subsidies in other trading partners. Europe, for example, has also passed legislation to develop and support semiconductors. China has a five-year investment plan in this field, approaching $150 billion. Even virtuous Germany has given in to subsidizing its companies to speed up their energy transition and compete in key strategic sectors.[14]

Another phenomenon supporting the development of industrial policies is the global geopolitical situation. The proliferation of conflicts is leading most nations to rearm. Traditionally, military investment has been controlled and subsidized by governments.

---

[12] Mounier-Kuhn, Pierre-Éric. L'Informatique en France, de la seconde guerre mondiale au Plan Calcul: L'émergence d'une science. Paris: Presses de l'Université Paris-Sorbonne, 2010.
[13] Although such policies may yet be amended by President Trump.
[14] Overall, most countries today invest between 0.5% and 1.5% of their GDP in industrial policy and, therefore, in subsidies of all kinds.

Geopolitics Interferes

This multiplication of geopolitical conflicts has taken on particular significance following the war in Ukraine, which began in February 2022, followed by the war in Gaza in October 2023, and then in Lebanon in September 2024, and Iran in 2025. Conflicts inevitably give rise to retaliatory measures in the form of sanctions against companies and individuals. These are often accompanied by restrictions on trade in raw materials, commerce, and technology.

These conflicts challenge the political and economic strength of states. Industrialized countries leverage their economic power to increase their political influence over others. This is the concept of extraterritoriality of the law. It enables a country to extend its jurisdiction beyond its borders, using its economic power as a weapon of retaliation in the event of non-application.[15] The US has a whole arsenal in this field (see inset).

An Arsenal of American Jurisdictions

The "Trading with the Enemy Act" of 1917 allows sanctions to be imposed not only on hostile countries, but also on companies and individuals who fail to comply with the Act, regardless of nationality or residence.

The Foreign Corrupt Practices Act (FCPA) prohibits US companies and their subsidiaries from engaging in bribery of foreign officials.

There are also numerous Foreign Account Tax Compliance (FATCA) provisions, which apply to foreign financial institutions that manage the accounts of US citizens even outside the country.

This can lead to complicated situations for companies. After the Russian invasion of Afghanistan in 1979, the US imposed retaliatory measures against the Soviet Union. I remember the dilemma faced by the head of the French subsidiary of a major American energy company that traded with Moscow. His CEO in the US ordered him to cease all contact, in line with the measures of the "Trade with the Enemy Act." Conversely, the French government ordered him to do the opposite, arguing that

---

[15] Extraterritoriality is not just an economic concept. It can be found in diplomacy, with embassies, and also in education. In 2024, the Turkish government came into conflict with France over the curriculum of French schools in Turkey. The French curriculum dealt with the Armenian genocide, but the Turkish curriculum did not.

a subsidiary, even owned by an American company, remained under French law and was not obliged to follow Washington's instructions. What was he to do?[16]

Chapter Takeaways

- Globalization can also be defined as transitioning from an export-based economy to a strategy relying more on foreign direct investment. However, such an approach entails greater complexity for companies. It implies an in-depth knowledge of the many host countries' economic, social, and political environments.
- Globalization developed in three phases: a golden age (1978–2018) when the world was open and efficient, followed by an age of vulnerability characterized by multiple geopolitical crises, and, currently, an age of fracturing in which many nations are developing parallel economic and business models.
- In this environment, protectionism and industrial policies increase. National security becomes more of a priority than job protection.

Where Next?

The influence of the three major economic blocs (the US, China, and the EU) is rising. They aim to impose their strategy on the rest of the world. Other nations are looking for counter-strategies.

The primary consequence is the weakening of the multilateral system, which has guaranteed the world economy's stability. It has provided an unbiased system for resolving economic conflicts. If multilateralism were to disappear, what would it imply for the world?

---

[16] Obviously, he followed the instructions of his American CEO. But, as a French citizen, he also received the wrath of his government.

17 | The Emergence of Multi-aligned Countries

As the world experiences a resurgence of empires or aspiring empires, many nations are choosing not to be satellites or remain non-aligned. A new trend is emerging: being multi-aligned. This new strategy implies maintaining political and economic relationships with as many countries as national interest requires, regardless of pressures from major blocs.

The Return of Empires
The Strategy of Multi-alignment
The Multilateral System in Peril

The Return of Empires

International political and economic relations are taking on a new dimension in this new environment. Very large nations continue to aspire to become empires. Consequently, relations with other countries are changing dramatically.

In an empire, relations between the central country and those under its influence are exclusive. In the past, empires relied mainly on their military strength.

Today, empires are also based on economic power. The United States accounts for 25% of global GDP, China for 18%, and Europe for 15%.

Traditionally, certain regions aligned with specific powers: Central and South America, Japan, and East Asia with the US; Africa with Europe; the Commonwealth with the UK; and communist countries with Moscow.

The purpose of empires is described thus by Henry Kissinger:[1]

> For most of humanity and the longest period of our history, empire has been the preferred mode of government. Empires have no interest in operating within an international system; they aspire to be the international system.[2]

The Strategy of Multi-alignment

Nations under the sway of empires face a challenging decision: align with one of these powerful blocs, maintain neutrality, or − as a recent development − seek cooperation with all parties. Some countries have sought to avoid these dilemmas, exemplified by the Non-Aligned Movement, established in 1961 at the Belgrade conference, now comprising around 120 nations. Their goal is not consistently to align with any major power.[3] Today, there is a new alternative: the emergence of "multi-alignment."

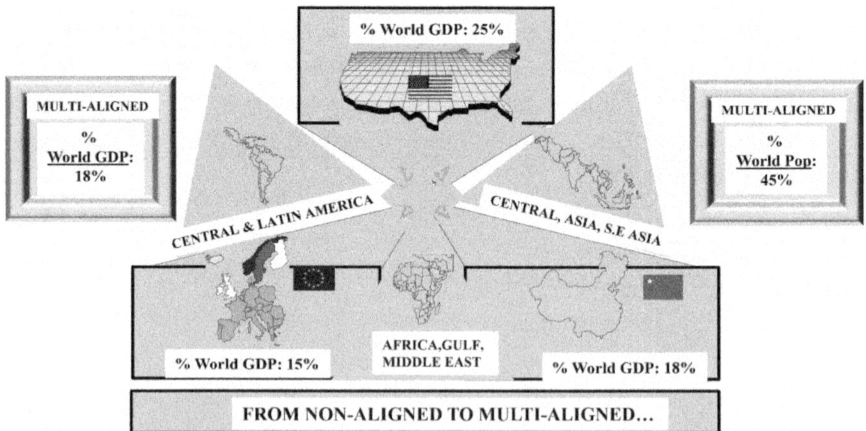

---

[1] Kissinger, Henry. *White House Years*. Boston: Little, Brown and Company, 1979.
[2] I only met him once, in Davos after the Soviet Union invaded Afghanistan in 1979. I remember what he said at the time: "We cannot accept that one country should have a conception of its security that makes all the other nations insecure." A particularly prescient statement for today.
[3] Čavoški, Jovan. *Non-Aligned Movement Summits: A History*. London: Bloomsbury Academic, 2022.

Multi-aligned countries want to emancipate themselves from political tensions between blocs. These countries span the Indian subcontinent, the Middle East, and Central Asia. They are growing in presence in Africa and Latin America. They represent 45% of the global population and 18% of its GDP, making them impossible to overlook. Among those countries refusing to enter the perimeter of a bloc is, for example, Turkey – which cooperates with Russia on nuclear energy but sends drones to Ukraine. India buys oil from Russia, but strengthens its ties with the UK. Saudi Arabia sells its oil to Europe, but negotiates with Iran and Syria.[4]

This strategy can irritate the major powers. In the case of Brazil, the US, its traditional ally, has expressed its resentment to President Lula over his remarks in China concerning the Ukraine and Western hegemony. Yet this overlooks the fact that 32% of Brazil's exports now go to China, compared with 12% to the US.[5]

In business terms, multi-aligned countries have decided to remain active in the international economy without necessarily sharing the same operating platforms or conflict resolution mechanisms.

A New Business Model

Until recently, the same international companies could be found in the US, Europe, Japan, and South-East Asia. They shared the same means of communication or payment transfer systems, such as Swift, and credit cards, such as Visa, MasterCard, and American Express.

Conversely, many multi-aligned countries aim to grow their own companies and create specific platforms for transactions like payment transfers (CIPS or SPFS) and credit cards. There is also an effort to reduce reliance on the dollar for global transactions. Currently, 45% of global trade uses the dollar, while over 58% of currency reserves are held in this currency. However, Chinese Renminbi transactions have doubled in recent years. Although this accounts for only 4.5% of global trade financing, the change is noteworthy. This is why Dilma Rousseff, the new president of the BRICS development bank (the NDB)[6] – and former president of Brazil – declared in 2023: "The NDB must become an alternative to the major international financing institutions, the IMF or the World Bank, which are dominated by the dollar and the West."[7]

---

[4] In 2024, Vietnam managed the feat of welcoming Presidents Xin Jinping, Biden, and Putin – separately, of course…

[5] Figures for 2023.

[6] "New Development Bank" created in 2015.

[7] She added: "Our objective is to achieve 30% of our financing through local currencies." Moreover, no conditionality would be attached to these loans, as she says, "We respect the policies of each country."

The boldness of these policies comes from the existence of an alternative to Western power, specifically China. China holds economic, military, and political influence. Additionally, the military strength of the West has diminished. Numerous US military actions in the Middle East and European interventions in Africa have been unsuccessful. The West no longer instills fear.

The Multilateral System in Peril

The decline in the influence of the multilateral system, represented by the United Nations and its affiliate organizations – and particularly by the World Trade Organization – can also be attributed to the ongoing conflict between different value systems. Small countries are the victims, but so are companies. They export more than just products; they also export practices linked to working conditions, environmental protection standards, and business transparency.

However, while often accepting the principle, many countries reject these practices as interfering with their sovereignty. Sometimes, it is even seen as a resurgence of colonialism. And yet, in their home countries, many companies face strict behavioral requirements that they are expected to apply in all the countries in which they operate.

Bridging the widening gap in attitudes and values between diverse nations is becoming a major strategic issue for companies, especially when these conflicts become political or military. All organizations, whether national or international, experience conflict. It is the norm, especially if they are competing with each other in an open world. The question is how these conflicts are resolved.

In the past, this was done by force of arms. A more civilized approach is to do it through discussion and negotiation. As President Ronald Reagan said:

> Peace is not the absence of conflict, but the ability to cope with conflicts by peaceful means.[8]

This is what we risk losing today if the world continues to fracture.

Chapter Takeaways

- The US, China, and the EU are increasingly adopting an empire mindset. They want to impose their conception of international order on the rest of the world. Not only are they in conflict with each other, but they are also putting additional pressure on other nations.

---

[8] Reagan, Ronald (1982). Commencement Address at Eureka College, May 9, 1982. Ronald Reagan Presidential Library. Accessed March 2, 2025.

- To counter this, some other nations have developed a multi-alignment strategy, which implies favoring economic relations with all partners with common interests, irrespective of geopolitical considerations.
- Large economic powers are probably not willing to allow this freedom. The temptation to recreate zones of influence and satellite countries is resurfacing. Consequently, an attack on the multilateral system, which aims to be balanced and objective, will have dire consequences for medium-sized or smaller economies with little geopolitical clout to defend their point of view.

Where Next?

In the next chapter, we momentarily leave the greater world of competitiveness to highlight the more direct consequences of a fractured international economy on business and work.

The changes in the working environment also stem from a profound shift in society's priorities. In parallel to the strategies of nations to ensure competitiveness, employees' expectations and companies' goals are evolving quickly. Why?

18 | Work in a Fractured World Economy

The workplace has been reshaped by changing value systems and advances in technology, influencing both company and employee expectations. This change has also impacted how companies view their economic and social responsibilities.

The Growing Impact of Civil Society
Profit Is Necessary but Not Enough
The Future of the Workplace
The Hybrid Company
A Management Model for Tomorrow

The essence of management is the management of efficiency and change. But today, the level of environmental interference in strategy is constantly increasing. These interferences include business models in the global economy, technological innovations, and changes in attitudes and value systems in society.

In 1968, significant student protests in the US and Europe led to a profound shift in societal mentality and structure, marking the emergence of "civil society."

The Growing Impact of Civil Society

"Civil society" is an old concept. Thomas Hobbes (1588–1679), for example, refers to it in his *Leviathan* (1651)[1] and sees its creation as a condition of peace and security resulting from a social contract. Today, civil society represents social structures and non-governmental organizations that operate autonomously from the state and the private sector. These include non-governmental organizations, associations, and pressure groups with societal objectives.

Its impact on corporate strategy is increasingly significant. Topics like climate protection, economic decarbonization, biodiversity, gender diversity, corporate governance, and social responsibility have made their way into enterprise (and its boards of directors) through civil society. Accordingly, Peter Drucker, one of the fathers of modern management, liked to emphasize:

> Changes in society today have more impact on companies than changes in management.[2]

From Employee-Citizen to Corporate-Citizen

The mobility of employees within and between the company and their homes has accelerated this process. By working outside the company, employees have become vectors of values that traditionally had no place in the company that hired them. A new generation of leaders has also accelerated this awareness. They often come from the committed young people who have helped society evolve over the last 40 years. Unlike their predecessors, they readily see themselves as ordinary citizens who return home at night, have families, and share the same goals and limitations as everyone else.

---

[1] Hobbes, Thomas. *Leviathan*. Edited by Richard Tuck. Cambridge: Cambridge University Press, 1996.
[2] Drucker, Peter F. *Management Challenges for the 21st Century*. New York: HarperBusiness, 1999.

The goal is to align the company's mission with the personal objectives of its employees. It goes beyond achieving work-life balance; it is about harmonizing different value systems. Consequently, companies must adjust their strategies, working conditions, and corporate culture to the societal expectations of employees.

The employee-citizen has created the citizen-company.

Civil Society Activism

While most companies are willing to acknowledge the influence of civil society on their strategy, the situation becomes more complicated when national value systems clash. Global companies are increasingly caught between the non-interference demands of governments in the countries where they operate and those of a more militant civil society "at home." They probably would also like to be multi-aligned, but this seems less and less possible.

Therefore, their strategy is to diversify assets to escape the increasing politicization and unpredictability of economic and political decisions. It is called "friend-shoring" when relocating to territories with good relationships with the home country. When production is relocated closer to the end consumer, it is called "nearshoring" or even "reshoring."

Although companies are increasingly becoming "pawns" in the geopolitical game, they remain one of the last links to peaceful cooperation between nations.

Profit Is Necessary but Not Enough

The most significant area of tension between business and civil society is the impact on profits. Societal demands are often laudable but also costly. Who is going to pay? Classical economic theory argues that companies carry global economic responsibility by holding people's savings through shares and funds. Losses or closures destroy these savings, making profit a social necessity.

To illustrate this debate, the fate of Emmanuel Faber, the former chairman of Danone in France, is emblematic. Danone was a forerunner of the "mission-driven company" status, created in 2019 by the PACTE law in France.[3] This provides for an independent committee to oversee the implementation of the mission – in Danone's case: "Bringing health through food to as many people as possible." Faber did not hesitate to claim that he had "debunked the statue of Milton Friedman." Unfortunately, Friedman took his revenge from beyond the grave. Or rather, the

---

[3] France. *Loi n° 2019-486 du 22 mai 2019 relative à la croissance et la transformation des entreprises. Journal Officiel de la République Française*, May 23, 2019. https://www.legifrance.gouv.fr/jorf/id/JORFTEXT000038496102/

activist funds Bluebell Capital and Artisan Partners did it for him. They decided that Danone's performance was lagging behind that of Nestlé and Unilever and that it was time to change priorities – and CEO.

Without being quite as extreme, the thinking of Larry Fink, BlackRock's Chairman and CEO, is just as interesting. He has been a key player in promoting Environmental, Social, and Governance (ESG) criteria in investment strategies. As the world's largest asset manager, BlackRock has heavily influenced corporate sustainability and social responsibility practices. It often urged companies to set targets for reducing emissions and report their progress. However, by 2024, Larry Fink was no longer discussing ESG with investors due to its ambitious nature, vague definition, and conflicts with client performance pressures.[4] The pressure exerted by the new Trump administration to abandon this concept has likely also been a contributing factor.

The Future of the Workplace

Today, in developing their mission, almost all companies want to demonstrate a positive impact not only on shareholder income but also on the well-being of their customers, employees, and society. They also want to attract young talent. As a professor, I was struck by the growing number of my students who told me they had turned down a well-paid and sometimes even very prestigious job at the end of their degree. They did not feel motivated by the corporate culture of the company or its contribution to society.

A new generation, whose parents have often accumulated some capital, feels freer to make choices. They have more leeway to find a job they like, even if it takes time. As for consumers, those who can afford it are becoming more interested in the non-financial standards of products, such as environmental impact and fair trade with developing countries or local producers.

Ever More Productive?

On August 3, 1923, the American Iron and Steel Institute announced the end of the 12-hour factory day (6 days a week, of course).

Although this resulted in a 15% increase in costs, it was offset by productivity growth. Across the US and Europe, the aim was to work less to produce more.

---

[4] Since then, and with the election of President Trump, many companies have also reduced their emphasis on this concept, as well as the related ideas of Diversity, Equity, and Inclusion.

> But the Soviet Union was about to try the opposite. In 1929, it introduced the permanent workweek (*Nepreryvka*). Workers were divided into five five-day shifts to ensure uninterrupted production.
>
> Of course, the result was a messy private life, as no one could plan any free time together. After 11 years without a weekend, the experiment was abandoned.

Working Less?

For many, this is the central question. Ultimately, companies and employees tend to work less but better.

Since the last century (see insert), shorter working hours have been the norm. According to OECD figures, Germans worked an average of 1,426 hours yearly in 2010. Before the pandemic, by 2019, this had fallen to 1,383 hours. Over the same period, Switzerland went from 1,611 to 1,549 hours worked.[5]

However, these figures should be treated cautiously, given the emergence of part-time work. The Netherlands, for example, works an average of just 1,440 hours a year. But it has one of the highest rates of part-time work in Europe: 36% of employment, compared with 26% in Switzerland and 13% in France.

In many countries, the employment rate is now preferred to the number of hours worked: it is over 75% of the working-age population in Switzerland, the Netherlands, and Germany, but only 65% in France. A country succeeds better when more people work.

Outsourcing Work

Relocation of work from a company site enables people to rethink their priorities for work. In Europe, two-thirds of employees favor a hybrid model where going to the office is no longer the only option. But there may be some drawbacks. One might consider whether the digitization of the economy is driving up working hours again.

In the European Union, half of employees work on-site or at home one Saturday a month. In the US, annual working hours have stayed consistent at 1,777; in Great Britain, they have risen by 30 hours to 1,537. These figures may not properly account for "intellectual" workers whose work-life boundaries are less defined.

---

[5] Organisation for Economic Co-operation and Development (OECD) (2024). Hours Worked. OECD Employment and Labour Market Statistics.

Even if some companies want to limit the obligation to answer e-mails or telephone calls after a particular hour, they cannot stop people from thinking about their work, even if they are away from work. Working better is an ambivalent concept: it implies quantifiable objectives, such as reaching a budget, and value judgments, such as fitting into a corporate culture. For the employer, it is a strategic necessity. For the employee, it is a professional skill that needs to be recognized.

In any case, the company needs a stable frame of reference. And therein lies the problem. Working hours and company presence structure the day. Not everyone necessarily feels more at ease when the conventional work environment is replaced outside the office by our body's circadian rhythm (getting up later) or family life's interference (however pleasant).

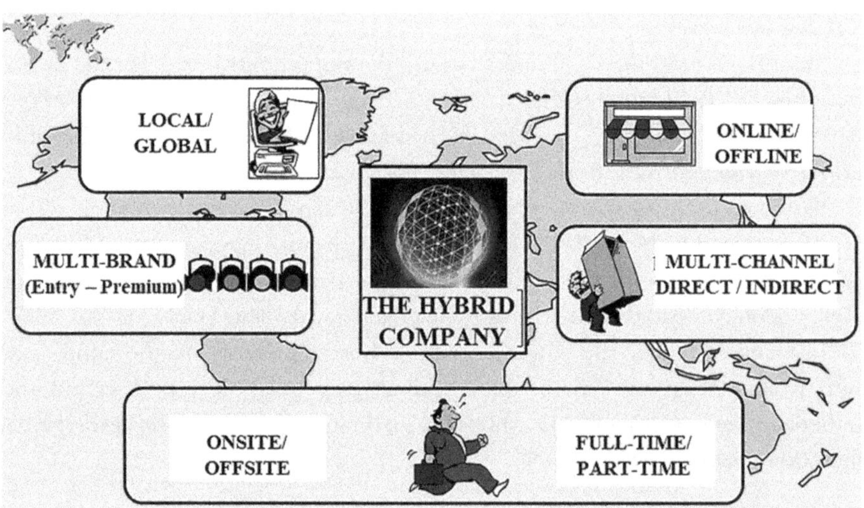

The Hybrid Company

As the global economy faces disruption, companies have shifted to hybrid structures, evolving from monolithic organizations to decentralized structures. Hybrid companies blend systems once seen as incompatible. For customers, this means accessibility both online and in-person, along with a balance of global strategy and local proximity. Hybrid companies frequently offer multibrand and multichannel options. For employees, this translates into flexible work arrangements, allowing on-site, remote, full-time, or part-time work.

In theory, this is relatively straightforward. In practice, it is somewhat more complicated. It requires a perfect mastery of an organization's management and structural processes. And not everyone can manage this level of complexity.

Thus, some companies frequently revert to "spin-off" strategies to address these challenges. This approach acknowledges the potential conflicts between differing business models and their profitability. It involves fully separating organizations legally and financially, each independently listed on the stock market. However, cross-ownership is often preserved, at least for some time.

Integrated hybrid structures are complex to manage and require exceptionally competent managers. And yet no company's survival can be based on the systematic use of geniuses. Such exceptional professionals include Harold Geneen at ITT, Percy Barnevik at ABB, and Jack Welch at General Electric. However, once these individuals leave, their companies struggle to recover.

This underlines that successful companies, in the long run, have good management "in-depth" and at all levels. They are not overdependent on one person, however brilliant. As Warren Buffet said: "I always invest in a company that can be run by an idiot because sooner or later, that is what happens."

The Risk of a Two-Tier Company

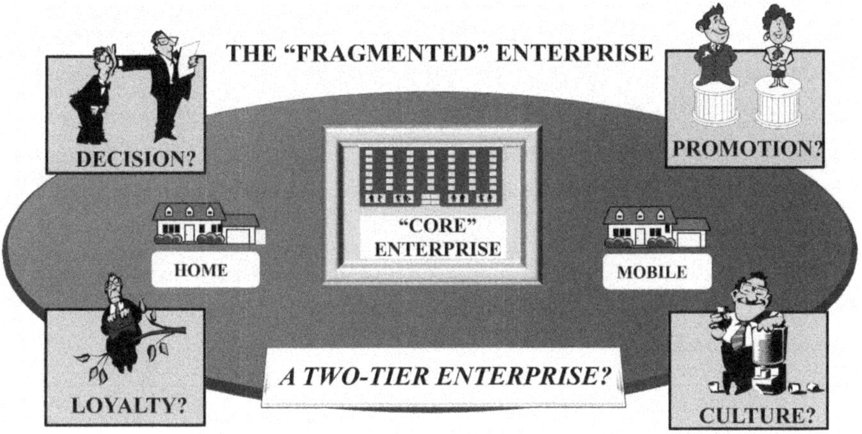

The consequence of a hybrid structure is often the creation of a two-tier company. At the heart of the company are the full-time, office-based employees who form the strategic core of the business. On the periphery are employees, sometimes part-time, who are mobile or work from home.

The distinction is not absolute. With the reduction in the working week, it is now possible for center employees to work one or two days from home. Similarly, to stay in touch with the company, remote employees are often required to physically come to the center to maintain face-to-face contact with their colleagues and experience the corporate culture first-hand.

This structure, which is becoming increasingly widespread, raises several problems, particularly for employees not located in the same location. The following questions may arise.

- Will important decisions affecting the future of the company or my work be made without giving me the chance to share my opinion?
- In case of a promotion, would I be at a disadvantage compared to colleagues who are in the office daily and can regularly interact with their superiors?

The Importance of Dress Code

Dress is a complex code with far-reaching consequences.

Traditionally, the business world was all about suits and ties. Some companies, such as IBM or TetraPak, even went so far as to recommend typical colors: white shirts, dark blue suits, red ties, and so on. This was to symbolize belonging to a group.

In Asia, companies often advocate uniforms. When I visited Sony's headquarters in Tokyo, I was struck by the fact that everyone wore the same tunic and badge, including the president (Akio Morita at the time), as if we did not know who he was…

Today, the hooded sweatshirt made famous by Meta founder Mark Zuckerberg has become the signifier of a whole generation: a bit of a protestor, a bit of a differentiator.

When visiting Zuckerberg, President Obama boasted that he was the only one who was able to get him to wear a tie. Today, it is the presidents who are taking theirs off…

- Would I be among the first affected by business restructuring since off-site workers might be seen as less crucial than those near decision-making centers?
- Could my commitment to the company be doubted because I have chosen to balance my work and personal life better or prioritize both career and quality of life?

These challenges impact employee motivation and disrupt the company's culture. A fragmented structure makes cohesion difficult. Companies must treat everyone equally and respect diverse career choices to address this. This includes ensuring equal information flow, such as teleconferencing meetings for all interested participants.

The employee who has chosen to live off-center also needs to be realistic. One rarely becomes a company manager while working, even partially, from the kitchen. Such employees can also miss out on opportunities and essential but informal information, such as what you hear over coffee with colleagues.

Ultimately, the hybrid corporate structure responds to changing consumer attitudes and employee motivations. The age of monolithic, hierarchical, mono-cultural companies is probably gone.

The Tiger, the Cat, and the Dinosaur

Employee expectations also evolve with time, age, and lifestyle. Companies must be sensitive to employees' changing attitudes about their work lives to retain the best talent. The theory below describes the evolution of the value system when working in a company or any other organization. It probably applies to all of us.

We pass through three stages.

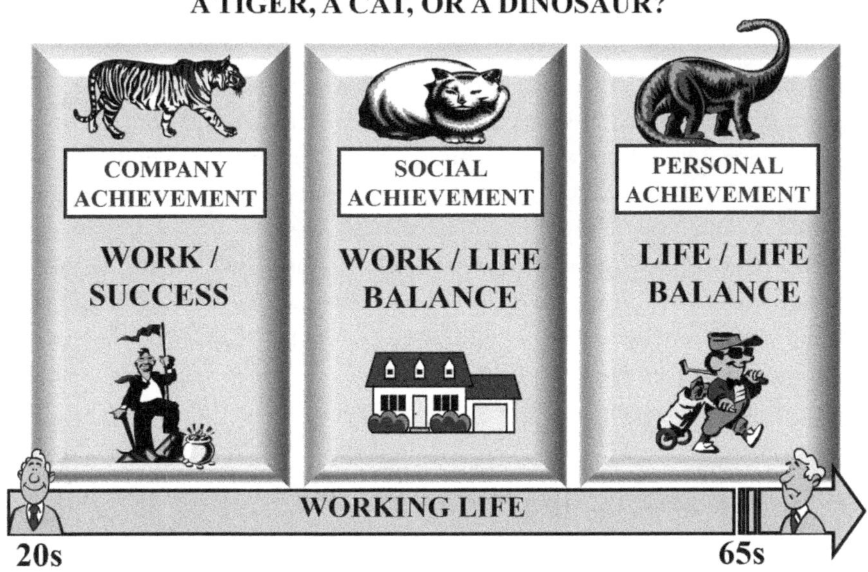

- *Tigers*: Are motivated by success and driven to climb the ranks swiftly. Working over 60 hours a week, they are highly mobile and take on global responsibilities. With no spouse or children, their company becomes their family and measure of success. They possess a "killer" instinct and can aggressively achieve their goals.

- *Cats:* With time, tigers become cats. The once-ambitious young executive settles down, marries, has children, buys a house, and gets a mortgage. They enjoy family life and struggle with their children's education system, working around 40 hours a week. They remain dedicated to their job, but seek to balance work and home.
- *Dinosaurs:* After many years with the company, the cat morphs into a dinosaur. Life beyond work becomes their focus. Their career is complete, ambitions either met or abandoned, and they no longer retain a tiger's drive or a cat's comfort-seeking nature. They wants to be left alone and leave the company at 5 p.m. Peter Drucker described this stage of development as follows: "There is an enormous number of managers who have retired on the job."

Another way to describe dinosaurs is that they introduced the idea of "life-life" balance. Despite what some might believe, dinosaurs are far from useless. They serve as keepers of corporate knowledge, retaining the company's history, the reasons behind certain practices, the successes, failures, and more. New managers can often bypass unnecessary repetitions and avoid numerous errors by paying attention to them.

Companies can lose their best executives because they do not recognize this evolution in employee motivation. Giving a "cat" a promotion in a faraway country will not go down well. They will not want to move their family and quit their living environment. They will often refuse the promotion and leave the company, convinced that no other promotion will be offered.

Some international companies, therefore, agree to move work to the employee (and not the employee to the site). For example, a human resources director for a large region can continue to live in a location of his choice, provided they travel regularly to all the subsidiaries under their management. Moreover, new technologies like videoconferencing make it easy to keep in touch.

The Globalization of Corporate Values

Globalization has also considerably impacted companies' value systems and the people who work for them. Howard Perlmutter (1925–2011), a professor at the University of Pennsylvania and IMD in Lausanne, created a typology that defines companies' attitudes concerning their managers' profiles.[6] It remains relevant today.

---

[6] Perlmutter, H. V., & Heenan, D. A. (1974). "How multinational should your multinational be?" *Harvard Business Review*, 52(6), 121-132.

In an "ethnocentric" approach, companies prefer managers from their home country, even for global operations. Many Asian (Japanese, Korean, Chinese) and some European (especially Scandinavian) companies do this. The benefit is maintaining a unified corporate culture and values. However, it can hinder hiring top talent from other countries.

The "polycentric" approach involves hiring managers from the host country for its subsidiaries. For instance, a German manager would manage a subsidiary in Germany, a Chinese manager in China, etc. This method helps the company integrate well with the local community, as the manager maintains strong connections with local government and institutions, benefiting the company. However, such a corporate approach can lead to divisions within the company, where a director might disregard central management and essential subsidiaries by thinking, "We are different from the others." It makes it harder to implement a unified global strategy.

Lastly, the "geocentric" strategy involves selecting the best candidate for a position irrespective of their cultural background. This method is becoming more common today. It is now quite common to see a foreign individual leading a major international corporation outside his nationality.[7] The disadvantage is that these managers generally do not stay in their positions long. Their ultimate goal is to rise to the top of the company. Sometimes, the companies themselves support "fast track" development programs, which identify future leaders by moving them from one subsidiary to another to give them global experience.

This typology provides a better understanding of how companies manage different value systems as a whole, but also indicates how employees adapt to these changes.

A Value System for Expatriates: The Third Culture

Expatriates, those who live temporarily (but sometimes for quite a long time) outside their own country, are experimenting with the "third culture" theory. It goes like this.

The "first culture" is that of the country of origin. It is easy to identify since it corresponds to a well-defined value system. A German, a Korean, a Swede, or a Mexican may have very different cultures, but they are easily recognizable. Some expatriates firmly refuse to deviate from their culture of origin. Abroad, they will form closed communities that are reluctant to integrate into the local environment. In extreme cases, they can create ethnic communities, sometimes within large cities like New York, with Chinatowns and Italian or Puerto Rican neighborhoods.

---

[7] For instance, a 2018 study by the consulting firm Heidrick and Struggles reported that 52% of CEOs at Switzerland's 50 largest companies were foreign nationals. Heidrick & Struggles. Route to the Top 2018. Chicago: Heidrick & Struggles, 2018. https://www.heidrick.com/-/media/heidrickcom/publications-and-reports/route_to_the_top_2018.pdf.

The "second culture" is that of the host country. This corresponds to the country where the expatriate works. Some love the country they are in so much that they almost totally absorb its culture. This is the case for those who go to the US, China, or Europe and integrate so well that promoting them in other countries is difficult. When this occurs, they often resign.

The "third culture" is a hybrid. It belongs neither to the country of origin nor to the host country. It is the result of globalization and the synthesis of many attitudes that create a new culture. It is a lifestyle that can be found just about everywhere. This third culture has developed with the internationalization of business and communications.

The individual belonging to the third culture has news outlets like CNN, the *Financial Times*, Bloomberg, and the *Wall Street Journal*. They share the same social networks, such as LinkedIn or X (formerly Twitter). They have their dress codes (jackets with or without ties) and favorite brands, which can be found in airports worldwide. The third culture also has its language, a hybrid, simplified English that horrifies every self-righteous professor at Oxford.[8]

The Right Time!

Good timing is one of the most difficult concepts to manage. As Montaigne said, "It is a mistake like no other to be right before everyone else." Examples include the following.

In August 1978, Freddy Laker launched Laker Airways, the first low-cost airline on the Atlantic. Despite initial success, the market was not ready for it. The business model was not perfect, particularly in its focus on long-haul rather than regional flights. Laker Airways ceased operations.

In August 1993, Apple launched the Newton, the first electronic diary and precursor of our cell phones. Again, it was a failure. Apple almost went bankrupt, and its CEO at the time, John Sculley, was forced to resign.

In both cases, the timing was not right, and consumers weren't ready. Yet today, low-cost flights and cell phones are part of our daily lives.

A good idea at the wrong time is still a bad idea!

---

[8] Nevertheless, it is essential when facing an audience where the English of the participants is not the mother tongue. In my teaching experience, I have often encountered teachers who spoke such perfect English that their international audience only partially understood it.

While this third culture has enabled the international community to communicate more effectively, it also generates an inevitable cultural impoverishment, like all common denominators. It must, therefore, be complemented by the culture of the country of origin or the host country to avoid becoming a superficial value system.

The Dilemma of Success: The Pyramid Theory

Most management theories focus on failure and its consequences. But success also creates problems. As Pablo Picasso (1881–1973) once remarked: "Success can be dangerous. You tend to copy yourself. That is more dangerous than copying others. It leads to sterility."

In other words, success has a numbing effect. It creates a false sense of security that immunizes against change. Why change a successful business or behavioral model?

Such an attitude also implies that the only way to get people to change is to have a crisis. Nothing is more complicated than changing mentalities before a crisis arrives. Afterward, it is simpler, but often too late.

This is where the pyramid theory comes in. It acknowledges that life is never a smooth ride, whether at work or home. Dealing with life's problems is always tricky. However, sometimes, it is worth creating your own problems. In any career that leads to rapid success, one climbs rapidly up a pyramid of responsibilities to reach the top. From there, the view is magnificent, the satisfaction of success is intense, and you relish the privilege of being visible to all.

What Is Next? Once you've reached the top of a pyramid, you are quickly struck by the obvious: it is impossible to go any higher, either in front, behind, or to the side. There are only two options: stay there and wait for degeneration, or climb back down to build another, higher pyramid.

For those brave enough to climb back down the pyramid, the experience is particularly frustrating. Losing one's power, work environment, and the comfort of success is an ordeal.

I was a young managing director of the World Economic Forum and, one day, I decided to move down the pyramid of success and discover new horizons. I had a large office overlooking the city of Geneva and the lake. I rubbed shoulders with the world's most influential government and business leaders. Sometime later, I found myself in a construction cabin on the grounds of the IMD business school (which was being rebuilt), all alone, with no office furniture and only a small electric heater. I wondered if I had made the right decision.

Yet, I never regretted it. My new life quickly resumed, and more pyramids were climbed. It was not easy. However, it is the price of a success that fits you – it makes all the difference. This kind of attitude allows one to manage success without falling victim to it. Generally speaking, when one door closes, several others open.

Does "Human Capital" Exist?

> ### A False Good Idea!
>
> The good idea was this: an employee who knows he or she has a market value beyond the company where he or she works is more flexible and willing to take risks. In the worst-case scenario, they can find another job.
>
> So we thought we would ask employees to assess not only their contribution to the company, but also their market value, in case they had a problem… To do this, they had to see whether their internal skills were also recognized externally.
>
> They had the help of a consultant and an employment agency. Of course, the approach was purely theoretical, but it turned out badly…
>
> "Come on, tell us the truth: you want to lay us off, don't you?" As is often the case in economics, the law of unintended consequences was unleashed. Instead of stabilizing and securing people in their jobs by showing them that they also had a market value, we had destabilized everyone.

A scene is repeated regularly all over the world and in every company. The CEO addresses employees: "You are the most important resource in this company." They believe it, and they are right. However, on the other side of the room, employees listen doubtfully. They know that the company's "most important resource" will likely be dismantled at the first sign of a crisis.

At the heart of the problem lies an accounting peculiarity.[9] A company's employees appear on the balance sheet as a cost, not an investment. In other words, they're on the wrong side of the operating statement. If a company employs 100 geniuses or 100 bells, they are accounted for similarly, i.e., as a cost. Such an approach completely underestimates the investments in the person's know-how and professional and individual development. It also ignores the loss of experience and skills when that person leaves.

Could it be done differently? From an accounting point of view, the approach makes some sense. Employees are very mobile. The company's "most important resource" leaves at six o'clock in the evening and perhaps returns at eight o'clock the

---

[9] Schiuma, Giovanni, and Daniela Carlucci. *Valuation of Human Capital: Quantifying the Importance of an Intangible Asset.* Cham: Springer International Publishing, 2018.

following day. This uncertainty explains why, historically, employees get paid at the end of the month. It is to make sure they come back. This mobility continues to increase as people work from home, by teleconference, or part-time. It is a reality that must be taken into account. Companies' control over their employees will continue to diminish.

Second, the central idea is that employees do not belong to a company. As such, they cannot be counted as an asset like a machine or a building. This is correct, but it cultivates a fundamental ambiguity regarding the value of people.

Some economists like to talk about human capital. But that is not how it is perceived in company valuations. Stock markets always favor companies with the smallest ratio between employees and sales. Generally, when a company lays off staff, its share price rises.

People are capital, but not in the accounting sense of the term. Instead, they are an asset to the company. This wealth is made up of skills and experience but also of attitudes and value systems. The problem is that it is impossible to put a figure on this wealth. Yet this value exists. It is up to the corporate culture and the managers who uphold it never to forget it or let it be forgotten.

A Management Model for Tomorrow

This model summarizes the various aspects seen in the figure. To succeed, a company needs a solid foundation in three areas.

- Management of efficiency for sustained productivity.
- Management of change for resilience.
- Management of complexity for excellence in customer relations.

Even when perfectly mastered, these three management areas are not enough without the component of human values or attitudes that constitute a competitive "mindset."

These are the following.

- An attitude based on imagination and "Why not?" All too often, companies confront a "Why?" mindset. In contrast, valuable employees are willing to consider and try out new ideas: "Why not do it?" For companies, this means accepting some failures. As Thomas Edison said: "I have not failed. I have just found 10,000 ways that won't work."

The Spirit of Competitiveness

Jean-Baptiste Charcot (1867–1936) was a French physician and polar explorer.

He led several expeditions to Antarctica, including the first French expedition in 1903–1905 and the second in 1908–1910, which led to the mapping of new regions and a better understanding of the polar regions.

His ship Pourquoi-Pas (Why Not?) has become emblematic of a spirit of adventure and curiosity. This applies particularly to many organizations, where negative, wait-and-see attitudes of "Why?" all too often prevail and lead to stagnation.

His ship sank in 1936 off the coast of Iceland. Legend has it that before sinking, he opened the cage of the ship's mascot bird, the seagull Rita, to give her a chance.

- An attitude of immediacy or urgency: "Why not now?" Putting a good idea off until tomorrow is rarely successful because the competition will get hold of it. Sometimes, managers have to stop analyzing and start moving forward, even if things are not clear-cut. A company president once told me: "We analyze a good idea until it becomes a bad one…"

- A "why not me?" attitude: some employees accept that an idea is good but not for them. "Why me? I haven't done anything." Good companies make everyone feel involved in a strategy and want to be part of its implementation.
- Finally, an attitude of legitimacy: "Why us?" What is the uniqueness factor and the company's added value for its customers and society?

In this model, all the elements are essential in their own right. However, their interaction creates the dynamic that leads to success and drives a company's competitiveness.

Chapter Takeaways

- The emergence of civil society has profoundly impacted fundamental business goals in a globalized world. Profit is recognized as necessary, but not sufficient, to meet people's aspirations.
- This has changed the work environment, whether in the office, on the move, or at home, particularly after the COVID crisis. Consequently, an office may not necessarily be located inside a company's premises. However, it is a concept that is not unanimously accepted today.
- The structure of companies is becoming increasingly hybrid, meaning they must combine very different business models, such as low-cost, premium, online, brick and mortar, direct, indirect, etc. Managing will become more complex and require new competencies and personal skills.

Where Next?

Work isn't everything. The impact of a fractured global economy on people's daily lives is growing. The rapid succession of generations has also led to a rapid change in life goals and societal expectations.

The traditional corporate life, the drive to succeed, or the thrust for power are no longer objectives entirely shared by the new generations. Companies must offer value systems and work structures that match these changing attitudes to attract and retain the best talents.

The challenge is also to enable different generations to work and live together. For top management, this means keeping in touch with new generations of employees who are also customers. How do you do this?

19 | Life in a New World

The fracturing of the global economy and its consequences on the structure of companies is significantly impacting people's lives. The boundary between work and private life is not as clear-cut as in the past. Attitudes and expectations are changing.

A New Generation and New Objectives in Life
Life Online and Its Consequences
Management Is Less Attractive
How Can Companies Keep in Touch with the Next Generations?

A New Generation and New Objectives in Life

Traditionally, new generations followed each other in a 30-year sequence. This corresponded, more or less, to life expectancy. Today, new generations follow each other at a much faster pace. They are determined by the technological innovations people use.

The use of television characterized the Baby Boomers (1946–1964). Generation X (1965–1979) surfed the infant Internet on the personal computer, Generation Y (1980–1996) on the smartphone. Finally, Generation Z, that of today, will be the generation of artificial intelligence.

Older generations may find it challenging to assess Generation Z objectively. Nonetheless, it's essential since increasing numbers of Generation Z professionals are joining the workforce and will influence business and politics in their countries.

UNDERSTANDING A NEW GENERATION

Self-fulfillment has become a fundamental objective. This does not exclude communicating or cooperating with others, but it prioritizes focusing on one's ambitions. Furthermore, we are experiencing an environment that prioritizes individual values. It is the "meism" phase we saw earlier in the self-realization phase of value evolution. From the point of view of motivation theories, it corresponds to the ultimate stages of Abraham Maslow's (1908–1970)[1] pyramid, when all other material objectives have been reached; then, people concentrate on higher goals.

Generation Z often demonstrates a pronounced *sense of entitlement*. It means they believe they deserve access to information about any company or organization that might affect their lives. Consequently, this can lead to actions that sometimes violate privacy or data protection regulations.

Generation Z *has few affiliations* and interests, either in religion or politics. For example, convincing them of the importance of voting and expressing their opinion in social debate is becoming increasingly difficult. This trend is particularly marked in industrialized countries.[2]

---

[1] Maslow, A. H. (1943). "A theory of human motivation." *Psychological Review*, 50(4), 370-396. 10.1037/h0054346

[2] Depending on the country concerned, the abstention rate among 18–24-year-olds varies between 35% and 45%.

On the other hand, they are very *concerned with the state of the world* and the major issues of the moment, such as global warming, biodiversity, gender diversity, and the decarbonization of the economy. As a result, they form communities of interest that extend beyond traditional religious or political boundaries, reaching a global scale and crossing borders.

Their idea of *ownership* differs from that of other age groups; they value sharing and prioritize using shared goods or services over owning them. Additionally, obtaining things for free is perfectly acceptable. For some, it even becomes a sport.[3] This concept of free access is, however, illusory. As Apple Chairman Tim Cook once said: "If you think a product is free, then you are the product." In other words, a product or service can be purchased by transferring personal information from the user's PC or phone to a service provider.[4]

Life Online and Its Consequences

The new generation is also characterized by its strong online presence. Most surveys suggest they spend more than 10 hours in front of a screen daily; 90% of them look at their smartphone within 15 minutes of waking up (if you do the same, it means you are young); 65% would rather have their car stolen than their phone (perhaps because the car belongs to their parents…); and 81% fear answering phone calls.[5]

Their attitude towards the protection of personal data is ambiguous. Everyone attaches growing importance to it, particularly in the context of cyber-attacks. However, some people like to share their lives on TikTok or Instagram and display their ideas and emotions with little or no restraint. It is yet another illustration of the famous paradox of the loner who needs to live in society.[6]

However, it is surprising that the deluge of communication through the Internet and social networks has not increased the sociability of this new generation. We have all seen groups of teenagers hypnotized by their cell phones, looking at nothing else, but doing it within a group of friends.

---

[3] I have often raised this issue with my students, "Yes, Professor, someone has to pay for the provider of a product or service to make a living, but not us…"

[4] This poses a problem for GDP statistics. Transactions in an entire sector of the economy are carried out without monetary exchange but through the acquisition of personal data that is later resold.

[5] We probably have all tried calling young professionals unsuccessfully and soon after receiving a text message asking "What do you want?"

[6] This is what the philosopher Immanuel Kant called "The Unsocial Sociability of Men."

Isolation and Loneliness?

Today's debate focuses on whether modern technologies contribute to the erosion of social interactions, thereby weakening the cohesion within our societies. While browsing the Internet or engaging with social networks increases awareness of global issues, it simultaneously raises the concern of individual isolation.

Vivek Murthy, the Surgeon General, has alerted public opinion to "an epidemic of isolation and loneliness" in the US. Social isolation, measured by the average time spent alone, has risen from 285 minutes a day in 2003 to 333 minutes in 2022. Half of all Americans surveyed said they had no more than three close friends. In 20 years, the time spent seeing each other "in person" has fallen by 70%.

In an article published in *The Atlantic* in August 2023, Hillary Clinton[7] wrote that this wave of isolation had engendered apathy and polarization, destroying the American political community. One of the most unexpected consequences of our society's hyper-connectivity is that a sense of isolation quickly spreads among large parts of the population.

Meanwhile, virtual "intimacy" forms between celebrities, YouTubers, or influencers and their isolated followers who feel connected and unique, although they are millions. This phenomenon is now referred to as "Prosocial." In addition, it seems that the possibility of communicating on a large scale with people on the other side of the world does not solve the problem of social ties in a local environment.[8]

Dissolution of Authority

In 1968, in the streets of Paris, the following slogan became emblematic of revolt: "Il est interdit d'interdire" ("It is forbidden to forbid"). Questioning established authorities, state, or religion was a significant hallmark in the emergence of civil society, marking the advent of a new generation and value system.

Authority can be defined as the ability to decide and to be followed. One might even add "without having to explain oneself." Queen Elizabeth II of England used to say, "Never complain, never explain." Another example is Pope John Paul II, who was asked by a journalist why he had a swimming pool built at Castel Gandolfo:[9] "Because I like to swim; next question."

---

[7] Clinton, Hillary Rodham. "The Weaponization of Loneliness." *The Atlantic*, August 7, 2023.
[8] In many countries, there are initiatives like "Neighbors' Day," where people rediscover the people who live in their immediate vicinity; for example, in the flat opposite to theirs.
[9] The summer residence of the Catholic popes.

In our societies, the concept of authority – considered from a sociological perspective and without moral implications – has evolved across five domains: the family, the state, the military, education, and business. In each of these areas, the idea of authority is being scrutinized.

Authority is ideally rooted in legitimacy, but this isn't always the case. The president of a nation or company might be elected or appointed legitimately yet still cannot exercise his mandate with full authority. Moreover, it's not just anti-system activists confronting authority; activism also appears in sectors like industry and finance, with shareholder motions questioning executive salaries and climate policies.

We are undoubtedly witnessing the end of unquestioned authority, or at least that which does not see fit to explain or justify itself. Communications such as "Move along, there is nothing to see" are no longer acceptable to a new generation (to be honest, they probably were not to the previous ones, either). An emerging sense of authority, necessary as it is, needs to be more inclusive. It relies on new principles: transparency, dialogue, empathy, and an awareness of new social challenges.

Yet the erosion of traditional authority is also accompanied by a need to rediscover another kind of influence based on personal credibility. While institutional authority frequently fades away, personal authority persists and is coveted. Thus, a key aspect of leadership is consistently living the values we promote and expect from others. A principle summarizes it: "Walk the Talk."

The New Role Models

Thus, people still need role models, "admirable" personalities who exemplify a value system and ambitions. They are essential for any new generation, which also learns by imitation. But who is admirable today?

Authority and Self-Confidence

There remains an irreducible part of the notion of authority that seems to escape analysis and the upheavals of time.

It was described by François de La Rochefoucauld (1613–1680):

> There is an elevation that does not depend on fortune: it is a certain air that distinguishes us…
> It is a price we imperceptibly give to ourselves; it is by this quality that we usurp the deference of other men…

(continued)

> *(continued)*
>
> But the opposite is also true.
>
> The Marquise de Sévigné (1626–1696) said of the Duke Charles de Longueville (1649–1672), who died at the age of 23 crossing the Rhine with his army:
>
>> Never before had a man had such solid virtues, and he lacked only the vices to be perfect. These vices were a little pride, vanity and self-love, with the help of which greater things are made.

Elon Musk, Kim Kardashian, Jeff Bezos, and Victoria Beckham are famous, but is that enough? Today, when surveys ask the question of who people admire, even among the youngest, the answers throw up other names: Nelson Mandela, Mahatma Gandhi, Martin Luther King, Mother Teresa, or Alexei Navalny. All these admirable personalities have something in common: they embody virtue, passion, and sacrifice for the good of others. Unfortunately, they have something else in common: they are all dead.

The current trend in social networks is increasingly to identify admirable people as those who "make" something, especially money, and are thriving. Much more rarely are they people who "embody" role models for the rest of society because of their personality or charisma. Today, a famous, wealthy personality often has more impact on society than an honorable one. Visibility and material success have taken over our value systems.

The Risk of Being Exposed

Given that perfect personalities do not exist, the new generation directs their efforts towards commendable goals like climate protection, energy transition, gender equality, poverty alleviation, and bridging the social divide. However, new ideas and ideals require individuals to embody them – think Greta Thunberg for climate activism – and such individuals may currently be lacking.

There are undoubtedly admirable and virtuous people in our societies. However, most do not want to be visible, perhaps because they belong to another generation that does not view success the same way. For these generations, fame is perceived as threatening to their private life. We ask too much of our role models and, in doing so, we discourage the best intentions. Not everyone has the soul of a martyr.[10]

---

[10] An Icelandic proverb sums it up very well: "It is when the whale comes to the surface that it gets harpooned!"

Management Is Less Attractive

The natural consequence of the change in authority seems to be a loss of appeal for management functions. A third of young professionals today say they are not interested in managing other colleagues.

There was a time when the measure of success was the number of people under your command. Titles gave the impression of being at the top of a hierarchy of colleagues and power and have long been sought after. In a letter to the *New York Times* in 2012, Goldman Sachs chairman Lloyd Blankfein mentioned that the company then had more than 12,000 vice presidents.[11] The American expression spread that in many companies, they had now "only Chiefs and no Indians." Today, a new generation often considers management as too stressful and too complicated, and it no longer corresponds to their ambitions.

Managing can disrupt a balanced personal or social life. Though some wish to switch off, an executive cannot. In turbulent times, the leader cannot afford to miss evenings and weekends. Work hours extend both in the office and beyond. In addition, managing often involves tough human choices, like laying off employees. This is even harder in flat-structured firms where subordinates are considered colleagues or friends.

Rejecting Uncertainty and Stress

Leadership means accepting uncertainty and almost constant crises. In a good company, the obvious decisions are taken at the bottom of the hierarchy. Only the most difficult ones make their way to the top. These are no longer solutions but choices. Yet, many young people have been raised in a comfortable, protected environment. They find it hard to cope with the stress inherent in a managerial role. They prefer peace and quiet.

This lack of interest in management can also be seen in the proliferation of start-ups, which seem to be the project of choice for many young professionals. If successful, the aim is to resell the company, not grow it. No one wants to be subject to the administrative and management constraints of a large operation.

Aversion to management responsibilities has led some companies to resort to lateral promotions. These consist of offering parallel jobs in other areas. They may be in other geographies, in different activities, but not necessarily with more human or operational responsibilities. Diversity has replaced responsibility.

Leadership entails being willing to face unpopularity. It is particularly challenging for a new generation accustomed to seeking "likes" on various social media platforms, particularly Facebook. For many, success equates to gaining approval. At best, it means becoming an influencer but not necessarily a leader.

---

[11] Blankfein, Lloyd C., and Gary D. Cohn. "Our Response to Today's New York Times Op-Ed." *The Guardian*, March 14, 2012.

As a CEO once told me: "The best way to dissatisfy everyone is to try to satisfy everyone."

A Financially Secure Generation

In industrialized countries, a new social class has emerged along with a new generation. It has family assets they will inherit, but do not derive immediate wealth or financial income from.

Words That Speak...

In 1979, the Dentsu Institute of Human Studies asked the Japanese what words best reflected their values. Result: *Effort, Perseverance, Thanks, Loyalty, Tenacity*.

In 1992, the same study was repeated. Result: *Effort, Sincerity, Freedom, Peace, Love*.

In just a few years, Japan has become a country where personal values have become increasingly important, just as they are in the West.

In 1995, the Gallup Institute asked the same kind of question to a selection of people living in major Chinese cities. The result: "Work hard and get rich!" for 68% of responses.

It is likely that at the same time in Europe and the US, the majority of responses would have been: "Get rich right away without working hard…," perhaps by becoming influencers. Today it might be *"Not necessarily get rich"* – our parents have already done that for us. All we have to do is wait…

They do not represent all of the population, but the phenomenon affects almost everyone to varying degrees. Over five decades of post–World War II prosperity has allowed numerous households to build up some capital. While this trend is well documented in the US and Europe, it is also fast-growing in Asia and the Gulf States. Family offices, which professionally manage a family's capital, proliferate.

Nowadays, the generations succeeding the Baby Boomers are part of families with increasing amounts of accumulated wealth, significantly altering their perspective on life. Once exclusive to the wealthy, family heritage is now common among the middle class. But, while the wealthy invest in stocks, arts, or leisure, the middle class prioritizes real estate, focusing on purchasing homes.

However, real estate does not generate regular income like a financial investment. This means that the new heirs of this middle class are capitalists without financial annuities. One day, they will receive their inheritance. Until then, the economic impact is non-existent. They are like farmers, rich in land but poor in income.

Having an inheritance "on standby" is a non-negligible safety net against the hazards of life. The proportion of children who leave home late continues to rise. In Italy, over 30% of 30-year-olds live under the family roof.[12] Others leave and return shortly afterward. It is the "boomerang" generation.

That Has the Choice to Work or Not

Having pending assets offers flexibility in job selection. Many students today reject well-paying jobs they dislike. With family capital, they can be more selective and wait for the right opportunity. Some more enterprising individuals use family capital as collateral to launch their own businesses. The importance of family capital in financing start-ups cannot be overstated. Young entrepreneurs prefer to borrow money from their parents or relatives before going to the bank.

For some, it is a way to support a meaningful cause. Many staff members of humanitarian and social organizations come from affluent families. Financial support at home allows participation in city demonstrations during midday while others work.

A family estate's most significant benefit, beyond financial gain, is the peace of mind and time it offers. Noted philosophers like Aristotle, Arthur Schopenhauer, and Ludwig Wittgenstein valued having time to write, think, or live without the pressure of earning a living. An estate enables this freedom. Securing retirement funds without extensive labor is a luxury unavailable to past generations, who often spent their lives earning retirement money. Today, this objective is shifting for a whole generation. It is vital to value this change, provided it does not encourage laziness or futility.

How Can Companies Keep in Touch with the Next Generations?

The rapid shift from one generation to the next results in diverse personal values within a company. It can be seen in the varied dress codes, from suits and ties to open-necked shirts and hoodies with jeans. Except for tech start-ups with a uniform culture, most company managers face intergenerational differences in value systems that can cause misunderstandings.

---

[12] Istat. "Number of Young Unmarried People Living in the Household with at Least One Parent in Italy in 2020, by Age Group (in 1,000s)." *Statista*, September 3, 2021.

Until recently, executives could easily disregard this, as the younger generation usually held minor roles and were not significant customers. Furthermore, their influence on the company's objectives was minimal. However, the emergence of new technologies and the rise of civil society have changed this. Young professionals are rapidly moving into positions of responsibility in areas such as IT and cybersecurity.

Through online purchasing, they also become customers. In addition, their presence on social networks enables them to influence the company's fundamental orientations in societal areas. Some aspire to become "whistle-blowers."

Corporate Intergenerational Initiatives

Executives have often relied on their children to understand the next generation. The benefit is getting an unfiltered message, free from corporate political correctness. However, this approach offers a small and potentially unrepresentative sample.

Direct contact with young employees can be facilitated through organized events. Some companies arrange regular lunches between management and new hires. The aim is to get their candid opinion of the company, its external image, and its strategy before corporate culture, internal politics, and ambitions distort the message.

Another possibility is to create an advisory board representing a crucial generation for the company. This board can provide advice and opinions and even test innovative products. The selection of members is essential. I once met a particularly astute business leader who had chosen the daughters and sons of his best customers or influencers for this board. It was a particularly effective way of building market loyalty.

A more advanced approach is to implement a "reverse mentoring" system. Traditionally, mentoring pairs a young executive with a senior manager to leverage their experience and network. Typically, the chosen young individual is within a "fast track" program, selecting managers with particularly promising career prospects within the company. This young executive is expected to ascend to senior positions quickly.

Reverse mentoring, on the other hand, reverses the roles. The young professional assists a senior manager in sensitizing them to the values and mindset of a new generation of customers. The American cosmetics company Estée Lauder has tested this approach.[13] Finally, the "ultimate" is when a young executive is chosen

---

[13] Estée Lauder Companies. 2023. The CEO Global Reverse Mentor Program. New York: Estée Lauder Companies. https://www.youtube.com/watch?v=uh0suX0KHtw.

to follow the entire agenda, including travel, of a senior manager or even the CEO for a more extended period. Adecco has tested this model.

In practice, the difficulty lies in anticipating the young professional's re-entry into the organization. After such an experience, his expectations are likely to be very high. On the other hand, having invested a great deal of management time in training him, the company will want to see a return on its investment. Sometimes, the two expectations do not coincide.

Companies today must navigate the integration of various generations within their organization. Relying solely on hierarchies is insufficient, as younger employees often bring skills and perspectives that older managers may lack.

Chapter Takeaways

- The changing value system of each new generation has an ever-increasing impact on companies and their strategy. New generations are technologically savvy customers, whose objectives differ greatly from their predecessors.
- "Meism" – the prime importance of individuals compared to their environment – is becoming paramount to understand changing motivations. The evolving approach to authority also considerably impacts corporate structures and management.
- The balance between work and private life also takes precedence for the incoming generations. They have inherited more economic capital than their predecessors, enabling them to choose their professional goals more freely.

Where Next?

Beyond its impact on work and daily life, competitiveness has also helped redefine the goals of a powerful civil society. Thus, the next chapter analyzes the influence of world competitiveness on society at large.

In a global world, each country may have different fundamental objectives. Yet, globalization has enabled nations and their people to live closer to one another, and societal objectives have become more aligned. However, one fundamental question remains: should the pursuit of happiness also be an objective for competitiveness?

20 | Challenges for the Future

How will a fractured world economy impact national prosperity and individual well-being? What are the economic and social challenges that nations will have to address? What are their fundamental objectives?

Freedom of Choice
The Imperative of Efficiency
Managing Expectations
Universalism Versus Tradition
The Importance of Social Capital
Happiness as an Economic Objective?

Freedom of Choice

As this book has shown, nations that have embraced the idea of an open world have experienced increased prosperity. The routes to such prosperity can vary significantly and sometimes be complex, influenced by each nation's history, geography, or culture. All are valuable because, in an open world, each country can learn from the other and benchmark new strategies.

What makes openness a driver of prosperity? A fundamental principle for citizens and consumers: *freedom of choice*. With this freedom, people can travel, educate themselves, communicate, and form opinions, becoming more knowledgeable. Through global logistics and e-commerce, they can purchase products worldwide at reasonable prices and compare their quality.

From 1978 to 2018, the opening of markets significantly increased freedom of choice, which greatly stimulated the global economy by enabling anyone to become a producer or buyer of goods and services. When people have freedom of choice, economic systems can function efficiently based on individual preferences. In contrast, denying this freedom causes distortions. It can lead to economic breakdown due to a lack of transparency and disruptive state interventions like protectionism and industrial policies.

Rules Are Necessary[1]

Most economies implement policies which prevent limitations on consumers' freedom of choice, such as actions against monopolies, misuse of dominant market positions, and insider trading in finance. However, there are exceptions. Strategic areas like national security, the military, or public utilities such as water and energy can be exempt from competition if this is in people's interest.

An issue arises when everything becomes strategic in a politicized global economy. For instance, China and India produce about two-thirds of the world's steel. Is this strategic? The US government believes so and wants to protect local production for military needs. Furthermore, nearly anything can become strategic: semiconductors, energy, agriculture, environmental protection, healthcare products, and even key companies. Every government sees different sectors as crucial for their national security.

The debate hinges on where to draw the line. An economic perspective favors open markets for growth, while a political viewpoint supports protective measures to safeguard strategic areas. For example, German automakers oppose tariffs on Chinese electric cars to maintain access to the Chinese market, whereas the European Commission and the US advocate for local market protection through taxes.

Ultimately, political priorities often overshadow economic considerations in today's fractured economy.

Companies Pushing Back the Boundaries

Companies often state that they support free competition but then act differently. Major technology firms, for instance, claim that bundling services into a unified suite benefits consumers by making them easier to use, which is partly true.

---

[1] Otherwise, as Paul Valéry (1871–1945) put it, a society can become a place for "The free fox in the free henhouse."

From time to time, competition authorities think this goes a little too far. For example, the European Commission required Microsoft to decouple its Teams videoconferencing service from its traditional[2] offering. Google faces pressure in the US to be partly dismantled.

Some companies contend that a few limitations on choice are acceptable if they ensure product safety. An example is the automotive industry, where manufacturers may require customers to use their dedicated maintenance services, claiming they benefit consumers by ensuring the safety of repairs.

Thus, businesses can implement various measures to protect consumers, such as upholding environmental standards, ethically sourcing materials, and safeguarding local wages and working conditions. Despite advocating for open markets, governments and companies often endorse certain restrictions or exceptions.

François-René de Chateaubriand (1768–1848) summed it up differently: "Institutions go through three periods: service, privilege, and abuse."[3] It is tempting to replace "institutions" with "governments" or "companies."

The Return of the Military

Political and economic tensions have increased armed conflicts, and public fear has pushed military rearmament to one of the top spending priorities of governments. Historically, empires exerted dominance through military strength. Joseph Stalin even questioned the Pope's military power. "How many divisions does the Pope have?"

After World War II, the focus shifted to economic competition and resolving conflicts through international organizations, reducing military spending. This decline accelerated after the Berlin Wall fell; as former German Chancellor Olaf Scholz noted: "Why maintain a large military force when all our neighbors seemed to be friends?"[4]

Until the 1980s, almost all Western countries spent more than 2% of their GDP on military affairs. It was the threshold set by NATO in 2006 to ensure Europe's military security. Today, for the first time in years, the UK (2.3%), Germany (2.2%),

---

[2] There is a difference here: a monopoly situation is generally always prohibited, unless it is a state monopoly. A dominant position is not prohibited if it is the result of internal growth (e.g., Google's search engine). On the other hand, it is restricted if it is the result of an acquisition. Finally, in all cases, abuse of a dominant position (e.g. forcing the purchase of one product in order to receive another) is prohibited.

[3] Wallis, Wilson Dallam. *Culture and Progress*. New York: Whittlesey House, McGraw-Hill Book Company, 1930.

[4] Scholz, Olaf. "Policy Statement by Olaf Scholz, Chancellor of the Federal Republic of Germany and Member of the German Bundestag, February 27, 2022, in Berlin." *Bundesregierung*, February 27, 2022.

and France (2.06%) meet this threshold. Poland and the Baltic states are all above 3%.[5] The goal is to quickly achieve a 3% target for all European countries. President Trump proposes aiming for 5%…

Europe pales in international comparison. The US invests \$860 billion in defense (3.3% of GDP), and China \$300 billion. The US and China account for almost 50% of global military spending.[6]

A major challenge is managing dual-use technologies with both military and civilian applications. Cross-subsidies from the military to private sectors are common.

US Army orders fund research in various companies, and NASA's missions have stimulated advances in computing and telecommunications. Such interference between the military and the economy occurs globally. However, European military firms are often public, while in the US, they are private. Increased militarization will continue to raise transparency issues regarding some business activities and their funding.

Blurring Economic Statistics

As noted earlier, GDP statistics do not separate state spending from appropriation. A country with heavy arms industry expenditures can appear to have a thriving economy. Currently, Russia exhibits this situation because of the war in Ukraine. In addition, one nation's military spending often prompts others to increase theirs.

However, most populations prefer hospitals, schools, social insurance, or infrastructure investments over military complexes. Governments did this before the remilitarization of many economies and redirected their military spending to social infrastructure. It was called the "peace dividend."

In 1989, healthcare and defense spending were roughly equal in the United States and Great Britain. Today, defense accounts for only 40% of healthcare spending in both countries. Defense used to rank 11th in the UK as an immediate concern, after health, immigration, and housing.[7] Only 1% of respondents in the US consider national security a priority.

---

[5] Stockholm International Peace Research Institute (SIPRI). (2024). *SIPRI Yearbook 2023: Armaments, Disarmament and International Security*. Oxford: Oxford University Press. Available at: https://www.sipri.org/publications/sipri-yearbook

[6] It has been calculated that if Europe dedicated as much as the US to military spending, i.e., 3.3% of its GDP, it would amount to \$2,800 billion, about the equivalent of the French GDP. Source: *Bloomberg Economics*, October 2024.

[7] YouGov. "The Most Important Issues Facing the Country." https://yougov.co.uk/topics/society/trackers/the-most-important-issues-facing-the-country (accessed May 15, 2025).

Consequently, funds previously allocated to the military were shifted to health, education, and pensions. This was sensible in the context of an aging population and was aligned with public desires. However, these expenditures have become fixed, creating a dilemma for countries needing to secure military spending today to confront geopolitical risks without increasing debt.

Many countries are in dire straits. They have a diminishing possibility of increasing their debt to face all their priorities, and even the wealthiest nations are reaching their limits.[8] So drastic choices must be made. People, particularly in wealthy nations, dislike making such choices. They want everything instantly and expect the state to provide it. Governments and populist parties sustain this illusion.

The Imperative of Efficiency

Numerous developed nations struggle with inefficiency. Previously, we observed that in the 19th century, a British administration with only 2,000 civil servants effectively governed India, with a population of 300 million. In contrast, the National Health Service today employs 2 million individuals.

Tony Blair, the former British Prime Minister, accurately articulated this issue:

> The challenge facing Western democracies is one of efficiency. Our politicians, in general, are not corrupt, but they do not deliver the services that citizens expect. Our system is expensive and does not produce enough.

There is also a real risk of institutional paralysis. Whether in the USA, Europe, or Japan, governments are becoming increasingly short-lived. Since 1945, Japan has had 33 prime ministers and Italy 31![9] Political instability hinders long-term decision-making, especially in election-heavy countries like the US. Additionally, the increasing influence of civil society and its varied opinions leads to fragmented viewpoints.

Social networks amplify this by allowing everyone to voice their opinions, and algorithms can create echo chambers where similar views dominate. Ultimately, it is not what is true that counts but how many people share the same opinion. "Likes" take precedence over reasoning. Reflex replaces reflection.

Decision-making in this environment is becoming increasingly difficult for political leaders and those running companies. The atomization of opinions and the

---

[8] While a country's principal debt can be paid over the long term, or even rescheduled, interest is paid annually and is having an ever-increasing impact on budgets.
[9] Figures for 2023.

multiplication of pressure tactics increase delays and blockages. In contemporary societies, balancing efficiency with the rising aspirations of the population is emerging as a crucial priority for future leaders.

Managing Expectations

With rising prosperity comes higher expectations. Managing these expectations is crucial for governments and businesses; leaders who over-promise or under-deliver create dissatisfaction. As wealth grows, these expectations become more important, personal, and immaterial.

- *Important*, because the modern state tends to be a universal safety net against all the hazards of life. It becomes responsible not only for the population's well-being, but also for ensuring that it continues. Numerous politicians have stepped in, making broad promises while ignoring the financial repercussions on public debt and household income.
- *Personal*, because everyone's private life is increasingly taking precedence over national ambitions. A budget deficit or negative trade balance means nothing to most people. What speaks to them is purchasing power, health and pension systems, and their physical and mental security.
- *Immaterial*, because when everyday material needs are guaranteed (food, housing, etc.), the population focuses on different endeavors such as promoting well-being, supporting the less privileged, and addressing issues like biodiversity and climate protection.

Moreover, a good leader must also have the courage to be unpopular. This can be challenging, especially in social networks, where everything revolves around popularity. Ultimately, managing expectations also relies on proper timing. This involves first being clear and realistic at the appropriate times and then, second, shifting to a positive outlook when needed.

In his famous speech to the House of Commons on May 13, 1940, Winston Churchill was in the first phase and showed his realism when he talked of "blood, toil, tears and sweat." But on June 4, he turned to motivation: "We will fight on the beaches, we will fight on the landing grounds, we will fight in the fields and streets, we will fight in the hills; we will never surrender."[10]

---

[10] Churchill, Winston. We Shall Fight on the Beaches Speech, June 4, 1940. House of Commons, London.

However, everything has its time. Following the war, Winston Churchill lost the July 1945 election, and the Labour Party achieved its first absolute majority in Parliament. Clement Attlee became Prime Minister. The British people now wanted hope and calm. Expectations had changed.

Equal Opportunities and Equal Results

The principle of equality is closely linked to managing expectations. In every nation, it is crucial to manage the expectations of all individuals equally. However, it is critical to distinguish between these two concepts that are frequently misunderstood.

Equal opportunities must be a priority objective, enabling everyone, regardless of their social origins, ideas, or gender, to have fair access to all a country's infrastructures, such as education, employment, or health.

Equality of outcome, on the other hand, is a false good idea. It holds that everyone should enjoy the same results and lifestyle regardless of effort or education. Simply put, someone who wakes up at 5 a.m. to bake or start a business after borrowing family money should earn as much as someone who stays in bed watching TV or gaming.

Economic prosperity leads to unequal results, assuming there is equal opportunity. This inequality drives younger generations to be inventive and hardworking, inspired by successful entrepreneurs like Bill Gates, Steve Jobs, and Elon Musk. Excessive equality can demotivate the most dynamic individuals. Winston Churchill gave a very political definition of this phenomenon:

> The inherent vice of capitalism is the unequal distribution of wealth. The virtue inherent in socialism consists in an equal distribution of misery.[11]

Universalism Versus Tradition

As value systems evolve with time and prosperity, they will compete between and within countries. The main divide arises from the coexistence of universalism and tradition.

Universalism, often linked to Western culture, is based on the idea that all humans equally share certain rights, values, and principles that should be universally adopted. Originating from Greek philosophers like Plato and Aristotle and later shaped by Enlightenment thinkers such as Diderot, Voltaire, Rousseau, and

---

[11] Churchill, Winston (1945). "Speech to the House of Commons," October 22, 1945.

Kant, it gained prominence through scientific advances. Just as scientific laws apply universally, so should principles in human sciences like sociology, economics, and politics.

Perceived as "natural," universalism leads to a principle of global "interference," where universal rights must be implemented globally. The most emblematic culmination of this principle is the "Universal" Declaration of Human Rights, adopted by the United Nations in 1948.[12] This was followed by international institutions aiming to set international standards acceptable to all. The International Labor Organization is a case in point in the world of work.[13]

Universalism is no longer accepted everywhere. What Europe or the US may see as legitimate can be viewed by other nations as colonial and intrusive. As the world becomes multi-aligned, different economic and value systems coexist.

An alternative is a value system that prioritizes respect for *tradition*, whether religious, philosophical, social, or historical, making it the superior standard. This applies to nations re-establishing themselves as global powers, such as China, Russia, India, Turkey, and Iran. In all cases, history is an essential reference for building the identity of the present.[14] This movement emerged from frustration with Western self-righteousness. Many nations are tired of guilt-inducing remarks from confident Western leaders and organizations.

Internal Tensions

The ongoing conflict between universalism and tradition is also evident within individual nations. In Western countries, we see the rise of populism aimed at reinforcing national traditions against foreign influences, which results in isolation. In some developing nations, the same trend leans towards religious or ethnic realignment.

Previously, multilateralism provided a peaceful means to address these differences, mainly through international organizations. However, their influence has diminished, leading to conflicts that are often resolved bilaterally or militarily. Similarly, corporate cultures aim to offer a set of principles equally applicable to all

---

[12] Taking further the text adopted by the French Revolution on the Rights of Man and Citizen voted in 1789.

[13] In fact, the ILO is one of the oldest international organizations. It was founded in October 1919 by the League of Nations. Its headquarters are in Geneva.

[14] For example, in China, it is a reminder of the values of Confucianism; in Russia, it is the "historic" borders; in India, it is the supremacy of Hinduism and the proposal to change the country's name to "Bharat."

employees of an international organization while acknowledging their diversity. Companies must also fragment their cultures due to new political pressures.

Both government leaders and corporate executives must navigate competing value systems, which can be potentially volatile when ideologies collide. In the context of a fracturing world economy and fragmenting societies, what are the priorities to ensure that the prosperity created by an open world does not disappear?

The Importance of Social Capital

Social Consensus: A Fundamental Objective

Our work on competitiveness shows that there can be no long-term prosperity unless a nation can build on a solid foundation of social consensus. Short-term economic growth that is undone by social upheavals holds little value. Some nations decide rapidly, only for new governments to reverse these decisions just as swiftly.

Social consensus is vital for a nation's prosperity and competitiveness, enabling long-term economic strategies. It refers to a general state of agreement or harmony within society regarding fundamental values, norms, and shared goals. This agreement can be partly imposed by law, but it takes on its full importance when it is freely accepted by the population and lived out daily.

An absence of social consensus leads to anomie, as we saw earlier with Emile Durkheim's theory, which describes a state of social disintegration or disorder resulting from the absence or breakdown of shared societal norms and values.

A Brief History

This is a familiar concept that was historically often referred to as the "social contract."

Thomas Hobbes (1588–1679), in his seminal work *Leviathan* (1651),[15] sought to elucidate how individuals create a social contract to avert the chaos and danger inherent in the "state of nature." According to Hobbes, escaping this state necessitates relinquishing personal freedoms in favor of an omnipotent ruler.

John Locke (1632–1704), another prominent English political philosopher, explored the social contract in his *Treatise on Civil Government* (1690).[16] Locke posited that government should rest on the consent of the governed and rely on representative institutions. His thought significantly influenced French Enlightenment philosophers such as Voltaire and Diderot.

---

[15] Hobbes, Thomas. *Leviathan, or the Matter, Forme, and Power of a Commonwealth Ecclesiasticall and Civil.* London: Andrew Crooke, 1651.
[16] Locke, John. *Treatise on Civil Government.* London 1690.

Montesquieu (1689–1755), in *L'Esprit des Lois* (1748),[17] articulated the principle of balance among the branches of the state – executive, legislative, and judicial – which must operate in harmony. He argued that social consensus arises not only from agreement among citizens but also from the symbiotic relationship between social institutions, laws, and local customs.

Jean-Jacques Rousseau (1712–1778), in his *Social Contract* (1762),[18] proposed the concept of an implicit contract between individuals and the state. Rousseau suggested that individuals unite and forfeit some personal liberties to create a "general will," embodying the collective aspirations and needs of the community.

The list is extensive, encompassing many 19th-century thinkers who contemplated the political implications of establishing a social contract.

In short, there are two approaches proposed by philosophers: some believe that social consensus should be enforced by the community, as proposed by Plato in the Republic or Thomas Moore in Utopia. More recently, communism could be perceived this way. Others argue that the social contract must be freely agreed upon by individuals, a view supported by John Locke, Montesquieu, and Jean-Jacques Rousseau, leading to the concept of liberal democracy championed by Alexis de Tocqueville.

Values in Everyday Life: Social Capital

Aside from ideologies intended to bind a nation through shared beliefs, an important concept concretely advances social consensus by merging social and economic responsibilities. It is known as *social capital*.

It encompasses the network of relationships that influence our daily interactions and foster trust and collaboration within a community. It motivates individuals to donate blood, return a misplaced wallet, or engage in charitable activities.

According to French sociologist Pierre Bourdieu,[19] there are four kinds of capital: economic, cultural, symbolic, and social. In examining competitiveness, the significance of social capital, which fosters robust networks within a community, has consistently proven to be a crucial factor for success.

In the 19th century, Alexis de Tocqueville noted that "the health of liberal democracies" relied on social capital. He praised American society for its

---

[17] Montesquieu, Charles de Secondat. *The Spirit of the Laws.* Translated by Thomas Nugent. New York: Hafner Press, 1949. Originally published 1748.

[18] Rousseau, Jean-Jacques. *The Social Contract, or Principles of Political Right.* Translated by G. D. H. Cole. London: J.M. Dent, 1913. Originally published 1762.

[19] Bourdieu, P. "The forms of capital." In J. G. Richardson (Ed.), *Handbook of Theory and Research for the Sociology of Education* (pp. 241-258). New York: Greenwood 1986.

engagement in discussions and community issues. Even today, this is reflected in the "Town Hall meetings"[20] that punctuate the electoral process.

Social capital is crucial for cohesion, survival, and prosperity. Without it, even economically wealthy nations can face social collapse due to a lack of trust and reciprocity among their people.

New Theories

Today, Harvard professor Robert Putnam, in his book *Bowling Alone*,[21] has brought this concept back into fashion. There are two kinds of social capital: that which creates links within the same community (family, friends, etc.) and that which builds bridges with more distant communities.

Religious phenomena have also played an essential role in a country's economic development and social consensus, as Max Weber demonstrated. More recently, Harvard professors Joseph Heinrich and Jonathan Schultz[22] have put forward the surprising hypothesis of a link between religious laws and entrepreneurship. They state that starting in the 500s, the Catholic Church's prohibition of polygamy and marriages between cousins or close relatives compelled men to find wives in distant communities. This practice promoted a healthier genetic diversity and fostered a spirit of adventure and entrepreneurship.

The "Croissant" Effect

In a company I knew well, 10 a.m. was eagerly awaited.

This was the time when management offered employees croissants and fruit, near the coffee machines.

It was a convivial moment when everyone got together.

(continued)

---

[20] Town Hall meetings date back to colonial New England in the 17th century. These meetings were held in town halls to enable citizens to participate directly in local decision-making. They were a key element of participatory democracy, where community members could discuss and vote on important issues such as local taxes, legislation, or community projects.

[21] Putnam, Robert D. *Bowling Alone: The Collapse and Revival of American Community.* New York: Simon & Schuster, 2000.

[22] Henrich, J., & Schultz, J. "The church, intensive kinship, and global psychological variation," *Science*, 2019, 366(6,466), eaau5141. 10.1126/science.aau5141

> (*continued*)
>
> It was also an opportunity to meet new employees, exchange ideas with colleagues, and have access to top management who were present.
>
> After 15 minutes, everyone headed back to work, having filled up on contacts, information, and positive energy.
>
> One day, a zealous accountant thought that savings could be made on this "stupid" practice. It was abolished. Some minor savings were made – but everyone felt that something more important had been lost.

Social Capital in Companies

In business, social capital is as crucial as financial capital. A company lacking a shared value system among employees faces troubles similar to those that do not have sufficient financial investment.

Among employees, simple daily actions like greeting each other when arriving, checking on one another, engaging with colleagues from various departments or levels within the hierarchy, or having conversations about non-work topics all contribute to building a company culture.

During a visit to a research center at a prominent company in Germany, I observed the typically uninspiring components of such a facility: pipes, scattered cables, and computers displaying complex mathematical equations. However, an authentic Irish pub stood out amidst this technical array. Complete with green leather sofas, Guinness on tap, a pool table, darts, and table soccer; it even featured a seat playfully reserved for James Joyce. My host amusingly noted that it was likely that more innovations were sparked in this pub than elsewhere.

Community Well-Being

Social capital undeniably expands into a more significant but related idea: it fosters *community well-being*. This concept thrives within neighborhoods, cities, or companies. The objective remains to foster attitudes that help community members live together peacefully and respectfully.

It is essential to underline that this concept does not solely result from law or tradition. It also derives from personal choices aimed at benefiting the community.

The ideas of social capital and living well together are interlinked. These factors create positive emotions that solidify a society's daily operations, promoting mutual understanding and solidarity. They help develop nations and companies into more resilient entities that face problems confidently. However, it also leads to a fundamental question: does a country's prosperity, the living standards of its population, the social consensus of a nation, or the social capital of a community make people happier?

Happiness is a complex subject traditionally explored by philosophers, sociologists, and psychologists. Over time, politicians also found it necessary to address the happiness of their people. Economists followed suit as well.

Happiness as an Economic Objective?

It is difficult to establish an "economic" definition of happiness for two reasons: first, everyone's conception of happiness differs. Second, policies aimed at managing happiness would necessarily involve intrusion into the private sphere of citizens, which represents a risk to individual freedom.[23]

On the other hand, there is an "economic" definition of *unhappiness* – or, indeed, several definitions. Unhappiness can result from poverty, unemployment, insecurity, environmental pollution, absence of medical care, a deficient education system, and various forms of discrimination. The list continues indefinitely.

Thus, it can be argued that an initial economic goal related to happiness is to eliminate these sources of unhappiness. Generally, this is a point of consensus. Nevertheless, is it sufficient? Does happiness just come from avoiding unhappiness?

An Age-Old Obsession

Happiness has always been a source of debate. Aristotle viewed it as the ultimate human goal, achieved through virtue. The Epicureans prioritized happiness and pleasure, seeing it as the absence of pain (ataraxia), similar to some Buddhist ideas. Stoics connected happiness with accepting external events and controlling emotions.

Enlightenment philosophers like Locke, Rousseau, and Bentham examined collective happiness. Jeremy Bentham's "principle of utility" states that an action is morally good if it increases happiness or reduces suffering for most people. Unlike moral theories based on individual rights, Bentham's utilitarianism focuses on collective well-being. He argues that actions should be judged not on their consequences for a single individual but on the overall effect on society.[24]

The reflections of 18th-century philosophers led to the establishment of happiness as a political objective. During the French Revolution, Saint-Just[25] made a

---

[23] It is what many dictatorial regimes in history have tried to do, when they aimed to make people happy, even despite themselves…

[24] Jeremy Bentham even proposed quantifying happiness with a "Calculus of Happiness" based on seven criteria: intensity, duration, proximity, certainty, purity, fecundity, and extent. Bentham, Jeremy. *An Introduction to the Principles of Morals and Legislation.* 1789. Reprint, Mineola, NY: Dover Publications, 2007.

[25] Louis Antoine de Saint-Just (1767–1794). Report to the French Convention, March 3, 1794.

statement that would become famous: "Happiness is a new idea in Europe." It was not quite right, but it did reflect a new priority for governments.

Today, this reflection continues. There is even a Gross National Happiness Index, which found international resonance in the 1970s when it was formalized in Bhutan on the initiative of its king, Jigme Singye Wangchuck.[26]

Confusion at the Origin

I believe there is a misunderstanding between two ideas: happiness as personal fulfillment and the "*pursuit*" of happiness as a *fundamental right* for everyone.

This distinction is clearly outlined in the US Declaration of Independence (1776), which declares that the pursuit of happiness is an unalienable right, equal to life and liberty. Here is the text:

> All men are created equal; they are endowed by the Creator with certain inalienable rights, among which are life, liberty, and the pursuit of happiness.[27]

Consequently, economics must address two aspects: first, a nation's goal should be to eliminate the negative impacts of growth on people's lives. The Industrial Revolution created unprecedented wealth for some but also brought widespread misery and exploitation in many factories and cities. Second, it should foster conditions that enable individuals to pursue their happiness freely without interfering with their private lives.

This doesn't necessarily imply grand strategies. For instance, someone who likes jogging will value the public authorities' effort to offer safe, green, and well-maintained city paths. We all too often underestimate the impact of small, sometimes emblematic actions that increase the general well-being of the population.

Companies and Happiness

As for companies, employee happiness was long considered separate from corporate responsibility, with a clear divide between profit goals and personal well-being. At best, some more enlightened entrepreneurs were willing to pay lip service to the idea that happy employees would be more productive. This led to economic

---

[26]This index is made up of 72 criteria grouped into 4 factors: sustainable and equitable economic and social development; preservation and promotion of cultural traditions; environmental protection; and good governance. It was enshrined in the Bhutanese constitution in 2008.
[27]The United States. *The Declaration of Independence*. July 4, 1776. National Archives.

paternalism and the construction of towns and social services around factories in the 19th and 20th centuries.[28] Furthermore, it kept employees loyal.

The line between professional and private life is now blurred. Workplace mobility and civic activism have started directly impacting company culture and strategy. Managing expectations within companies involves more than just economic issues; it includes employees' living environments and values.

Even if some question this attitude nowadays, companies must respect the private lives of their employees inside and outside the company. Demanding total alignment with a company's objectives without respecting personal values is outdated. Consensus between companies and employees on social values will shape tomorrow's work environment.

Chapter Takeaways

- A nation's competitiveness cannot succeed if it is not aligned with the expectations of its society and population. Among these expectations are government efficiency and the freedom of people to choose the economic and social model they favor.
- While competitiveness has developed globally, it must also be sensitive to its implications at the local level. The quality of the social fabric must not be jeopardized by global economic imperatives, which the population would perceive as an attack on their value system.
- In addition, it is not up to competitiveness strategies to define happiness. On the contrary, the aim is to enable everyone to pursue their personal objectives by creating an economic and social infrastructure that eliminates the sources of unhappiness. In doing so, it should allow individuals to identify their own goals.

Where Next?

The book's conclusion considers whether the fracturing of the global economy is an inevitable outcome or a passing eruption. Will the world's opening up of which nations' competitiveness was a fundamental element, remain a short 40-year episode between 1978 and 2018, or is it a fundamental course that will resume?

One element of the answer may lie in the extraordinary resilience of humanity, which, through war and epidemics, has always been able to overcome the most formidable challenges and resume its march towards an open world.

---

[28] As we've seen before, with the "Company Town" concept developed in Illinois by George Pullman, or, in Germany, in Leverkusen by Bayer, Wolfsburg by Volkswagen or Sindelfingen by Mercedes-Benz.

Conclusion

Societies, often mirrored by economies, do not evolve in a straight line. Growth and decline come in cycles; a recurring theme in this book.

Still, over time, the trend has been towards openness. A sense of adventure or curiosity has always spurred people to travel, meet, and exchange ideas and goods. We have inherited this legacy; it remains within us and is probably partly in our DNA. For example, it explains our strong urge to travel, seen in the popularity of "low-cost" airlines, and our desire to communicate through technologies like the Internet and social media.

The journey towards openness has been long and chaotic, often paused by wars, pandemics, or human follies, but it has always resumed. History shows people's remarkable resilience in adversity. The Black Death led to the loss of nearly 50 million people in 14th-century Europe.[1] Nevertheless, a century later, the Renaissance in Italy initiated a formidable burst of intellectual, scientific, and artistic innovation that spread across Europe. And 400 years later, the Industrial Revolution in England transformed economics and generated unprecedented wealth.

Another prevailing theme is the relentless pursuit of happiness as an ultimate objective for people and nations. This idea is not new. For centuries, philosophers have linked prosperity and the pursuit of happiness. From 1968 onward, my generation was merely revisiting this enduring concept. This endeavor is not about enforcing a uniform standard of happiness, as authoritarian regimes have historically attempted. Instead, it is about nations providing the conditions that enable people to pursue their own idea of happiness. This is what prosperity should provide.

---

[1] Benedictow, Ole J. *The Black Death, 1,346–1,353: The Complete History*. Woodbridge, UK: Boydell Press, 2004.

During my university days, we were told that economics should avoid moral issues like right or wrong, justice or injustice, which belonged to philosophy or religion. However, this is not what people want today. At the very least, people expect the economy to eliminate sources of unhappiness and, ideally, foster those ideas that instead lead to towards happiness. Economics cannot just focus on the intricate balances of supply and demand based on complex mathematical equations; it also needs to address questions about daily life, such as purchasing power or the economic impact of a divorce.

Understanding the mechanism of prosperity implies merging economics with other disciplines like anthropology, sociology, or psychology. In addition, society's aspiration means that economists must now address not only the "how" but also the "why" of their actions.

Maybe it is time to conclude this journey with an essential purpose. In my opinion, Wen Jiabao, the former Chinese prime minister, has done just that:

> The aim is to enable everyone to pursue a happy and dignified life, to feel secure, and to have confidence in the future while living in a society of equality and justice.

Unfortunately, the road ahead remains full of obstacles. Openness has created a sense of vulnerability and fear for many. While curiosity and travel are innate, the survival instinct is equally fundamental. The two feelings are often conflicting.

Various forms of nationalism and economic protectionism have exploited this fear. Though the terminology – sovereignty, industrial policy, or immigration – has shifted, the consequence remains the same: global fragmentation is once again on the rise.

In 1835, in *Democracy in America*, Alexis de Tocqueville[2] had the premonition that, with prosperity, nations would find it increasingly difficult to progress or reform:

> I cannot help fearing that men will reach the point where they regard every new theory as a danger, every innovation as a painful problem, every social advance as a first step towards revolution, and absolutely refuse to advance.[3]

We are living in such a time. The openness of the world is waning, and doubt is setting in. But not everywhere. Many countries worldwide are also enjoying a new-found prosperity and have no doubts about their future. They remain havens of hope.

---

[2] Tocqueville, Alexis de. *Democracy in America*. Translated by Harvey C. Mansfield and Delba Winthrop. Chicago: University of Chicago Press, 2000.

[3] An analysis made even more remarkable by the fact that it was written by a 29-year-old man.

Confidence in the future, progress, and our ability to solve problems rather than suffer or avoid them is undoubtedly a nation's greatest competitive advantage.

To achieve that goal, we need to stay positive.

When Mark Twain was asked, after listening to an opera by Richard Wagner, what he thought of it. He replied:

It is not as bad as it sounds.[4]

It is the same for the world; and we must believe it.

---

[4] Twain, Mark. *Mark Twain's Notebook*. Edited by Albert Bigelow Paine. New York: Harper & Brothers, 1935.

Acknowledgments

This book is also dedicated to my brother Christian, who has reviewed the various versions and, out of modesty, chose not to be prominently acknowledged.

About the Author

Stéphane Garelli is a leading authority on world competitiveness, where he has pioneered research and theory. He is Professor Emeritus of World Competitiveness at the University of Lausanne and IMD, where he continues to teach.

He founded the World Competitiveness Center, one of whose activities is to rank the competitiveness of nations each year.

Stéphane Garelli was, for many years, the managing director of the World Economic Forum and the Davos Annual Meetings.

He was, among others, Chairman of the Board and shareholder of the newspaper *Le Temps*, as well as Chairman of the Board of Sandoz Financial and Banking Holding and a member of the Board of Directors of Banque Edouard Constant.

He is a member of the International Olympic Committee's Commission on Sustainability and Legacy. He is also part of several international institutions and boards and continues to advise governments.

In 1999, he was also elected to the Constituent Assembly of the Canton of Vaud, Switzerland.

Author of numerous articles and studies, he has published two best-selling books: *Top Class Competitors – How Nations, Firms and Individuals Succeed in the New World of Competitiveness* and *Are You a Tiger, a Cat or a Dinosaur?*, which have been translated into several languages.